Ethics in International Affairs

Ethics in International Affairs

Theories and Cases

edited by
Andrew Valls

ROWMAN & LITTLEFIELD PUBLISHERS, INC.
Lanham • Boulder • New York • Oxford

ROWMAN & LITTLEFIELD PUBLISHERS, INC.

Published in the United States of America
by Rowman & Littlefield Publishers, Inc.
4720 Boston Way, Lanham, Maryland 20706
http://www.rowmanlittlefield.com

12 Hid's Copse Road, Cumnor Hill, Oxford OX2 9JJ, England

British Library Cataloguing in Publication Information Available

Library of Congress Cataloging-in-Publication Data

Ethics in international affairs : theories and cases / edited by Andrew Valls.
    p. cm.
   Includes bibliographical references and index.
   ISBN 0-8476-9156-X (alk. paper)—ISBN 0-8476-9157-8 (paper: alk. paper)
    1. International relations—Moral and ethical aspects.   I. Valls,
  Andrew, 1966–
JZ1306.E88   2000
172'.4—dc21   99-057384

Printed in the United States of America

♾ ™ The paper used in this publication meets the minimum requirements of American
National Standard for Information Sciences—Permanence of Paper for Printed Library
Materials, ANSI/NISO Z39.48-1992.

Contents

v

Acknowledgments

This volume began with a conversation I had with Jennifer Knerr, my editor at Rowman and Littlefield, over three years ago. I wish to thank Jennifer for all of her work on the project since that time. At every stage of the process, Jennifer's suggestions improved the volume substantially. I also wish to thank others at Rowman and Littlefield for their contributions to the volume, including Brenda Hadenfeldt; Janice Braunstein, the production editor who guided the manuscript through its final phases; and Elisabeth Graves for an excellent job copyediting the manuscript.

Thanks to Genese Brooks, political science secretary at Morehouse College, for her assistance and especially for typing chapter 9 on a very tight deadline.

I also wish to thank Debra Kornblau and Piibi-Kai Kivik at Indiana University for their help in facilitating the project while I was at Indiana in the summer of 1999.

For their comments and suggestions on chapter 5, I wish to thank Fred Whelan, Fran Harbour, Nick Fotion, and Christopher Wellman. Versions of the chapter were presented at the 1998 meeting of the International Studies Association, where Fran Harbour was my discussant; the Sam Nunn School of International Affairs at Georgia Institute of Technology; the Department of Philosophy at Morehouse College; and the Department of Political Science at Tartu University in Estonia. I thank all those who participated in these forums.

For her careful and thoughtful comments on the whole manuscript, I thank an anonymous reader.

Thanks also to the contributors to the volume for their timely and high-quality work, which made my job as editor much easier than it might have been.

Finally, I thank my wife, Joanne Cono, for her comments on the introduction and chapter 5; for listening to me talk, sometimes incessantly, about my work; and for all of the other forms of support that she so generously gives me.

Andrew Valls
Tartu, Estonia

Foreword

Among the most serious moral problems that call for attention are those concerning international affairs, ranging from when and whether the use of violence by states and groups can be justified to how the economic gains and burdens of the world should be divided. When two colleagues and I published the edited collection of essays *Philosophy, Morality, and International Affairs* in 1974, it was one of the few treatments of ethics and foreign policy available at that time. Among other aims, we sought to provide a largely missing philosophical and moral critique of the U.S. pursuit of the war in Vietnam. In that heyday of what was called "realism" in thinking about international affairs, policy makers, political theorists, and students of foreign policy were preoccupied with considerations of the national interest divorced from morality, and philosophers were preoccupied with metaethics, wondering whether any moral positions on any matters whatsoever could be justified. The contributors to our volume recognized that we shared moral responsibility, in varying degrees, for the views held and the actions and inactions indulged in by our governments and fellow citizens.

As the essays in this new collection make clear, the division between what is in the national interest and what can be morally justified is often questionable. One reason is that the citizens who vote for the governments that make and carry out policy are not indifferent to the moral justifiability or lack of it of those policies. Another reason is that the conception of morality that sees it as completely divorced from what is in the interests of a state that serves the interests of its citizens is a faulty conception.

If the views of some philosophers today prevail, philosophy will once again remove itself from actual moral problems, leaving them to practitioners and journalists and valuing only the metaethical components of such discussions. But many others, among them philosophers, recognize that moral problems are inescapable and demand responsible attention by moral philosophers as well as others. To decide well what we ought to do requires a combination of moral and other theory, a wide knowledge of relevant facts, and sound moral judgment.

And the work done in dealing with actual moral problems—those in international relations are a good example—then makes possible the improvement of normative theory at every level, even the most general. I argue in *Rights and Goods: Justifying Social Action* (1984) that philosophical ethics are needed to responsibly address the moral problems confronting us in all domains and that philosophical ethics will be improved by its encounters with social scientists and others also working on such problems, which are rarely merely empirical. This collection of essays in international affairs is a good example of the fruitful outcome of such cooperation.

In the last couple of decades, the development of concern for human rights on the part of scholars, activists, and governments has greatly affected the discussion of international affairs and has contributed to the willingness of participants to deal with the moral aspects of foreign policies and intergroup interactions. More recently, greater attention to the claims of groups other than states—ethnic and cultural groups for instance—has broadened the discussion in useful ways.

This volume contains helpful essays on the justifiability, or not, of the use of violence by states and by groups that are not states but may have legitimate claims to self-determination of various kinds. There is appropriate criticism of the double standard often involved in holding that violence only be used as a last resort: It has often been wrongly supposed that it is relatively easy for states to meet this requirement and almost impossible for nonstate groups that use violence to do so. The volume makes a substantial contribution to the responsible discussion of terrorism, exposing the unreasonableness often characterizing descriptions and evaluations of it. Contributors argue that if states can satisfy the criteria of just war theory, so can some nonstate groups, and if certain acts carried out by nonstate groups are cases of terrorism, then so are similar acts carried out by states. The volume makes fundamental and eminently important points about the need to develop nonviolent alternatives through which groups and states can press their claims.

Arguments around "humanitarian intervention" are also clearly at the forefront of what responsible scholars and citizens should concern themselves with these days. The discussion in this book of the motives and mistakes involved in the breakup of the former Yugoslavia and the international responses to it is highly instructive. Humanitarian principles and a respect for sovereignty that can also be defended on moral grounds can conflict in ways that cry out for analysis and evaluation. Much about the possibilities for peace, order, and justice will continue to depend on the answers arrived at to the questions involved.

Finally, global economic justice should be high on the list of moral issues to which scholars and citizens devote sustained attention. The essays in this volume provide needed arguments and calls to conscience, as well as disheartening analyses of the economic, political, and ideological reasons for past failures.

Andrew Valls notes in his introduction to this book that the field of international ethics is now thriving. This development, and the kind of work offered in this collection, can give us some hope that gradually the policies of states, groups, and persons in the international arena will be less morally indefensible than in the past.

Virginia Held
Distinguished Professor of Philosophy
City University of New York

Introduction

Andrew Valls

International ethics is a field that has been coming into its own for some time, and evidence that it is thriving can now be found in a number of quarters. The Carnegie Council on Ethics and International Affairs has had a journal devoted to international ethics for over ten years. The International Ethics section of the International Studies Association sponsors a number of lively panels at the association's annual convention. Every year more and more articles and books are published on some aspect of international ethics, such as just war theory, humanitarian intervention, human rights, global justice, or any number of other topics. Courses on international ethics are now commonly taught in departments of international affairs, political science, and philosophy.

The current state of international ethics can be attributed to the confluence of a number of factors. The advent of nuclear weapons and the nuclear arms race raised fundamental moral issues that were debated from the end of World War II and throughout the Cold War. The American experience in Vietnam prompted a number of philosophers to think seriously about the justifications for going to war and the ethics of fighting a war. The ever growing interdependence of the countries of the world has raised issues of global justice, issues that are increasingly difficult to ignore.

The end of the Cold War has only accelerated the growth of interest in international ethics. For example, it has led to an increased willingness of the international community to violate norms of state sovereignty in order to protect human rights and bring violent conflicts to an end. The breakup of the former Soviet Union, and of some of its former satellite states, has renewed interest in the ethics of secession and the basis of national self-determination.

Developments within the academy have paralleled these events, both reflecting them and, in turn, contributing to debates about their significance, theoretical basis, and policy implications. Two early important contributions to international ethics are Michael Walzer's *Just and Unjust Wars* (1992; first edition 1977) and Charles Beitz's *Political Theory and International Relations* (1979b), and their publication was an important event in the development of the field. Interest in international ethics also has been supported by the growth of political theory and applied ethics in the last generation. Philosophers have shown an increased interest in first-order ethical questions in recent decades, and political theory, once pronounced dead, is now very much alive and well. Though international ethics was not a central part of the "rebirth" of political theory, it is clearly now an important aspect of the latter, and its centrality only grows. No political theorist or philosopher working today can ignore the international dimension of the issues that concern them.

This book attempts to cover and take stock of the field of international ethics with attention to both theoretical issues and their application to cases, all at a level that will be both accessible to newcomers and of interest to scholars. The contributors come from a variety of disciplinary, theoretical, and national backgrounds, reflecting the diversity in the field itself. The volume is organized topically, with four of the five sections leading with a theoretical chapter that covers the general issues, followed by two case studies that apply and engage the theoretical debates.

The volume begins by considering a threshold question for international ethics: Does ethics apply to international affairs at all? Many would argue that it does not. A central tenet of "realism," long the main school of thought in international relations theory, is that morality does not and should not apply to international affairs. It does not because, as an empirical matter, international actors are not motivated by moral considerations, and it should not because when moral concerns do intrude into international events, the results are usually worse than if they had not done so.

David Welch takes on this position in his chapter on morality and the national interest. The notion of "the national interest" has played a central role in realist thinking, as it is often contrasted sharply with moral considerations. Against those who argue that morality plays no part in the reasoning or motivation of political actors, Welch argues that human beings are intrinsically moral creatures, in that we cannot help but think in moral terms. Further, he argues that "the national interest" is itself a moral concept, appealing, if only implicitly, to "stakes, goals, and values." But because invoking the national interest usually obscures precisely which goals and values are at issue, the concept does more harm than good. We would be better off, Welch concludes, if we dropped the false contrast between morality and the national interest and directly addressed the question of what considerations are and ought to be behind the behavior of political actors at home and abroad.

If we cannot help but think about international relations in moral terms, the question arises, How are we to do so? Where are we to start, and what framework are we to use? One place to start is just war theory, which is perhaps the oldest and most developed framework for thinking about the morality of relations among states. Just war theory as it is practiced today is largely a product of the Christian tradition, though there is significant overlap and convergence between this tradition and non-Christian, non-Western schools of thought. Intimations of just war theory can be seen as early as St. Augustine, who argued that war can be just and that a good Christian can kill for the state without imperiling his soul. The theory was further developed during the late medieval and early modern periods by Aquinas, Vattel, Suarez, Vitoria, and Grotius, among others, and today stands as a secularized and widely used set of criteria that shapes both public and scholarly debate over the ethics of war.

Some of the richness as well as the ambiguity of just war theory is brought out by Nick Fotion's chapter. Fotion locates just war theory as a middle position, between pacifism and realism. If pacifism maintains that war can never be morally justified, and realism that it need not be, just war theory holds that war both can be justified and must be justified. Relations among states are not amoral, but they do allow for the use of violence when certain criteria are satisfied. More than this, Fotion brings out the diversity of positions possible within pacifism, realism, and just war theory. He suggests that moderate forms of pacifism and realism may, in some ways, converge on the position of just war theory. If pacifism admits of exceptions, just war theory may help us think about those exceptions; and if (as a realist can concede) it is often in the interest of amoral actors to respect norms, just war theory may provide those norms. Even if just war theory does constitute a kind of overlapping consensus, however, it will not settle every question because the theory itself allows a number of interpretations. On almost every criterion, Fotion shows, there is a range of possible positions available to the just war theorist.

The ambiguity of just war theory is further brought out by Tony Coates in his treatment of the Persian Gulf War. Whether discussing just cause, legitimate authority, proportionality, discrimination, or almost any other criterion of just war theory, Coates shows that in the case of the Gulf War, it is difficult to be certain whether the requirements were met. Part of the difficulty lies in the standards of the theory themselves, the ambiguity about what they require, in concrete terms, in a particular situation. The other part of the problem is that even if the criteria themselves were quite clear, we would require a great deal of empirical evidence to apply them correctly. As Coates shows, that empirical evidence is often simply not available to observers of the Gulf War. In attempting to be fair to the arguments of both the critics and the defenders of the war, Coates often finds that the evidence is either mixed or absent. He shows that each side of the debate over the war fills the gaps in the record in ways that support its preferred position. Coates resists this and therefore resists the temptation to come to a clear, morally unambiguous conclusion. His conclusion is more nuanced, but it is clear that Coates finds good reasons to be skeptical about the humanitarian and cosmopolitan interpretation of the war.

Fran Harbour's chapter also explores the meaning and the limits of just war theory, focusing on proportionality and discrimination, the requirements of *jus in bello* (justice in the war). Her case is the use of nonlethal chemical weapons during the Vietnam War, in particular the use of "harassing agents" and defoliants. The former were used during air rescues and to flush both civilians and combatants out of protective bunkers. The latter were used to destroy both jungle canopy that provided cover to the enemy and food crops. Though nonlethal, these weapons raise fundamental questions about proportionality, discrimination, and double effect, Harbour argues. What emerges from Harbour's discussion, and from the chapters by Fotion and Coates, is that while just war theory provides a framework for discussion about the morality of war, it does not provide clear and easy answers. It is a place to start the discussion but does not by itself conclude it.

Still, in many ways, just war theory is the best starting point that we have in thinking of the morality of relations among states. It is not surprising, then, that many arguments about those relations—even those that do not pertain to war—involve extending just war theory into other realms. In addition, it may be that just war theory can also provide some guidance in assessing the morality of political violence even when that violence is undertaken by entities other than states. Such violence is usually called terrorism and is often committed by groups or peoples that aspire to have their own states. While terrorism is usually condemned as morally reprehensible, such condemnation without argument is too quick. The chapters in the following section explore the morality of terrorism and investigate the questions of whether it can ever be justified and, if so, under what circumstances.

The section begins with my discussion of terrorism and just war theory. I argue that, in principle, terrorism can satisfy the requirements of a just war. Despite the usual application of just war theory to interstate violence, stateless groups may have the same moral basis to commit violence, and they may do so within the constraints that just war theory imposes. I rely on the idea of self-determination to argue that stateless groups may have a just cause and also argue—against those who see terrorism as inherently random—that terrorism both may be proportionate and may discriminate among targets. I conclude that if interstate war can be justified, so too may terrorism. The implication is that if most cases of terrorism deserve condemnation, this is not because nonstate violence is intrinsically wrong or because terrorists necessarily are the amoral monsters that they are so often portrayed to be.

In the following chapter, David George also uses just war theory to assess the morality of terrorism, focusing on the case of the Irish Republican Army (IRA) in Northern Ireland. George utilizes four criteria from just war theory—legitimate authority, just cause, right intention, and discrimination—arguing that, on all four, IRA terrorism utterly fails. By tracing the historical development of the IRA, George argues that its claim to be the legitimate representative of the Irish people is implausible, especially in light of the splintering of the IRA into rival factions since the late 1960s. George also argues that the IRA lacks a just cause to commit violence, for its goal of self-determination is "ideological." Hence, while George agrees with me that just war theory can apply to terrorism, he disagrees about whether self-determination can give rise to a just cause. Lacking a just cause and a good claim to be a legitimate authority, the IRA's terrorism, George concludes, is private violence and therefore is properly understood as crime rather than war.

Neve Gordon and George Lopez then take up the case of terrorism in the Arab–Israeli conflict. They trace the development and activities of Palestinian terrorist groups from 1948 to the late 1980s and use these data to critique the definition of *terrorism* maintained by the U.S. Department of State. In particular, they criticize the feature of the definition that holds that only nonstate actors may commit terrorism, arguing to the contrary that it is a mistake to focus on the identity of the actor when defining *terrorism*. State sponsorship of terrorism, Gordon and Lopez argue, significantly complicates the issue of who is responsible for terrorism when nonstate actors commit it with state support. Furthermore, one must reckon with the phenomenon of state terrorism itself. Indeed, after their treatment of Palestinian terrorism, the authors go on to discuss Israeli terrorism, committed both outside of its borders and within them. After establishing that terrorism has been a tool used by both sides of the conflict, Gordon and Lopez conclude, among other things, that arresting terrorism requires addressing its roots in injustice.

One prominent theme in the chapters on terrorism is the tension between the competing claims of states and individuals. This theme is continued in the following section on state sovereignty and humanitarian intervention. The tension between the prerogatives of states and the claims of individuals is a fundamental one in international ethics. Most views hold that—despite the state-centric nature of international relations theory and just war theory—the rights of states are derivative of the rights of the individuals within them. State sovereignty is a norm of international relations, but at some point violations of the rights of individuals within a state warrant intervention into the affairs of that state by others. Almost no one maintains the extreme position that state sovereignty is entitled to no consideration or, at the other extreme, that no considerations can justify violating a state's sovereignty. The debate, then, is about where the line is to be drawn, when and how intervention is justified. The trend, both in international politics and in scholarly debates, is toward lowering the hurdle that must be cleared before intervention may be undertaken.

The analysis in this section is framed by Simon Caney's discussion of the philosophical debates over humanitarian intervention. Caney explicates the assumptions on which the case for humanitarian intervention rests. He then reviews the main arguments for and against humanitarian intervention, and on the whole he finds that the objections raised by intervention's opponents do not withstand scrutiny. At best, critics of humanitarian intervention point out difficulties that intervention may face but do not raise fundamental objections to the idea that, in principle, humanitarian intervention can be justified. Caney goes on to discuss the circumstances under which intervention is justified, arguing in particular that, if it is to be legitimate, intervention should be undertaken by a "legitimate authority," meaning that multilateral interventions are preferable to unilateral ones.

George Kieh offers an analysis of the interventions into civil wars in four African countries—Somalia, Rwanda, Liberia, and Sierra Leone. He places each conflict in its historical context and by so doing points to the difficulties that each intervention faced. Kieh presents a dismal assessment of these interventions, all of which were multilateral. Indeed, of the four, only the intervention into Liberia can be considered a (qualified) success. In the others, some crucial factor was missing, whether it was basic knowledge of the country (as in Somalia); or simply the political will to remain long enough for a stable peace to be established (as in Rwanda); or the ability to stay above the fray of the conflict itself (as in both Somalia and Sierra Leone). Kieh's analysis clearly shows that, whatever theorists may conclude about the justifiability of humanitarian intervention, it is political leaders and organizations that must carry it out. If they are to do more good than harm, they will be wise to consider the lessons of past interventions.

The other case study, by Emil Nagengast, on Western policy toward the former Yugoslavia, is no more of a cause for optimism about the politics of intervention. Nagengast details the developments that led up to the declaration of independence by Croatia and Slovenia and the subsequent events that led to the civil war. He focuses particularly on German policy toward these events, arguing that, contrary to critics of German policy, German recognition of their statehood was guided by the ethical norms of self-determination and by opposition to violence as a means to settle disputes. Nagengast contrasts German policy with that of other Western powers, in particular the United States, which spent years threatening, equivocating, and hesitating before finally intervening in the civil war. Although it appeared to many that Germany was engaging in dangerous unilateral policy by its recognition of Croatia and Slovenia, Nagengast argues that, compared with the policies of its allies, Germany's was the more ethically defensible course.

International ethics is not, however, all about violence and its regulation. Indeed, perhaps the fastest growing area of interest in the field is global justice. As noted above, increased economic interaction and interdependence have led many scholars to argue that the kind of cooperation that gives rise to considerations of justice in domestic society now exists on a global scale. The implication is that we must now take seriously the idea of global distributive justice. This leaves open the question of which theory of justice one ought to embrace. What we find is that scholars inevitably think about global justice by extending theories of justice developed in the domestic sphere. Hence, to a certain extent, the debate over global justice reproduces the one about domestic justice, the main issues being whether redistribution is justified and, if so, how much and according to which principles.

As Peter Jones notes in his survey of the topic, much of the debate over global justice takes place within a Rawlsian framework, which invites us to think of the current distribution of resources and assets as "arbitrary from a moral point of view" and asks us to arrive at principles of justice from behind a "veil of ignorance," which deprives us of knowledge of our own positions and endowments. Rawls argued in his theory of domestic justice that this reasoning would lead to the "difference principle," which requires that inequalities benefit the least well off. Some theorists of global distributive justice argue (against Rawls himself) for a global difference principle. After discussing this line of thought, Jones goes on to treat other issues pertinent to global justice, such as whether states or individuals are the proper subjects of distribution, whether respecting political communities argues against global redistribution, and whether the ideas of "basic needs" or "humanity" are able to ground claims for global justice. What emerge from Jones's discussion most clearly are the many issues and wide variety of positions that exist in the debate about global justice and the fact that the debate, like that on domestic justice, is unlikely to draw to a close any time soon.

One of the major actors shaping the global distribution of wealth is multinational corporations, and one of the issues within the debate about global justice is the moral responsibilities of multinationals, particularly toward developing countries where they extract natural resources. This issue is taken up by Gerard Elfstrom in his study of North American aluminum companies in Jamaica. Elfstrom provides background on this case as well as reviewing some prominent theories about the responsibilities of multinationals, demonstrating how one sheds light on the other. On the one hand, the theories certainly provide ways of thinking through the moral issues involved in this case. At the same time, however, the case of aluminum in Jamaica indicates the limits of those theories, which are often ill-equipped to handle the complexities of an actual case with its own particular features. Elfstrom concludes that multinationals do in fact have moral obligations to the states in which they operate, but there are limits to those obligations, some of which are a function of the requirements of capitalist enterprise.

Finally, Jeff Cason offers an assessment of the fate of the New International Economic Order (NIEO), the only serious attempt to publicly discuss issues of global distributive justice on a broad basis. The heyday of the NIEO was the 1970s, and Cason explains why this period was especially friendly toward such claims. Unfortunately for those pressing these claims, the window of opportunity shut by the early 1980s. According to Cason, a number of factors contributed to this, but they can be reduced to two: changes in the global economy and the ideological triumph of neoliberalism, which was hostile to redistributive policies both within and between states. While an opportunity to press for global redistribution could arise again, Cason is not optimistic about this. His analysis raises the question, then, of how global justice, if it requires redistribution, might ever be achieved.

The volume may be said to conclude, then, on a pessimistic note. Indeed, many of the cases examined here no doubt will strengthen the conviction of some that, even if "international ethics" is not an oxymoron, there is little hope of ever establishing something approaching a just international order. The skeptic might suggest a contrast in the volume, between well-worked-out and plausible philosophical positions on the one hand and actual cases with generally disheartening outcomes on the other. Still, despite the support for pessimism some will find here, there may be grounds for optimism as well. As Virginia Held points out in her foreword, philosophical theories can and do have an impact on public debate and policy makers and citizens are not immune to the moral dimensions of international affairs. The gap between normative theories and cases in international affairs may often be larger than one would like, but they undeniably interact with and inform one another. This mutual dependence is reason enough to study both theories and cases in international ethics—and to study them together. Perhaps this volume will contribute in some small way to this worthwhile endeavor.

PART I

DOES MORALITY APPLY TO INTERNATIONAL AFFAIRS?

1

Morality and "the National Interest"

David A. Welch

What, exactly, is the relationship between morality and "the national interest"? This straightforward question has anything but a straightforward answer. Over the course of the long history of international relations thought and practice, thinkers and practitioners have staked out various positions on the issue. Broadly speaking, it is possible to identify four.

For some, these are fundamentally different imperatives. On this view, to the extent that morality informs foreign policy, "the national interest" cannot, and vice versa. The very same act or policy might, in some circumstances, serve the national interest *and* gratify our moral impulses, but that would be entirely fortuitous. There is no necessary relation between these concepts whatsoever. Perhaps the best-known proponent of this view is George Kennan (e.g., 1985–86).

For others, there is not, and cannot be, a tension between the two. What is in the national interest is ipso facto the moral thing to do. On this view, the national interest is itself a moral concept of such power and cogency that it overwhelms all other moral considerations. Perhaps the best-known proponent of this view is Hans Morgenthau, who argues, in a famous essay, that the statesman's highest moral duty is to ensure the survival of the state and that this *is* the national interest in a nutshell (1950).

A third view is that while morality and the national interest are logically different considerations—one, after all, concerns what is right or wrong, whereas the other concerns what is advantageous or disadvantageous—nevertheless, as an empirical matter, the two coincide. If we truly understand what will conduce to the national interest, we will see that in the long run the best way of securing peace and prosperity is always to seek to do what is right. This view is less firmly identified with specific thinkers than either of the first two, but it has an ancient

3

and venerable pedigree. It represents a common ground between Christians and utilitarians (particularly rule utilitarians) and commanded general assent among nineteenth-century liberals, idealists, and utopians. The Manchester School embraced it, and both William Gladstone and Woodrow Wilson professed it (perhaps honoring it in the breach as often as not; see generally Nardin and Mapel 1992).

Finally, a fourth view holds that while the national interest is a concept with moral content, nevertheless a foreign policy grounded in the national interest will sometimes fail a test of morality. The security and welfare of the body politic is a prima facie good, and leaders shoulder a moral obligation to promote it when they take up the reins of power. Nevertheless, there are times when a diligent pursuit of one's own country's security or welfare would contravene higher moral duties. Sometimes one simply must risk one's own comfort to prevent great evil or to relieve the sufferings of others. The world is not a perfect place; there is an irreducible element of tragedy in international affairs. We see this view reflected in the thought of Reinhold Niebuhr (1958; 1962), Arnold Wolfers (1965), and Stanley Hoffmann (1981), among others.[1]

My purpose in this chapter is not to choose among these various schools of thought. Instead, it is to examine the very question for which these represent possible answers. I will suggest that it is not a very good question. Before we can even begin to debate the relationship between morality and the national interest, we must establish that these are concepts with clear referents. They are not.

In a very general sense, we all know what the word *morality* means, but when we bring the concept to bear on real debates about real foreign policy choices, we see that we cannot speak of it sensibly without wrestling second-order questions to the ground—questions about the various ways in which we might go about seeking to identify the principles to guide our moral choices, about the proper scope of moral judgment, and about how to interpret the general concept in specific circumstances. These are questions that scholars of international relations rarely (and practitioners virtually never) critically examine.

Morality, at least, is a concept with a future, I shall argue. "The national interest" is not. I shall contend that the phrase does more harm than good in thinking about international affairs, that to the extent that it has any value at all it is wholly superfluous, and that it is unsalvageable. Hence, we need not, and should not, bother to ask about the relationship between morality and the national interest. We should only ever ask, "What is the right thing to do?"

MORALITY

Human beings are creatures with a natural moral faculty. That is to say, it is normal for people to think in terms of right and wrong and to take guidance from their moral judgments when they act (Eisenberg, Reykowski, and Staub 1989;

Folger 1984; Gibbs 1991; Greenberg and Cohen 1982; Kahneman, Knetsch, and Thaler 1986; Lerner and Lerner 1981; Maxwell 1990; McGuire 1991; Thomas 1989). Some people do this more regularly and more rigorously than others, of course. Mother Theresa springs to mind. Other people's moral faculties are severely stunted: Adolf Hitler's, for example. If Mother Theresa and Adolf Hitler define the end points of the spectrum, most of us fall somewhere in the middle. We take guidance from moral principles or at least try to, but in the face of strong temptation, we sometimes choose to do what we acknowledge to be wrong.

It would be very convenient if everyone everywhere agreed both on moral principles and on their interpretation in specific cases. There is some reason to believe that at a certain level, people everywhere *do* agree on certain crucial things—for example, on the abstract meanings of key words such as *right, wrong, just,* and *unjust*. There is also reason to believe that when we take into account situational context, people everywhere tend to make very similar kinds of moral judgments (for example, that murder is wrong, that lying is wrong, that one should treat the elderly with care and respect, and so forth).[2] Nevertheless, it is plain that people disagree about the proper way to rank moral values, how to manage trade-offs between them, and even how to go about reasoning morally. Culture, religion, ideology, life experience, and even personality can have a profound influence on people's moral judgments.

We live, as it were, in the concrete not in the abstract, and so when scholars, political leaders, and citizens try to decide what is the moral thing to do in international affairs, inevitably disagreements in values, principles, and prescriptions emerge, even in the most homogeneous societies. On a global scale, the disagreements are typically very serious indeed. This raises the question, How do we know *who* is right about *what* is right? Most of us do not ask this question very often because we have strong moral views of our own. If I am a hard-core communitarian who insists that a liberal cosmopolitan conception of human rights is Western moral imperialism—a kind of conceit that insufficiently values cultural heterogeneity and national sovereignty—then I am unlikely to experience the angst of wondering whether my liberal cosmopolitan interlocutor is right. I am far more likely simply to lose my temper.[3]

The chief difficulty with thinking about the "morality" side of the question is deciding whose morality to credit. In the real world of moral debate about international affairs, the majority view among the policy community, politically active citizens, and the media tends to win out. In the United States in recent decades, the center of political gravity in debates about morality and foreign policy has drifted somewhat from what we might call liberal internationalism to conservative exceptionalism. But there is a certain bedrock consistency in American moral discourse no matter what the general tenor, and we find it in a strong commitment to individualism: hence the American emphasis on civil and political rights (including property rights) and on the spread of democracy. It hardly needs to be said that the center of political gravity in a place such as China is quite different, even if some Chinese embrace liberal individualism (Ames 1997).

The politically dominant view at any given time and in any given place is unlikely to be very systematic. That is to say, it will rarely be possible to articulate it in terms of a coherent and consistent set of principles. Perhaps this should not surprise us, for even individuals who have very fixed notions of what is right and wrong can almost never articulate a systematic basis for their judgments. In part, this is a function of the fact that most people tend to think in two dimensions at once when they engage in moral deliberation: they think in terms of rules, and they also evaluate consequences (see, e.g., Nye 1986). For example, we generally keep our promises and tell the truth if doing so only has minor negative consequences, but if the consequences are severe, most of us will break our promises or lie. Or, to use an international-political example, most of us tend to think that we should respect the sovereign independence of a state if it experiences only minor civil unrest but that we should intervene where possible to prevent wholesale slaughter or genocide. We tend to judge when consequences outweigh principles impressionistically, which makes it difficult to think about morality and foreign policy systematically.

The fact that moral debates about foreign policy are a kind of political debate—that is, that the moral judgments that inform policy tend merely to be the vector sum of the weighted individual moral preferences of influential people—is both a moral and a political problem. It is a moral problem because the right thing to do is not necessarily what most influential people just so happen to think is the right thing to do. It is a political problem because it generates discord, resentment, and conflict. We see this on a global scale not just domestically: The moral preferences of powerful states tend to steamroller the moral preferences of weaker states in debates over the design of international institutions, the rights and obligations of their members, terms of entry and accession to international regimes, and the content of international law.[4]

Unanimity in moral judgment would be very nice. It would satisfy everyone's moral impulses and would avoid generating conflict. While unanimity is clearly a vain hope, nevertheless it is possible in principle to approach it over time asymptotically through a process of intergenerational moral socialization that encourages the tendency to make moral judgments with reference to a relatively explicit and widely shared set of principles. Elsewhere I have argued that this leads to an endorsement of the conventionalist project (Welch 1994): The world will become a more satisfying place morally, and a more pleasant place politically, as leaders and individuals alike increasingly make moral judgments in terms of ever-more-detailed international agreements specifying the rights, duties, and obligations of both state and nonstate actors. The evolving international human rights regime offers an illustration of the process. If we look over the broad sweep of history, we see a gradually thickening and deepening consensus on the minimal standards of treatment governments owe individuals. Obviously, politics is at work in this process, too. It is no accident that an essentially liberal individualist conception of human rights is gaining sway globally in an era of U.S. hegemony. Nevertheless, if we take a primarily pragmatic attitude toward moral discourse, we will embrace any specific doctrine that can, in fact, command broad and deep assent.

Where does this leave us in the meantime? It leaves us forced to acknowledge that moral debate about foreign policy is both haphazard and parochial and that the outcomes of moral debates are the results of political forces as well as philosophical deliberation. Acknowledging this forces us to do two salutary things. First, it forces us to think explicitly about the bases of our particular moral judgments. Second, it forces us to recognize the rhetorical power of moral discourse in a politically charged debate.

THE NATIONAL INTEREST

"The national interest" is a fixed feature of both diplomatic and scholarly lexicons. We use the phrase so routinely and so comfortably that we tend to believe that we understand what it means. We do not.

The concept of the national interest came to the English language relatively recently, but it has deep historical roots.[5] The ancients spoke freely of the good of the community, or the *polis*. Medieval thinkers spoke of the health of the body politic, sometimes conceived quite literally as a corporate entity (e.g., John of Salisbury 1963). Sixteenth-century Italians spoke of *ragione degli stati* (or *ragione di stato*), popularized later by Cardinal Richelieu as *raison d'état*.[6] Rousseau (1974) speaks of the "general will." In other times and places, people spoke of the interests of the fatherland, the motherland, the people, the *Volk* (folk), and so forth. What unites these notions is that they denote a common good, something that benefits a collectivity as a whole even though it might not benefit any particular individual member. They differ primarily in the nature of the community whose common good they denote. Quite naturally, as the dominant institutional expressions of political community have changed over time, the denotation has evolved. When we now speak of the national interest, we almost always mean the common good of the members of political communities organized as sovereign states not the common good of "nations"—that is, imagined communities of people united by ethnicity, language, history, culture, mythology, or kinship (Anderson 1991).

The intellectual hegemony of realpolitik in nineteenth-century European diplomatic thought, if not practice (Schroeder 1994), pulled the phrase "the national interest" into what we might now call the realist orbit, where it took on strong power-political connotations. It caught on in the interwar period in the United States, where it has enjoyed a hegemony of sorts ever since (Peffer 1945). It is difficult to find two consecutive pages of prominent journals such as *Foreign Af-*

fairs, Foreign Policy, and—of course—*The National Interest* on which the term does not appear. But what, exactly, is the content of the common good it is meant to convey? Alas, the lineage of the phrase does not help us answer this crucial question.

In modern realist discourse, "the national interest" denotes at the very least the survival of the state. As Benjamin Frankel puts it, "There is no debate among realists . . . that, at a minimum, states are worried about their security and that they act vigilantly to enhance that security in an environment which offers them no choice but to do so" (1996, ix). While this may well be *a* national interest, however, it does not seem an adequate understanding of *the* national interest. In the first place, the survival of the state is almost never at stake in international politics. States may shrink, grow, split up, or change their names and flags on occasion, but they rarely die, and when they do it is more often the result of internal disruption than international politics. Yet people routinely invoke the national interest in support of their preferred policies. It may or may not be in the U.S. national interest to contribute to open-ended peacekeeping operations in the Balkans, but the reason why or why not cannot be that the very existence of the United States hangs in the balance. What, then, *is* at stake in this decision? Money, certainly, is at stake and perhaps the lives of some American soldiers; perhaps the U.S. reputation and credibility as a world leader, and hence its future influence; perhaps American "power" (another notoriously difficult concept to pin down); possibly the vitality of international security institutions and the robustness of international norms of civilized behavior; and perhaps even Americans' self-respect. The phrase "the national interest" is elastic enough to cover any and all of these.

And that, in a nutshell, is the problem. Both as an analytical tool and as a guide to foreign policy making, the term *the national interest* is useless. In fact, it does positive harm. It has four practical and philosophical drawbacks. First, except in the rare case when the very survival of the state is at stake and the sole appropriate means of redress is obvious, the concept provides indeterminate policy guidance. No government has ever confronted an important foreign policy choice without advocates of competing and irreconcilable options managing to muster a defense of their view in terms of the national interest. Unless the concept is specified clearly enough in advance to enable us to decide which of two diametrically opposed policy options it prescribes, it can help us neither explain, nor predict, nor guide foreign policy choices. At most, it can perform a rhetorical legitimating function.

Second, the concept prevents us from asking hard questions about *whose* interest the phrase actually denotes. Most foreign policy options threaten to harm certain segments of society but also to benefit others. Whose interest counts as the "national" interest? that of the majority? the elite? right-thinking people? whoever just so happens to prevail in the political process?

Third, interesting foreign policy problems threaten certain values that leaders and citizens hold and at the same time present opportunities to promote others. They require leaders to make trade-offs among security, welfare, order, justice, reputation, and a multitude of other important things. The phrase "the national interest" masks exactly which values leaders are attempting to promote and which they are willing to sacrifice. It encourages neither decision makers nor analysts to confront value trade-offs explicitly and scrutinize them closely.

Fourth, and finally, the phrase is superfluous. We can always do without it. We can describe the stakes, goals, and values implicated in any foreign policy choice in plain language, and we can do so in a way that is more precise and more helpful than if we subsume all of them under the rubric of a single generic term. At no point in the description, explanation, prediction, or advocacy of foreign policy do we need to invoke "the national interest," and never do we gain by doing so.

IMPLICATIONS

It is plain that the national interest cannot stand in any particular relation to morality unless we specify the meanings of each more precisely. I would argue, however, that the common view that the two somehow stand in opposition to each other is the least plausible view of all, both as a matter of logic and as a matter of historical usage. "The national interest" can rarely be understood as synonymous with "amoral selfishness" or "egoism." Whatever we mean by it in any given case, we use it to denote things that people (we or others) do, in fact, value or things that we feel people ought to value. When we say that state leaders *ought* to be guided by the national interest, we are saying that this is the moral thing for them to do. When Hans Morgenthau and George Kennan argue that the national interest ought to guide American foreign policy, they are arguing merely that an unsentimental realism is the surest road to the statesman's highest *moral* goal: the preservation of the state. On this view, Woodrow Wilson was not wrong because he sought guidance in his foreign policy from "morality." He was wrong because he pursued an unattainable moral goal. Used in this way, the phrase "the national interest" is itself a moral concept, and it cannot stand in opposition to "morality" (Kersch 1995).[7]

But both the concept of the national interest and the notion that it stands in opposition to morality are ideas central to historical and contemporary foreign policy discourse. We might be better off abolishing the one and using the other both more reflectively and more precisely, but usage is not something particularly amenable to change by fiat. What is to be done?

We can, at least, bear witness to the tragic consequence of current usage: namely, that it prevents us from acknowledging the role that morality (and *whose* morality) plays in foreign policy—in both our own foreign policy and that of other states. This masking effect makes it more difficult for states to pursue moral goals and also represents a permissive cause of international conflict.

There is a curious tendency for scholars, politicians, and the interested public alike to interpret the actions of state leaders through the lens of instrumental rationality and to assume that the goals they pursue are narrowly self-interested. Typically, when we attempt to understand the foreign policy of a state, we begin by asking, "How is it that this particular policy promotes the power of the state, its economic interest, or the personal political power of its leaders?" When Argentina invaded the Falkland/Malvinas Islands in 1982, for example, the natural tendency in the English-speaking world was to assume that the purpose of the invasion was to divert the attentions and political energies of the Argentine people from their economic plight and to bolster the Junta's public standing, not to correct a 150-year-old historical injustice that had simply become intolerable, as the Junta claimed (e.g., Calvert 1982; Dobson, Miller, and Payne 1982; Eddy et al. 1982; Levy and Vakili 1992). Yet if the vast majority of human beings constantly make moral judgments and act on them, and if moral judgment is part and parcel of human nature, why should political leaders be different? There is no compelling reason to suspect that they are somehow immune to moral impulses or that when they invoke morality, they do so disingenuously. In fact, the evidence now shows conclusively that moral motivations drove Argentine policy in 1982 (Freedman and Gamba-Stonehouse 1990; Welch 1997). The fact that most people in the English-speaking world did not sympathize with the Junta's moral judgments does not mean that they were insincere.

Supposing that leaders of states make moral judgments and act on them does not, of course, imply that they are indifferent to their own political fortunes or to the welfare and security of their states. We all know from our own experiences that the opportunity for personal gain often stands in tension with our moral commitments and that the desire to do the moral thing is not always the more powerful motivation. Most people at one time or another have been given more change than they are owed when they make a purchase at the store. Some return the difference; others quietly pocket it and walk away. Nevertheless, we are likely to err very often if we always cynically interpret the behavior of leaders as narrowly self-interested.

The tendency to interpret political action as narrowly self-interested and to dismiss the moral claims leaders make in defense of their actions as rationalization or as cant leads to systematic errors in judgment. An effective foreign policy—one that serves whatever ends leaders choose to pursue—requires accurately identifying others' goals, grievances, and desires; accurately determining what will or will not satisfy them; and, perhaps, accurately gauging what threats or actions will deter them or inflame them. Presupposing that no matter how much one's adversary articulates his or her demands in the language of morality or justice he or she is *really* motivated by the opportunity for gain can lead to a disastrous policy response in cases in which the adversary is being entirely honest. It will lead to errors in judgment about the kinds of concessions that will satisfy demands or about the kinds of threats that will quiet them. This is because people, while generally willing to accept side payments or compromises in cases in which they are seeking simple advantages, are categorical in their demands that the requirements of morality or justice as they conceive it be fulfilled and are easily enraged when these are not. They become more strident and take greater risks in the face of resistance and threats when they are driven by moral impulses. They do not become more cautious (Lerner 1975; Welch 1993).

If it is crucially important that leaders accurately identify the motives and objectives of other states when they craft foreign policy, they and the analysts upon whom they rely for expert judgment must overcome the prevalent tendency to interpret all state behavior as narrowly self-interested. This is a difficult task given the extent to which realist and rationalist assumptions about human nature and state behavior dominate the analysis of international relations. Unlike sociologists, anthropologists, and psychologists, scholars of international politics are relatively insensitive to moral motivations, and our conceptual armamentarium is ill-equipped to deal with them.

Of course, there will always be cases in which we would be right to be suspicious about the moral professions of political leaders, as well as cases in which the error of crediting those professions could lead to disasters at least as severe as the error of failing to credit them when they are sincere. Neville Chamberlain's credulity in the face of Hitler's repeated claims that he merely sought to correct the injustices of Versailles must be accounted one of the principal reasons for the failure of appeasement (Rock 1977; Welch 1993, 141–47). But the historical record seems to suggest that the error of *underestimating* the sincerity of states' moral claims is much more frequent than the error of *overestimating* it, possibly because we are naturally inclined to suspect the sincerity of claims with which we do not sympathize.

Once we become aware of the fact that virtually all leaders of states routinely make decisions on the basis of moral motivations, the practical value of attempting to promote common understandings of the requirements of morality becomes apparent. Universal moral consensus is unlikely even over the very long term, but short of this there is ample room for a useful narrowing of differences. Disciplining the invocation of "morality" is thus itself a moral imperative. It is one we can better pursue if we strive to purge moral debate of hopelessly vague rhetorical phrases that mask the true nature of leaders' motives and goals.

I come therefore not to praise the national interest but to bury it.

NOTES

1. "Realists" of different stripes variously embrace the first, second, and fourth positions, a point that emerges from a close reading of Nick Fotion's excellent discussion of realism in the next chapter (Fotion uses the term *self-interest* instead of *the national interest*, but the two are equivalent).

2. Duncker writes, "The same act, being the same with regard to all meanings involved, has never been observed to incur different valuations. That is to say: within the same pattern of situational meanings only one of two contrary behaviors can lay claim to the same ethical quality and valuation. There are, then, general 'inner laws' of ethical valuation, the independent variables of which are meanings" (1939, 50).

3. This dynamic was poignantly illustrated in the international reaction to the recent NATO intervention in Kosovo. See, for example, Wines 1999.

4. It is no wonder that China so deeply resents resistance to its joining the World Trade Organization, for example. China has the world's third-largest economy, and yet Western countries insist that China first satisfy Western moral demands before taking what the Chinese consider its rightful place in the world trading system.

5. See Pangle 1976. For more extensive examination of the evolution of realism, for which the national interest has become a central concept, see Pangle and Ahrensdorf 1999. My comments in the next several paragraphs have been greatly informed by debate about the origins of the concept on the listserv H-DIPLO, August–October 1998, and in particular by the very helpful remarks of Brian Etheridge, Dane Hartgrove, Reid Rozen, and Sérgio Rodriguez.

6. Meinecke (1962) traces the notion back to Thucydides' *Melian Dialogue*.

7. Although Morgenthau would disagree vehemently with my criticisms of the concept of the national interest, he would endorse my second point wholeheartedly: "The equation of political moralism with morality and of political realism with immorality is itself untenable. The choice is not between moral principles and the national interest, devoid of moral dignity, but between one set of moral principles, divorced from political reality, and another set of moral principles, derived from political reality" (1950, 853–54). Indeed, Morgenthau goes even further: "The antithesis between moral principles and the national interest is not only intellectually mistaken, but morally pernicious. A foreign policy derived from the national interest is in fact morally superior to a foreign policy inspired by universal moral principles" (1950, 854).

PART II

JUST WAR THEORY

2

Reactions to War: Pacifism, Realism, and Just War Theory

Nicholas Fotion

War has had its horrors, even from its inception when the main weapons available were the spear, dagger, mace, sling, and bow (Ferrill 1985, 189). The bloody business of hacking someone to death at close quarters may have enthralled some, but others wearied of or were repelled by such acts. Often the aftermath of war, such as the slaughter of the elderly, women, and children in a besieged city that had just fallen, had its own horrors. Then there were the horrors that followed in the wake of war, starvation and disease, which often put more people in their graves than the war itself.

These horrors were not, and still are not, occasional human experiences. The threat of attack may in fact have been one of the main motives for people coming together to live in communities—fortified ones (Ferrill 1985, 27). There have been thousands of wars since the Bronze Age, and even as early as the age of the Mongols the killings were in the hundreds of thousands and, at times, the millions (Kwanton 1979, 121). In this century, World Wars I and II caused 10 and 55 million deaths respectively (Addington 1984, 157, 248). And even today there are scores of little, but nonetheless shockingly bloody, wars in progress throughout the world. Thus, it is not surprising that people have been thinking about war almost as soon as it came into existence and ever since. Some of this thinking, such as Sun Tzu's *The Art of War* (1983) and Clausewitz's *On War* (1976), focuses mainly on how to wage war. Because war is such a nasty business, these and other writers, such as Jomini (1974) and Mahan (1957), were presumably encouraged to make sure that their sides did not come out second best. Others were concerned with the right and wrong of war. The horrors of war encouraged them to think about what role, if any, morality has to play in war. Over the years, this thinking has yielded three lines or branches of thought: pacifism, realism, and just war theory. It is these lines of thought that will be the focus of attention in this chapter.

PACIFISM

The first of these lines, pacifism, is both easy and difficult to understand. It is easy because experiencing, observing, and even learning about the horrors of war tempt almost all of us to the conviction that war is immoral and, thus, should be forbidden. After all, war seems to allow just about everything that ethics forbids. In war there is killing, maiming, torture, rape, theft, lying, and so on—all in wholesale proportions. But pacifism is not easy to understand because it is surprisingly difficult to find honest-to-goodness full-bodied pacifists.

Full-bodied pacifists argue that because of war's underlying immorality, people should choose not to participate in war under any circumstances. So they will not participate in a war in which their nation is the aggressor or when they and their nation are under attack. In addition, as full-bodied pacifists, they will urge those around them not to participate in any war effort. They will urge them not to kill, even if by not killing an aggressor, their lives and the lives of their family members and their friends are put at risk. Pacifists will also encourage their government not to enter any wars and urge it, as well, to back away from any war in which it might already be involved.

Initially, the appearance that full-bodied pacifists give is of passivity. But this is misleading. Pacifists, even of the full-bodied variety, could resist war; but they would do so without resorting to violence, that is, without using weapons to kill or physically harm others. A country of pacifists might, for example, be conquered because its members would not have resisted the aggressor's attack. But once conquered, they could engage in work slowdowns, civil disobedience, and other troublesome practices that would make the lives of the occupiers miserable and costly. Such practices would be consistent with their pacifism, as would be various love-thy-neighbor policies.

One can see why it is difficult to find full-bodied pacifists. It would take a rare kind of moral strength to act on such convictions. Of course that strength might be more readily sustained if pacifists understood the "why" of their own position. So far the discussion has focused on the content of pacifism: namely, to be a pacifist, one does not resort to violence under any circumstances. The why gives us the reasons behind the position. The why for one group of pacifists might be religious. Their God or their Teacher commands, urges, or invites them never to resort to violence (Hauerwas 1986).[1] They may not understand any further why, that is, why they have been given these commands. But if they have faith in their God or Teacher, their pacifism would have all the justification they require. It would now, for them, be only a question of whether they were strong enough to carry out their leader's commands and thereby follow the pacifist doctrine consistently.

Other full-bodied pacifists might accept a different "why" account. Intuitionists in ethics might appeal to moral insights having absolute status (i.e., ones without exceptions) such as the idea that it is wrong to kill innocents. Knowing that wars always kill innocents, they would then oppose all wars. Quite naturally they would express their views by saying that their conscience forbids them to participate in any way in any war (Holmes 1989).[2] Other pacifists might take a different tack. They might point to the bad consequences of war. This justification usually dwells on the horrors of war in the form of reports, photos, or videos of row upon row of the dead, weeping widows, wounded children, starving civilians, burned villages, and destroyed cities. It is also often supported by one-liners such as "War never solves any problems" and "Violence breeds more violence." But in the end, this consequentialist (most likely utilitarian) view of full-bodied pacifism makes the claim that when all the consequences of war are taken into account, wars always do more harm than good. Therefore, when all things are considered in a situation in which wars might take or are taking place, the moral or ethical thing to do is never to take part in such activity.

As was noted already, part of the difficulty many have with understanding pacifism is just the difficulty of living the doctrine. Only angels, it seems, could actually be full-bodied pacifists. The other part is with understanding non-full-bodied pacifists. These pacifists hedge their moral commitment in opposing war. They usually offer to those who will listen claims that war is evil, wrong, inhuman, and the like. On the face of it, these claims leave us with the impression that we are dealing with full-bodied pacifists. Supporting this impression are, perhaps, negative statements they make about one war after another. Looking at their stance on just about any particular war, they are on record as opposing it. Often their stance is backed by claims that a corrupt government, big business, and the military have all manipulated the nation into a war frenzy. So, for them, what seems like a justified war is in reality not. The war rhetoric is, perhaps, just a cover for another oil grab. Yet in spite of all this, our non-full-bodied pacifists make no explicit claim that going to war is in principle out of the question ethically for them. They do not, as the full-bodied pacifists do, deny that some war could be found that they would (ethically) support. As we will see shortly, the difficulty is that these "de facto" pacifists sound very much like very cautious just war theorists. The same can be said for nuclear pacifists who adopt a "never-never" posture about the use of nuclear weapons but no such posture concerning conventional war.

REALISM

In contrast to pacifists who say war is immoral, what can be called full-bodied realists say it is nonmoral.[3] This claim will be qualified in a bit, but for now we can take their nonmoralist stance about war as involving two claims. First, there are no significant moral relationships between nations the way there are between people who live within a society.[4] People can morally help or hurt one another in a variety of ways. When they, for example, keep their promises, we praise them; when they fail to do so, we condemn them. But promise keeping and other moral relationships do not apply between nations because they are in a state of nature with respect to one another. Thus, when a nation is considering going to war with another nation, it does not have to consult moral reasons that take that other nation into account. Even if it decides to start an aggressive war, it does no moral wrong.

Second, once a war starts, moral considerations are again inappropriate. Thus, warring nations cannot be criticized for how they fight the war. If they kill wounded enemy soldiers, shoot at enemy sailors in lifeboats, kill prisoners, attack civilians, "liberate" enemy property, and do other such things, they do no moral wrong.[5] They certainly harm the enemy by doing all these things, but they do no moral harm to them.

Full-bodied realists might summarize their position by saying that ethics and war do not mix.[6] It is an oxymoron to talk about starting and fighting wars ethically. That, then, represents the "what" or the content of the position. But what about the "why"? What reasons do these realists give for holding to their position? Like the pacifists, they are not united when the why question is raised. Some will present a why account as follows. There is no real moral or legal authority over nations to tell them how they ought to behave on an international stage filled with mean-spirited actors.[7] To survive on this stage a nation has to look after its own interests and nothing else. If one nation attacks another in order to harvest the abundant oil supply in that other nation, the only question the attacker should ask is, Will the attack profit us? If the nation under attack is weak militarily, if no one is willing to come to its aid, and, further, if there are few political costs to attacking, then, yes, it is profitable. On such an account, the world stage is obviously a jungle, not a garden of Eden.

Other realists give us variations on this why account. As full-bodied realists they still insist that self-interest animates what nations do, but they add that it is not a matter of choice as to how nations act. The realists discussed in the previous paragraph could in theory allow for ethical considerations to affect their behavior. They could say that if ethics actually played a role on the international stage (which, of course, for them it does not), they could in theory choose to act in accordance with ethical rules and principles. They probably still would not so choose, but the possibility of choosing is there. In contrast, the realists we are now considering say that the threat of war and war itself make it physically and psychologically impossible for a nation to do anything but act in its self-interest. These "inability" realists say that the stakes in war are so high that no nation can (is able to) sit down and rationally consider what the right and wrong of going to war and fighting are. If a nation faces an invader, it can lose everything—

including its people and its cultural heritage. Thus, it has no choice but to fight on a "no holds barred" basis.[8] If, as philosophers tell us, we are obligated to do only what we are able to (can) do ("Ought implies can," as it is often expressed), then we cannot be obligated to act ethically if it is literally beyond our means to do so.

Actually there are two versions of this inability realist position. The first limits our inability to act ethically to serious matters such as wars. The second generalizes our limitations by claiming that we cannot help but (try to) act exclusively in our self-interest in all our dealings with other human beings both in war and peace.[9] For our purposes, it will not matter which version is adopted by realists, for it all comes to the same thing in war. In calculating what they should do, both kinds will omit making moral calculations, and, thus, both will not consider the welfare of the enemy in whatever calculations they make.

There will be differences, however, in dealing with non-full-bodied realists. These are the thinkers one usually meets in the political science literature (Rosenthal 1991).[10] They might, semiseriously, be called weak-kneed realists, for, unlike their full-bodied brethren, they do not "go all the way." They normally talk tough by saying that nations must act in their self-interest, but it is not always clear whether they mean "act in their self-interest exclusively" or "act in their self-interest but, at times, take the interests of others into account."[11] If their position is the latter, then, we will shortly see that, as with some "weak-kneed" pacifists, it is difficult to tell them apart from certain just war theorists.

Before turning to a discussion of just war theorists, three comments on realism are in order. First, even if realists do not follow moral principles, they can still act in accordance with them. Sun Tzu recommends to his ruler that he treat prisoners well. He then adds that there is profit in doing so because well-treated prisoners can then be used to augment the size of the ruler's army (1983, 14). Here Sun Tzu is not following a moral rule. He is involved instead in a recruitment program. Indeed, he is probably not even thinking morally at all. Rather, he is recommending actions that are merely in accordance with moral principles, that is, actions that just happen to run parallel with morality at least in some situations. It is not clear what Sun Tzu would say and do if the prisoners refused to take the recruitment bait and, worse still, represented a burden to the ruler.

Another way a "ruler" might act in accordance with, but not follow, moral principles is as follows. Assume our ruler has no interest in acting morally, for whatever reason. But he knows that other nations have an interest in it, and some of these other nations are either friendly to his nation or allied with it. He cannot afford to alienate these nations. So he pretends to follow the moral path, all the while waiting for that moment when he can get away with leading his country down the nonmoral path of profit to his nation—and probably to himself.

Insofar as realist rulers can mimic moral behavior (for reasons of self-interest of course), they will not necessarily give the appearance of "heavies" on the international stage. They may look for all the world like morally decent actors.

Presumably, if they had the military strength of Genghis Khan, Napoleon, or Hitler, there would be less need to mimic. At least up to a point, these rulers would simply employ their power overtly and probably not act in ways that are even in accordance with the principles of morality.

The second comment pertains to the claim that realism represents a nonmoral stance with respect to war. This claim, I said, needs qualifying. The reason it does is that some realists claim that their recommendations actually fall within the ethical domain. If a distinction is made between the ethics of individuals and the nation (or state), their claim is that their position on war is compatible only with the latter (Niebuhr 1932, 83).[12] The form that national ethics takes is just that of the rulers doing their duty to protect the state and the people within it. In theory, this position could be expanded to say that overall more good is done within the state, and even throughout the world, if rulers make it their business to take care of their own people first and foremost. In this expanded form, then, these realists could claim that they are indirectly taking account of the interests of "foreigners." But this is a dubious claim because in carrying out their duties to their own, rulers could order attacks on and even the elimination of those who are not their own. In the nonexpanded form, this position is a variant of ethical egoism. It says that we have duties only to our own. But insofar as it, too, ignores the interests of others (by definition), its recommendations are, in principle, no different from those of the full-bodied realist. It might be said, then, that although technically this position is a moral one, in practice it is nonmoral.

The third and final comment on realism has to do with more variations on the position. Because realism is a two-part theory, dealing with conditions for starting a war and those for fighting it, the possibility arises that there are realists about one part but not the other. Henry Kissinger sounds like a realist with respect to diplomacy when he says, "In the next century, America's leaders will have to articulate for their public a concept of national interest" (1994, 810). But nowhere does he suggest that if diplomacy leads to war, America should fight the way realists might allow a nation to fight, by, for example, encouraging the killing of prisoners, raping of women, and pillaging. In contrast, William Tecumseh Sherman seems to assume that morality in the form of a social contract has a place during peacetime. But once the war starts, the transgressor must pay. In his classic statement about these matters, he says,

> You cannot qualify war in harsher terms than I will. War is cruelty, and you cannot refine it; and those who brought war into our country deserve all the curses and maledictions a people can pour out. . . . You might as well appeal against a thunderstorm as against these terrible hardships of war. They are inevitable, and the only way the people of Atlanta can hope once more to live in peace and quiet at home, is to stop the war, which can only be done by admitting that it began in error and is perpetuated by pride. [1892, 126]

In sum, realism is a highly variable position that one way or another rejects or diminishes the role of ethics in war. In is extreme form, what it says is that anything is fair when it comes to war, which is a roundabout way of saying that fairness (justice) and war have nothing to do with one another.

JUST WAR THEORY

If pacifism represents one extreme in saying wars are immoral, and full-bodied realism represents the other in saying that they are nonmoral, just war theory sits someplace in the middle between them. It says that some wars are, while others are not, immoral. Sitting in the middle makes the position vulnerable to attack from both sides. It is vulnerable for another reason. Pacifism and realism proved to be difficult to understand because each represents not one but several related but distinct positions. We will see that what is true about the extreme positions is even more true about just war theory.

The tradition of just war theory is a long one. The most familiar part in the West goes back to the Christians and especially, during the fourth and fifth centuries A.D., to St. Augustine (1984).[13] Faced with the reality of supporting a recently Christianized Roman Empire, Augustine found that he had to come to terms with war. He could not easily adopt a pacifist stance toward war as some of the earlier unempowered Christians did. Because, during his time, the empire was under attack from various "heathen" peoples, he had to consider urging Christians to go to war. So he faced this reality and, in the process, articulated some of the principles of just war theory as we know them today. These include the principle of just cause (i.e., a nation or empire must have good reasons for going to war) and proper authorization (i.e., only certain legally situated officials can take a nation to war) among others. Later, in the thirteenth century, St. Thomas Aquinas (1974) developed just war theory still more,[14] but he did so, as did Augustine, within the framework of the Church. Still later, especially with the work of Hugo Grotius (1925), that tradition became secularized.

However, the just war tradition is much older than the part most familiar to us. Before St. Augustine, St. Ambrose writes on this subject, but before him there is a tradition of just war theory that goes back to the Romans and even to the Greeks. Cicero among the former and both Plato and Aristotle among the latter write about the moral issues facing leaders and soldiers when they go to war. But the just war tradition is not wholly a Western one. In China, Mo Tzu and Mencius both write about the injustices facing people and the necessity, at times, of taking up arms to remedy these injustices. And in India we find a discussion of war and the ethics of war in *The Laws of Manu* (1991) and the *Bhadavad Gita* (1968). So the tradition of just war theory is truly intercultural.

As we know it today, just war theory possesses a certain amount of uniformity. Most contemporary followers of the theory agree on what the structure of the theory is and what the principles that make it up are. About the structure, a division is made between *jus ad bellum* (justice of the war) and *jus in bello* (justice in the war). This distinction corresponds roughly to the one we found in the discussion of realism. Recall that full-bodied realists say that morality has no role to play with respect to both starting a war and how the war is fought. Corresponding to this distinction, just war theorists argue that there are principles for helping a nation determine when it is morally justified in going to war (justice of the war) and how that war is to be morally fought (justice in the war).

JUSTICE OF THE WAR

The principles or criteria related to justice of the war usually come to six. The first, already anticipated in the earlier reference to Augustine, is just cause. This criterion can also be called righteous cause, the justification or the "very good reasons" criterion. None of these names is especially helpful in understanding what concrete reason will morally permit a nation to go to war. Realizing this, just war theorists give more content to this criterion by saying that any one of the following subcriteria will satisfy. If nation A aggresses and thus victimizes nation V in the sense that A's military forces cross the border into V uninvited, engage in wholesale destruction and occupy parts of V, then V is justified in responding. So national self-defense counts as a very good reason for entering into war. Or if A aggresses against F, a friend or ally of V, then V can justifiably enter into the war even if it has not been attacked itself. Another subcriterion concerns A's aggressive behavior against its own people. If the government of A, in consort with a large ethnic group in that nation, savages one of the other ethnic groups in A to the point that it is practicing genocide, then again V can justifiably enter the war on humanitarian grounds. This, of course, is the criterion appealed to by NATO when it attacked Yugoslavia (Serbia) over what was happening in Kosovo in 1999.[15]

Another subcriterion is often presented by just war theorists, but this one is more controversial. It is said that preemptive strikes are justified. If, for example, V is living under a clear and present threat of attack from A, it can strike first (Walzer 1992, 80–85). In part it can do so because if it were to wait to be attacked before responding, it would risk suffering mortal damage. But this subcriterion requires that there be a clear threat. This means that V must have evidence that A is going to attack. This evidence can be in the form of documents, satellite reports, various other intelligence reports, announcements from A that it will attack, and so on. But this subcriterion requires that the threat be a present one as well. This means that the attack must be imminent. It will happen in a matter of hours or days. A preemptive strike in war is a bit like the good cowboy who shoots first but only because the bad cowboy has reached for his gun first.

Although a preemptive strike counts as a good reason for entering a war, a preventive strike does not, according to just war theory. A preventive strike deals with a threat that is not imminent (or present). Rather, it is months or years away.

We will see shortly why preventive strikes fail to satisfy the just cause criterion. But it is useful at this point to note some other subcriteria that fail to meet the just cause standard. One large group deals with selfish reasons for starting a war. If A starts a war because it wants V's or F's oil, uranium, land, technologies, people, or other resources, then it starts war wrongly. These kinds of wars, started by A, are classically the ones we call wars of aggression.

Under the just cause heading, just war theory also condemns what can best be called ideological war. This kind of war starts because one side is convinced that it has the truth about life and how society should be structured. It also desires to spread the truth. This messianic spirit might be in the hearts of some powerful Communists, capitalists, followers of Islam, Christians, or others. Whatever the ideology being preached, the followers believe they are acting morally. After all, they are spreading the word in order to save the world from some evil. To be sure, there will be some individuals and groups within the "saved" society so corrupted that they will have to be destroyed. That is to be regretted. But, thank goodness, most will be saved. Still, in the process of spreading the truth, the true believers realize that they might very well have to go to war, possibly a war that others will label aggressive.

The reason just war theory condemns this sort of thinking is not easy to explain. In part it has to do with the tolerant attitude toward religion and political ideologies built up in the liberal Western tradition that goes back at least as far as the eighteenth century. An older tradition of tolerance is found in the East in such religious traditions as Buddhism, and that plays a role here too. Whatever the historical source of the argument, the argument itself often is presented against a background of skepticism. Karl, Robert, Mohammed, or Peter may each fervently believe in his own ideology, but none can easily present evidence to prove that his ideology is correct. Lacking such evidence, so the argument goes, one should be reluctant to practice coercion to try to bring about true belief among all.

As a general criterion for determining when wars are just and when they are not, then, just cause cuts both ways. It tells us positively what conditions need to apply before one can seriously consider war as a moral option; and it tells us negatively what conditions must not apply. If one of the negative conditions fits the situation, then the nation to which it applies is automatically disqualified from starting a just war. However, if one of the positive conditions fits the nation involved, it is not automatically justified in starting a just war. If one of the subcriteria (e.g., self-defense) applies, this only establishes a necessary condition for going to war under the banner of just war theory. This criterion is needed, but other criteria are needed as well.

A second, needed, criterion is called good intentions. In the past this criterion was read as saying that a nation should not enter a war with hate in its heart. Nowadays, good intentions usually means something a little easier to measure and a little less demanding. It now means that the nation enters a war with the intent to act in accordance with the just cause that prompted the war. So if V responds to A's aggression, the good intention of V will be to simply stop the aggression and, perhaps, punish the wrongdoers. V will not use the start of that war as an excuse, later, to gain territory it has always coveted. In the 1990–91 Gulf War, the United States and its allies could be said to have acted with good intentions because they repelled the Iraqi aggression against Kuwait and then went home. The United States and its allies, for instance, did not use the war as an excuse to occupy Kuwait and those parts of Iraq that they overran during the war.[16] Although the criterion of good intentions is listed under the justice of the war heading, it should be clear that it "bleeds over" onto the justice in the war heading. After all, it is only after the war is well under way and, in some cases, after it is over that we can tell how good the intentions of the good nation really are.

A third criterion is proportionality. Speaking roughly, this means that the anticipated cost of fighting the war should not be out of line with the benefits. But, in turn, what this means is not often made clear. Does it mean that a war is just only if the anticipated benefits are greater than the anticipated costs? Or is a war just if the costs and benefits are about equal? Of course, there is the other problem of how costs and benefits are to be measured. How, for instance, are the benefits of going to war in order to deter future aggressors to be measured? In truth, because of the ambiguity of the criterion and the measurement problem, the principle of proportionality is not a very powerful criterion. It is also not powerful because it is often difficult to predict just how long wars will last and how nasty they will get. The only good this criterion does is to remind us not to go to war when the anticipated costs of doing so are obviously overwhelmingly greater than the benefits. Thus, during the Cold War it would have been a violation of this principle to start World War III, nuclear weapons and all, in order to free Estonia from Soviet oppression. So even if the just cause criterion would permit another world war, the principle of proportionality would act as a veto in theory. It commands, instead, that some other means besides war be found to bring about Estonian freedom.

The fourth criterion is likelihood of success. This and the previous criterion are somewhat related because they both deal with consequences. This criterion says that if no good consequences result from going to war, usually because the country thinking about going to war is overmatched militarily, then that country should not go to war. The classic example here is Luxembourg. Squeezed as it is between France and Germany, when it is invaded by one or the other, there is not much point in resisting. Only bad consequences will come from resisting with the end result being inevitable. This criterion is like proportionality in another respect, in that it is not very powerful. The situations to which it might apply are minimal. Still, as it occasionally helps guide nations in deciding whether to fight, it has a proper place in the justice of the war portion of just war theory.

The fifth criterion, last resort, is more important. Some take this principle as urging the move to war only after no stone has been left unturned. But expressing last resort in this way is probably more hyperbole than good advice because the process of looking at all the options is literally endless. There is always another negotiating move, sanction, political maneuver, boycott, and so on, to be tried before firing the guns and unleashing the missiles. So probably last resort should be taken as meaning something like last *reasonable* resort. In effect it discourages trigger-happy responses when one is provoked or when some other situation that could be taken as a just cause for starting a war applies. The principle favors cool over hot heads.

The sixth and final criterion under justice of the war, legitimate authority, is a bit different from the rest in that it does not directly tell us how to deal with an impending war. Rather, it tells us that only certain people are authorized to make the decision whether to go or not go to war. The authorized ones are not private citizens, private organizations, generals, business leaders, or political science professors but, rather, only those governmental leaders who have the legal authority to send a nation to war.

JUSTICE IN THE WAR

In contrast to the justice of the war criteria, which do their work before the war starts, the justice in the war criteria do their work after it starts. Usually two criteria are cited. The first is proportionality, once again, only now with respect to costs and benefits of doing things in war. Thus, battle plans to cross a particular river are condemned by the principle if they lead to a victory but do so with high costs that could have been avoided had some other plan been adopted. But the principle also condemns killing enemy wounded in battle, or later for that matter, because the cost in human lives (to the enemy) is not balanced by any significant military gain. The same holds true for harm done to prisoners. Mistreating and even killing prisoners does not normally lead to an end to the war the way killing armed enemy soldiers does.

The second principle of justice in the war is called discrimination. Somehow or other those in war are supposed to discriminate so that some of the enemy are targets of a legitimate attack while others are not. A not wholly satisfactory, but still serviceable, way of discriminating is in terms of who is and who is not in uniform. If an enemy force attacked only those in uniform, it would attack chaplains and medical personnel as well as fighters, but at least it would leave the aged, (civilian) women, and children alone. In short, if followed, this principle would significantly curtail the slaughter of war. However, some have argued that not only should chaplains and medical personnel not be targeted but certain groups who are not in uniform should be. These might include guerrilla fighters but also those who work in factories that directly produce military equipment and supplies. Railroad workers who help bring this equipment and supplies to the front lines are also said by some to be legitimate targets.

So it might be suggested that a better way to discriminate is in terms of the degree to which individuals and groups participate in the war effort. This suggests that there is no bright line between those who can legitimately be targeted and those who cannot. And that seems right. To some extent, then, it will depend on the circumstances. In a very short war, for example, it would be unjust to attack even munitions workers. Although their contributions to the war effort are direct, the timing is such that the war would be over before the munitions they are producing when they are attacked would reach the front line. It would be another matter in a serious and protracted war. Attacking these workers, and perhaps attacking as well their means of transportation to work, might now be legitimate. Here is another example that shows that the line between those who participate and those who do not is not bright. In the 1990–91 Gulf War the coalition forces attacked bridges that were jointly used by civilians and the Iraqi military. Some of these bridges probably should have been attacked, and others should not have been. Bridges both near the front lines and used heavily by the military were no doubt legitimate targets. But others far from the front lines and used mainly by civilians probably should not have been targeted—especially because it was quickly obvious that the war was not going to last very long. However, surely there were other bridges in between the extremes for which it is difficult to say what should have been done.[17]

One way, then, to deal with the moral issues inherent in fighting a war is in terms of the dual principles of proportionality and discrimination. There is another way. Instead of identifying two very general principles, some prefer to identify a series of less general rules or guidelines. These intuitively inclined thinkers might produce for us an almost random list of rules that would include the following:

1. Double tapping (i.e., shooting a wounded enemy soldier as one moves through the battlefield during battle—in order to keep from being shot in the back) is not permitted.
2. Looting civilian homes and other property is forbidden.
3. Taking personal property (e.g., Rolex watches) from prisoners is forbidden.
4. Rape of either civilian or enemy military women is forbidden.
5. It is forbidden to attack any enemy medical facilities.
6. Religious institutions are not to be attacked.
7. Enemy prisoners are not to be tortured, brainwashed, or deprived of food, clothing, medical treatment, and housing.
8. Enemy prisoners are not to be used for doing military work.

The list could go on.

Whichever way one chooses, the principles or rules in the justice in the war portion of just war theory restrict the horrors of war to a significant degree. Further, the content of these principles and rules is supposed to be clear enough to act as a guide for those who are willing to be guided by the theory. Together with the justice of the war portion of the theory, the guidance the theory gives us is complete. That is the claim. But in another sense the theory is surely not complete. In focusing thus far on the content (the "what are you supposed to do" portion) of the theory, very little has been said about the why (the justification) portion. Indeed, some would argue that there is no theory without the why. Theory involves, it is said, not only pulling together many aspects of the subject matter but also giving an explanation as to why the parts pulled together, and not some other parts, belong in the theory.

But, immediately, when talking about justifying a theory we face a problem. When reading in the literature on the topic of just war theory it becomes quickly apparent that there is little agreement on the why question. One writer justifies a version of the what portion of just war theory by appealing to the tradition of the Church (U.S. Catholic Bishops 1986), while another takes a rights-based approach (Walzer 1992). Still another appeals to some medium-level "intuitive principles" (Childress 1986),[18] while yet another appeals to some version of a contract theory (Rawls 1993a). There are also utilitarian defenses of just war theory (Brandt 1979; Fotion 1997; Hare 1979a). One consoling aspect of this problem is that it is not one that plagues just war theory alone. Pacifism has the same problem. As we have seen, some pacifists arrive at their convictions by appealing to tradition, others to rights, others to general principles, and still others to utility. Beyond that, this why problem plagues all of ethics in a way that it does not plague science. Listen to Annette Baier on the subject: "Where do we have genuine and useful theories? Primarily in science—but there we find a plurality of them primarily over time, rather [as in ethics] at a time. We certainly do not find some engineers building bridges or spaceships by application of one theory, while others at the same time are applying another different theory" (1989, 33–34). Baier concludes that the variety of available theories at any one time means that theories are worthless. But one need not draw this conclusion. The fact that several general justification-type theories of ethics converge on just war theory (or pacifism) no more shows that they and just war theory are worthless than the fact that several highways converge on New York City shows that they are worthless. Theories are useful instruments for ordering our thinking, and we do not need to insist that only one theory does this best. So just war theory (and pacifism) can be justified or explained in many ways, one way emphasizing one aspect of just war theory, another emphasizing a different aspect.

SOME CONCLUDING COMMENTS

Four final comments about just war theory help to give a better sense of how the theory is to be used and what it can and cannot do. First, it should be noted that the principles in both the "of" and "in" portions of the theory are not ordered in any significant way. There are no clear statements within the theory that tell us whether one or another principle should receive priority or extra weight because it is more central than other principles. It is true that just cause and perhaps last resort receive more attention than the rest. Still these principles have no more than a checklist status when it comes to theory application. The leader who is thinking about going to war checks off whether there is a just cause leading to war and then moves on to the other principles in the "of" portion of the theory. The key here is not satisfying any one principle more than another but, rather, making sure that each one is satisfied before the leader orders the guns to be fired. As we have seen already, at least in the "of" portion of the theory, each principle acts as a necessary but not sufficient condition for war. The necessary and sufficient condition is achieved when a positive answer favoring war has been arrived at for each and every one of the criteria. The situation is somewhat different for the "in" portion of the theory. There will, of course, be situations in the war in which commanders and fighters will have to decide to shoot or not shoot by taking account of both the proportionality and the discrimination principles. But there will be times in war when the principle of discrimination will have no application. A sea battle between two naval forces is an example here. Another example is a land battle in the desert as in World War II between the British Eighth Army and General Erwin Rommel's forces. Most of the land portion of the Gulf War was also fought in settings where the principle of discrimination had no application. In all of these situations it was mainly the principle of proportionality that needed to be consulted.

Second, there is a significant difference between just war theory and pacifism that makes life difficult for advocates of the former theory. In terms of content, pacifism is a simple theory. In its full-bodied version it tells us in absolute terms that war is forbidden. It may be difficult psychologically to follow pacifism's edicts, but the edicts themselves are relatively clear. They come down to the following: Do not engage in violence, and, thus, do not engage in any way in any war. But just war theory does not enjoy this kind of clarity with respect to its content. The criteria can be applied with greater or lesser severity such that just war theorists can sincerely and sharply disagree with one another about the justice of particular wars. We already noted that several of the criteria in both "of" and "in" the war portions of the theory are degree concepts. Last (reasonable) resort, for instance, can be applied after six major efforts to avoid war—or seven, eight, or nine. Cautious just war theorists might even think that it is reasonable to make still another effort, a tenth one, to avoid war. And for these cautious theorists each resort might be lovingly lingered over—each taking more and more time. A less patient just war theorist might pull the trigger after the fifth.

In the same way, the principle of discrimination allows for great variation in how it is applied. Some just war theorists would be horrified if even a few nonparticipants (noncombatants, innocents, etc.) were harmed under any circumstances, whereas others would countenance many such harms in a protracted and serious war. Disagreement about how to apply the principle of discrimination might also result because of the role of technology. If a high-tech nation with smart weapons is fighting a medium-tech nation, it may be held accountable to a higher level of discrimination. It seems, that is, that the principle of discrimination is context sensitive and that sensitivity naturally leads to more disagreement about how that principle is to be applied. So, it now appears that just war theory is not especially designed to yield agreement when it is applied in concrete situations. Application can vary so much that it might be difficult at times to distinguish a strict just war theorist from a non-full-bodied pacifist. Both might agree, war for war, that the guns should not be fired. On the other side, some more lax just war theorists might agree, war for war, with some realists that the guns should be fired.

Third, contrary to what is commonly supposed, just war theory has applications for nonparadigmatic war settings, once some adjustments are made to the theory. Paradigmatic settings have to do with nations that threaten to or actually cross one another's borders with uniformed soldiers, bomb each other's military facilities or cities, and/or sink each other's ships. Nonparadigmatic settings include civil war, guerrilla war, various forms of low-intensity wars, and blockades. One of the adjustments that needs to be made is with the criterion of proper authorization (or legitimate authority) in the justice of the war portion of the theory. If a civil war is being fought, one side may not have a government in place to do any authorizing. Indeed, early on in the war the rebels may have the look of bandits. The same applies to guerrilla fighters who strike, run, and then fade away— who in the eyes of the regular military forces opposing them are fighting dirty. Lending credence to this view is the perception that many rebel and guerrilla groups have a preference for civilian rather than military targets. Although this perception may be correct in fact, it is not correct in principle. Guerrilla fighters need not attack schools, religious institutions, and market squares any more than regular fighters do. To be sure, they probably will not be in uniform. And if that constitutes a violation of just war theory, then they are to that extent in violation. But fighting in uniform is not a key component of just war theory. Besides, the guerrilla fighters can be excused for not being in uniform given their inferior military status relative to their opponents. For them to fight in uniform is to court disaster. In most any other ways, however, the guerrillas can be held to account. Presumably in starting the war they could and should cite the principles of just cause, last resort, and the rest of the principles as justification for their actions. Further, they could cite proportionality and discrimination once the war starts and be cited themselves just like any other armed force for not following these principles. The basic idea is that because each principle of just war theory serves the purpose of putting some constraints on the horrors of war, as many principles that can be cited should be—even if all cannot be.[19]

Many of these same points apply to blockades, even though this form of military action is classically between two fully recognized nations. Blockades are nonparadigmatic war settings nonetheless, for they need not result in violence of the sort we associate with war or they result in only very sporadic violence. Think here of the U.S. blockade of Cuba during the 1962 missile crisis, during which no damage was done to anything or anybody except U.S.S.R. pride. Certainly one common just war argument against blockades is that they violate the principle of discrimination. If blockades were thought of as weapons, they certainly would be classed as area weapons. By cutting off not only weapons supplies to the block-aded nation but also fuel, food, and medical supplies, blockades indiscriminately hurt everyone. That fact begins to show that just war theory has application here. But just war theory applies to blockades in other ways. Before a blockade is in-stalled, it is perfectly appropriate for the blockading nation to run through the list of justice of the war criteria. Certainly the heavy harm done to the blockaded nation demands that a just cause be present to justify the blockade. Good inten-tions, likelihood of success, and proportionality all also have application. The only criterion that might be suspect is last resort simply because all out war would be the last resort rather than a blockade. Still, in a somewhat modified form, even that principle has application here. Recall that the spirit of this princi-ple is to avoid acting on the saying "Fools rush in where angels fear to tread." In this spirit the modified last resort principle would insist that the blockade not be installed as a first resort (because it represents military action perilously close to war)—or second, third, or fourth resort. So just war theory works pretty well with blockades. Indeed, the theory works well even with severe economic sanctions, policies that represent two steps away from war just as blockades represent poli-cies one step away.

Fourth, it should be noted that there are issues falling under the heading of military ethics that have not been discussed thus far. Most of them arise in peace-time, but some actually arise during war. One group of these issues pertains to personnel. Should, for instance, women be allowed to participate in all, some, or no forms of combat? What about "gays in the military"? Another group of issues pertains to hardware. Should, for instance, the United States develop and then deploy its terribly expensive and very advanced "air superiority" F-22 fighter plane (Huber 1997)? Should it develop the capability of shooting down satellites (Broad 1997)? There are good military reasons for doing these and other such things. Modern high-tech wars are not too kind to those nations whose technol-ogy is second best. Yet when new weapons are developed too fast there is a ten-dency not only to escalate military spending but also to encourage a rat-race men-tality among potential U.S. enemies and competitors.

This fourth and final concluding point contributes toward putting just war the-ory in perspective. It reminds us that as important as it is to the area of concern we call military ethics, this theory deals with only part of that concern. Beyond what other limitations just war theory possesses, it is simply not designed to deal with all the ethical problems that face the military.

NOTES

1. His title ("Pacifism: Some Philosophical Considerations") notwithstanding, Hauerwas's most basic justification is from within the religious tradition based on the life of Christ. In effect, he asks, Are we willing to train ourselves to the virtues (the way of life) that Jesus exhibited for us when he visited the earth? (1986).

2. See especially Holmes's (1989) chapter 6 titled "The Killing of Innocent Persons in Wartime." Holmes comes as close as anyone to the positions I am characterizing as full bodied and "intuitionist."

3. Notice the difference between the terms *nonmoral* and *amoral*. The latter usually applies to an individual who lacks a sense of moral right and wrong. Typically, realists do not lack such a sense. They can and do make moral judgments all of the time. Rather, they argue that it is inappropriate to use moral terms on an international level, even though it is appropriate to use such terms on the national and interpersonal levels.

4. Many in history have held such a doctrine. The Legalists in ancient China both advised and helped administer the Chin dynasty in this spirit. Alexander the Great acted and probably thought along these lines. Genghis Kahn and the Spanish conquerors of the Americas belong to this line of thinking as well. In modern times, Hitler, Stalin, Saddam Hussein, and the Serb leaders of the former Yugoslavia also belong to this line.

5. Here are some comments by Genghis Kahn on these matters—notice how little ethics has to do with what he says: "The greatest joy a man can have is victory: to conquer one's enemy's armies, to pursue them, to deprive them of their possessions, to reduce their families to tears, to ride on their horses, and to make love to their wives and daughters" (Time-Life Editors 1989, 13).

6. In Gilbert's *Nuremberg Diary* Herman Goering is quoted as saying, "What the devil do you mean, morality?—word of honor? Sure, you can talk about word of honor when you promise to deliver goods in business.—But when it is the question of the interests of the nation. Phooey! Then morality stops" (1947, 339).

7. Treitschke writes, "It is a further consequence of the essential of sovereignty of the State that it can acknowledge no arbiter above it, and must ultimately submit its legal obligations to its own verdict" (1968, 417). Actually Treischke's statement sounds more like a prescription than a description of how things are. In some sense of "should," he thinks the state should not allow a higher authority to make decisions for it.

8. During a visit to Israel in 1995 an Israeli official said to me, "We would have no choice if we were attacked. We would do anything and everything to keep Israel from going under." For me this is the best example I have found of the inability realist position.

9. This may be close to the position Thrasymachus, the Sophist, holds in book 1 of Plato's *Republic*.

10. Rosenthal's (1991) book gives a good general account of the ethics involved in the realist position. As to the realists themselves, see Carr 1964, Kennan 1951, and Morgenthau 1952. I am indebted to Fran Harbour for alerting me to the point that there is a moral dimension to the position. In this volume, Welch discusses several versions of realism that are compatible with ethics. The closest he comes to describing full-bodied realism is in his discussion of the position he associates with Kennan. As I say above in note 4, history gives us better examples of full-bodied realism.

11. Holmes calls some of these thinkers "soft realists." These realists "honor morality

when they can [b]ut . . . believe that when it is expedient to do so, morality should be abandoned" (Holmes 1989, 57).

12. Niebuhr (1932) seems to be arguing that the rules of the collective (the nation, state) transcend those of the individual.

13. See especially book 19 (chapters 11 and 12) of Augustine's *City of God* (1984). For commentaries on Augustine's role in developing just war theory in the West, see Christopher 1999, especially chapter 3. See also Holmes 1989, chapter 4. Inclined as he is toward pacifism, Holmes's account of Augustine is understandably negative.

14. See especially Aquinas 1974, volume 2, part 2, question 40.

15. For a discussion of earlier Western interventions in Yugoslavia, see Nagengast's contribution to this volume.

16. For a detailed discussion of the justice of the Persian Gulf War, see Coates's contribution to this volume.

17. For more on the problematic nature of "dual use" targets in the Gulf War, see Coates's contribution to this volume.

18. Childress (1986) appeals to what he calls midlevel principles such as nonmaleficence (do no harm), beneficence (help others), and justice to generate the principles of just war theory.

19. For an application of just war theory to the nonparadigmatic case of terrorism, see the chapters by Valls and George in this volume.

3

Just War in the Persian Gulf?

Anthony J. Coates

According to the eminent military historian John Keegan, "The whirlwind victory of the forces sent to punish Iraq and deprive it of its illegal sequestration of territory . . . was the first genuine triumph of just war morality since Grotius had defined its guiding principles at the height of the Thirty Years' War in the seventeenth century" (1993, 384). The sweeping and enthusiastic tenor of this moral endorsement of the Gulf War is sufficient in itself to cast doubt on its claim to a just war pedigree. Such verdicts are too neat and final, too packaged, to do justice to the moral complexity and ambiguity of war.

Keeping that complexity and ambiguity very clearly in view is a condition of the moral regulation or containment of war, and it is the containment of war rather than its justification (much less its glorification) that just war theory attempts. Restraining rather than empowering a belligerent is the aim, curbing rather than inflaming the enthusiasm that the prospect of war so often arouses. In the moral theory, at least, the appropriate emphasis is a negative rather than a positive one. The moral presumption on which the theory rests is a presumption against war, and even when the moral permissibility of war has been reluctantly conceded, the theory is still at pains to strengthen rather than weaken moral inhibitions over the use of force.

The simpler the moral perception of war (the more clear-cut the moral verdict), the more uninhibited the war threatens to become. In the ideology, to which just war theory is often reduced in practice, the theory's negative emphasis and moral presumption against war are in danger of being reversed. During the Gulf War moral rhetoric was dominant in allied presentations of the conflict, particularly in President Bush's public portrayal of it. Presidential utterances were notably free of any hint of moral complexity or ambiguity: "For me it boils down to a very moral case of good versus evil, black versus white" (Wayne 1993, 40). Such a partisan or unilateral view of the conflict did little to promote the spirit of self-criticism and self-restraint that just war theory seeks to encourage.[1]

Moral assessments of the Gulf War are in fact much more varied than the simplicity and finality of Keegan's (or President Bush's) characterization might suggest. Moral approval of the war is matched in equal measure by its moral repudiation. Morally speaking, the Gulf War was a controversial war, and people have always held conflicting views about its justifiability. Far from abating, controversy has heightened with the passage of time. This was a war that, in the opinion of many critics, violated both just recourse *(jus ad bellum)* and just conduct *(jus in bello)*. Moreover, the moral deficiencies of the war itself are seen to be greatly compounded by the peace that the victors imposed on the vanquished. For such critics this was a "just" war in name alone. The reality was that of an imperialist war, a manifestation of power politics or realpolitik, in which the unprincipled pursuit of national self-interest made nonsense of the war's moral image.

That the war should be so contrarily assessed is hardly surprising. In the first place, analysts or critics often differ fundamentally in their moral understanding of war. Some who find the Gulf War wanting would feel the same about any war. Gordon Zahn's (1991) moral denunciation of the war, for example, purports to be based on just war principles. Zahn, however, is a pacifist for whom just war principles are always inapplicable. This weakens, if it does not invalidate, his criticism. Clearly, in his case the Gulf War was bound to fail the moral test right from the start.

At the same time, even among those who share, at least in principle, a moral acceptance of war (genuine just war theorists for example) differences abound. The reason for this is not hard to find. It has to do with the very nature of the ethics of war and with the way in which moral understanding and moral judgment are contingent upon the facts: "The question of whether this or that use of force is morally justifiable is not simply a moral question. It depends on a whole complex of political causes and effects, a set of facts" (Vann 1939, 28).

Uncertainty about the relevant and key facts clouds moral assessment of the Gulf War: Was Iraqi aggression unprovoked? Did the United States and its allies engineer the war through the deliberate entrapment of Iraq? Was a diplomatic solution to the crisis spurned in favor of war? Were noncombatants directly attacked? Did the target list for the bombing campaign include purely civilian sites? Was excess force used and unnecessary suffering inflicted on Iraqi ground forces? Affirmative answers to questions like these (all of which engage key just war criteria) would make a mockery of Keegan's claim that this was a "triumph of just war morality." But is an affirmative response justified? At best, the evidence, in some if not in all cases, appears mixed.

Because the relevant facts are often in dispute (in many cases they simply cannot be known with certainty given the secrecy in which war is typically shrouded), moral assessment of war seems bound (in some instances and in some aspects at least) to take a conditional or hypothetical form. In practice, however, moral certitude is everywhere to the fore in moral analyses (pro and con) of the Gulf War. In such cases what tends to happen is that a certain version of the "facts" is chosen that best supports the moral position favored by the critic in question, a position seemingly arrived at independently, or in advance, of the facts. A more fruitful and honest approach would be to acknowledge factual uncertainty where it exists and to allow that uncertainty to be reflected in the hypothetical or conditional form of the moral analysis and assessment.

THE RECOURSE TO WAR

What has inclined Keegan and others to accept the Gulf War's moral or just war credentials is its cosmopolitan and humanitarian image, according to which this was a war fought by the appointed agents of the international community to uphold international law and to undo an act of unprovoked and naked aggression against one of the international community's weakest and most vulnerable members. This, so it is claimed, was a case of international law enforcement and peacemaking motivated not by national interest or imperial ambition but by humanitarian impulse and respect for the rule of law.

The "cosmopolitanism" of the war, if real, would greatly strengthen the "just war" claim. All just wars are, in a sense, "cosmopolitan," being fought on the universalistic moral premise of a community of mankind subject to a common law and ordered to a common good, so that "even when an individual state acts ostensibly on its own behalf, if it acts in defence of its legitimate interests or in vindication of its rights, it acts at the same time as the agent and representative of the international community" (Coates 1997, 128).

Was the Gulf War's cosmopolitan and humanitarian reputation justified? For some critics this all-too-moral representation of the war constituted a gross distortion of the truth (at best naive, at worst cynically manipulative or propagandist).

In the first place, it is argued, the cosmopolitan image of the war is belied by the usurpation of legitimate authority that took place soon after the Iraqi invasion of Kuwait. Despite U.N. sponsorship, the war had little to do with the international community. The real prime mover throughout was the United States. Far from upholding the authority of the United Nations, the United States and its allies (principally Britain) did their best to undermine the efforts of Secretary General Javier Pérez de Cuéllar to maintain U.N. control and to achieve a diplomatic solution to the crisis. The aim, and the reality, was one of autonomous action by the United States and its subordinates.

Second, not only was the authority and leadership of the U.N. undermined, the cosmopolitan and humanitarian purposes for which the war was ostensibly being fought were contradicted by the West's real agenda, namely, securing and promoting its own strategic interests. As one critic of the war and its aftermath has written, "The reality is that the Western powers are pursuing a strategic policy, linked to the control of Gulf oil, that has nothing to do with support for human rights or condemnation of military aggression" (Simons 1998, xvii).

Third, in the opinion of the severest critics, the case is even worse than it seems. Not only was the West taking advantage of an opportunity presented to it by Iraq's foolhardy aggression, but, in true Machiavellian fashion, the West had itself engineered the Iraqi invasion of Kuwait with a view to furthering its own interests (see Campbell 1993; Clark 1992; Heikal 1992; Simons 1998). According to one version of events, for example, the U.S. government laid a trap for Iraq by simultaneously encouraging (or not discouraging) the Iraqi move against Kuwait while bolstering Kuwaiti and Saudi Arabian resistance to Iraqi claims for boundary changes, a reformed oil pricing policy, and financial compensation for losses incurred during the Iran–Iraq war (Campbell 1993). These criticisms, which strike at the heart of the question of just recourse, will be considered in turn.

Legitimate Authority

First is the issue of legitimate authority. That executive power in the Gulf War lay with the United States is indisputable. Given the realities of power and of international politics that existed at the time, it would be wholly unrealistic to expect it to have lain anywhere else, as the secretary general himself has acknowledged.[2] The question is whether that executive responsibility was abused. Did the United States use its position of leadership to work against the expressed will of the international community?

On the whole,[3] the evidence suggests that it did not. The charge of usurpation and subversion assumes a division of opinion that, arguably, did not exist at the time (though it has emerged subsequently). The accusation ignores the remarkable moral and political consensus that encouraged the United States to act decisively in the first place and to the preservation of which American policy remained committed. The consensus was, of course, a fragile and in some respects artificial construct, a creature of circumstance rather than a permanent reality. Its very fragility, however, helped it to exercise a restraining influence on the coalition leadership (see Schwarzkopf and Petre 1992, 497–98).

Whatever the truth of the matter, the relation between the international community and those who claim to act as its agents or representatives remains an issue of grave concern. Ensuring that that relation is a sound and secure one should be a primary consideration. Postwar events have reinforced that conviction. The tendency of the more powerful states to take authorization for granted or to interpret U.N. Security Council resolutions too permissively needs to be firmly resisted if the criterion of legitimate authority is to exercise its proper, restraining, role in such cases.

Just Cause and Right Intention

The second criticism, that the cosmopolitan image is either naive or duplicitous in its characterization of the war as a disinterested or altruistic war, seems, in part, well founded. That there was always more to the war than the defense of Kuwaiti sovereignty and the vindication of international law is undeniable. *Of course* the war was about oil, regional security, and the balance of power. To believe otherwise is to reveal a remarkable ignorance of the workings of international relations. The question so far as the ethics of war is concerned is, What follows from that admission?

For moral puritans the admission is sufficient to invalidate just cause for war: a "just" cause (at least in a cosmopolitan or humanitarian war) is precisely a "pure" or "disinterested" cause, so that the intrusion of an "interest" is seen to be morally undermining. This "Kantian" view of morality, which forces duty and inclination apart, seems entirely alien to just war thinking. The mere presence of an interest (or incentive) is not invalidating. Right intention is, in just war theory, a condition of just recourse, but a "right intention" does not have to be incentive free: the performance of duty for its own sake is not required (see Coates 1996).

The issue is whether the interest is legitimate and relevant to the case in question. If it is, then, far from weakening (much less invalidating) just cause, it might be thought to strengthen it. Of course, whether an interest (like the protection of oil supplies) is sufficient on its own to justify the use of force is another matter. All that is being argued here is that its mere presence does not invalidate a cause, which is considered worthy or sufficient.[4]

From a just war standpoint, the third criticism—that the Western powers procured war with Iraq to advance their own interests—could not be more damning, reversing as it does the primacy of peace over war that is at the center of just war thinking. The evidence of deliberate entrapment, however, seems largely unconvincing. It is, of course, not inconceivable that the intelligence services, even of a democratic state, should resort to such measures. In the continued absence of hard evidence, however, it is difficult not to sympathize with Makiya's albeit harsh assessment of one version of this criticism: "These are not arguments; they are undocumented assertions, resting on a conspiratorial view of politics and motivated by an emotional antipathy to the West" (1994, 256).

The matter, however, does not end there. Though the accusation of deliberate engineering of the war by the West may appear unfounded, the evidence far from absolves the Western powers of any responsibility for the war. Even a cursory examination of Western–Iraqi relations prior to the war indicates that the issue of agency and responsibility ought not to be viewed unilaterally. Talk of Iraq's "unprovoked aggression" (like some bolt from the blue) is a considerable oversimplification of events and one that simply does not do justice to the complex, and in this case very murky, world of international politics.

The record shows that the Western powers had been tolerant of, and even party to, Iraqi aggression for many years. In its protracted war with Iran (1980–88) Iraq received the political, economic, and military support of the Western powers. Military assistance included the supply of arms, the supply of machine tools for the manufacture of arms, help with Iraq's ballistic missile program, the supply of "dual use" materials and technology (including nuclear technology) with potential application to the weapons of mass destruction program, and the supply of military intelligence regarding the disposition of Iranian forces (see Campbell 1993).[5] Though this assistance came to an end with the conclusion of the Iran–Iraq war, this recent history of Western dealings with Iraq was hardly designed to incline Iraq to peaceful dealings with its neighbors or to convince Iraq that any future use of force would be met with military opposition by the West.

Clearly, the West was guilty of more than mere negligence, but negligence is part of the story. As in the case of the Falklands War and so in the case of the Gulf War, there are strong grounds for thinking that the war might have been averted if Britain and the United States had been more alive to the possibility of war. Had the United States made clear its commitment to the defense of Kuwait, the Iraqi invasion might have been prevented and war avoided. This is a view that the U.S. military command at the time seems to have shared (see Powell 1995, 461–62).

Just as the issue of agency and responsibility for the war is more blurred and complex than the simple moral image of the war would suggest, so is the matter of just cause as a whole.

The official line was straightforward and seemed intended to assuage any moral anxiety and to silence any emerging criticism or opposition. Both President Bush and Prime Minister Thatcher (whose influence was crucial in the key early stages of the crisis) set out to forestall such criticism and to construct a military alliance against Iraq. Theirs was the political and moral equivalent of the preemptive strike. The crisis was personalized. Saddam Hussein was portrayed in the worst terms possible. The analogy with that twentieth-century archetype of evil, Adolf Hitler, was frequently drawn. The divide between justice and injustice was presented as an absolute one. This unilateral conception of just cause was an unpromising basis on which to pursue a peaceful solution to the crisis.

Another view was possible and, in the opinion of critics, justified. The invasion of Kuwait was not a simple case of "unprovoked aggression" driven by the megalomania of a tyrannical ruler but, rather, an action that was better seen in rational-instrumental terms. Iraq had grievances, which were not without substance and which deserved to be addressed: the redrawing of long-disputed territorial boundaries; the cancellation or rescheduling of debts to Kuwait (incurred during the war with Iran, a war that Iraq claimed was as much in Kuwait's interest as it was in its own and which Kuwait had been happy to have Iraq fight on its behalf); the repair and future prevention of the damage to the Iraqi economy caused by the Kuwaiti and Saudi Arabian lowering of the price of oil and Kuwaiti exploitation of the Rumaila (and mainly Iraqi) oil field. These were among the grievances that led the leader of Iraq's Christian churches, the Chaldean Patriarch Raphael Bidawid, to uphold the justice of Iraq's cause and to depict its "invasion" of Kuwait as an act of self-defense (*The Tablet*, 26 January 1991, 110).

In this and every case, just cause can be, and ought to be, viewed bilaterally or relatively and not unilaterally or absolutely. Not only is "bilateral" or "relative" justice more likely to accord with the reality of interstate relations (which state can ever truthfully lay claim to absolute justice?), but the adoption of such a standpoint by potential belligerents seems likely to have a more moderating and restraining effect than assumptions of unilateral or absolute justice. The recognition of relative justice (and injustice) leaves the way open to negotiation and reconciliation and to that mutual recognition of rights, interests, and responsibilities that is a moral imperative in any authentic just war.

It does not, however, at least in just war thinking, preclude recourse to war or to the threat of war (even though it may improve the prospects of avoiding war). There are those who seem to think that it does. Vaux, for example, appears to take this view of the Gulf War: *"For a war to be fully justified there must be an unmitigated aggression committed against an innocent party"* (1992, 8). This notion (that when justice is relative, war is prohibited) looks like another example of the moral puritanism referred to earlier. As such it ill accords with just war theory. What the criterion of just cause requires is not absolute or unilateral justice but a balance (or, more accurately, *im*balance) of justice, a preponderance (but not a monopoly) of justice on one side and of injustice on the other (see Coates 1997, 146 ff.).[6]

Last Resort

Just as the recognition of relative justice promotes the prospects of peace, so the assumption of unilateral or absolute justice breeds further hostility and intransigence. The evidence suggests that the unilateral moral stance adopted by coalition leaders, by Britain and the United States in particular, made a peaceful resolution of the conflict improbable. In the view of those leaders, an act of unprovoked aggression and unmitigated evil could only be undone by force or the threat of force. Again, the analogy with Hitler was to the fore: negotiation would constitute a form of appeasement, a collusion with evil, which would have the effect, in the long if not in the short term, of exacerbating conflict.

Starting from this assumption, the idea that Iraq should be given any incentives to vacate Kuwait was bound to seem distasteful. And yet without some incentive, even if only of the presentational kind, Iraq's voluntary withdrawal seemed unlikely. Far from making it easier for Iraq to extricate itself from Kuwait (which some critics have argued Iraq was keen to do as long as it did not involve the loss of too much face),[7] U.S. diplomacy seemed intent on making it more difficult, on forcing Iraq not only to withdraw but to withdraw abjectly. It is this suspicion (strengthened by subsequent events) that lends the strongest support to what was perhaps the charge most frequently leveled at allied leaders at the time, namely, that their resort to arms violated the criterion of last resort.

In some of its forms this criticism seemed wide of the mark. Criticism informed by a "literal" conception of "last resort" was not persuasive, indifferent as that criticism always is to the real efficacy of alternative methods of resolving conflict as well as to the needs and constraints of effective military action. For such critics the point of last resort could never have been met, and the criterion was being used simply as a way of postponing war indefinitely. From a just war standpoint, such use appears improper: the criterion is meant to raise the moral threshold of war, but it is not intended that that threshold should become virtually insurmountable.

By no means all of the criticism was as indifferent as this to political and military realities or as reluctant to accept the potential use of force. Much criticism relied for its force on assumptions regarding the efficacy and moral superiority of economic sanctions. For example, Archbishop Roach, the chairman of the United States Catholic Conference International Policy Committee, invoking the just war tradition (as well as the views of experts like ex–National Security Advisor Zbigniew Brzezinski, ex–Defense Secretary James Schlesinger, and ex–Chairman of the Joint Chiefs of Staff Admiral William J. Crowe), advised the Senate Foreign Relations Committee, "The embargo needs time to work. . . . Before war can be justified, all peaceful means must be fully pursued. Thus far, I do not believe the principle of last resort has been met" (quoted in Johnson and Weigel 1991, 126).

That the assumptions about the efficacy and moral superiority of sanctions, on which this criticism was based, are open to very considerable doubt has become clearer with the passage of time. In the postwar period the continuing sanctions policy, while failing to achieve its strategic objectives, has inflicted enormous suffering on the civilian population of Iraq, suffering that seems both disproportionate and misdirected. Even at the time, however, both assumptions were sufficiently dubious to make the choice of sanctions over war less than morally compelling. It was not at all evident that sanctions constituted an effective and more morally acceptable means than war of resolving the conflict. That being so, the refusal to rely on sanctions (or to give sanctions longer to work) did not in itself constitute a violation of the criterion of last resort.[8]

Much more persuasive is the criticism that the conduct of allied diplomacy (by America and Britain at least) ran counter to the spirit of last resort, relying too heavily on the threat of force to achieve a peaceful resolution of the crisis. Allied diplomacy, it seems, was always too "hawkish" to persuade Iraq to depart Kuwait without a fight, as the U.S. field commander General Schwarzkopf appears to verify in his memoirs. When informed that the State Department was resisting a Soviet peace proposal (which envisaged an immediate and unconditional Iraqi withdrawal from Kuwait) because it did not require Iraq's unconditional surrender, Schwarzkopf opined, "That kind of ultimatum does not work with Arabs: they will die first" (Schwarzkopf and Petre 1992, 441). Later he concluded, "There had to be a contingent of hawks in Washington who did not want to stop until we'd punished Saddam" (Schwarzkopf and Petre 1992, 443).

Diplomacy of this kind looked more like a preparation for war than an attempt to avoid war by resort to peaceful means, and in considering its course it becomes clear how the conception of "just cause" can have a determining effect on the dynamics of just recourse. The more bipartisan the understanding of just cause, the more conciliatory potential belligerents are likely to be in their overtures to one another. Diplomatic initiatives informed by a spirit of moral bipartisanship are more likely to bear fruit than those conducted in a spirit of self-righteousness and retribution based on assumptions of absolute justice.

Proportionality

The moral preference for sanctions over war owed much to the assumption (perhaps unfounded in this case) that sanctions were a more proportionate response to the invasion of Kuwait than war. Proportionality is a key criterion of just war theory, and it is one that was frequently invoked in debate about the justifiability of this war. Even those who were convinced of the justice of the cause balked at the prospect of war and its predicted consequences. Those consequences were thought by some to include mass casualties on both sides, ecological disaster, and the collapse of the world economy. Given such apocalyptic expectations, many concluded that war was bound to be a disproportionate and, therefore, unjustifiable response.

The fact that the very worst of these consequences did not materialize is not in itself an indication that the recourse to war complied with the criterion of proportionality. The issue is whether the projection was realistic and, most importantly, whether those charged with the responsibility of deciding whether or not to go to war thought it to be so. The evidence suggests that (at the least) they did not regard these fears as so utterly groundless as to be unworthy of consideration. In that case, in the face of such horrendous risks, were they justified in choosing war?

It is a question that some moral analysts are reluctant to put to any war. Michael Walzer (1992, xv–xvi), for example, argues that the question is inappropriate because the demands of proportionality cannot be met: the costs and the benefits of war can neither be known in advance nor be expressed and compared mathematically or exactly. The problems to which Walzer alludes are real enough, but they are insufficient reasons for excluding from moral analysis an idea that appears so central to moral reflection and moral conduct. At the same time the principle of proportionality should not be asked to carry undue moral weight. It should not be applied in a form that implies a foresight that is beyond any human agent or in a form that achieves commensurability only by suppressing those nonmaterial elements of the moral equation that are not quantifiable. When used with a proper restraint, however, the idea of proportionality forms an essential part of the moral assessment of war.

Restraint often seemed lacking in the manner in which the principle was employed by critics of the war at the time: the very worst scenario was assumed; its probability was exaggerated; those ends of war that might have been expected to provide moral compensation were demeaned or neglected. The application of the principle in this form seemed designed to exclude war from the start rather than to subject the question of recourse to critical moral analysis.

THE CONDUCT OF THE WAR

The inadequacy of the simple "moral" image of the Gulf War is evident not only in respect of the recourse to war (*jus ad bellum*) but also in respect of the conduct of the war (*jus in bello*).

The key to the war, morally as well as militarily, was the air campaign. It is the area of greatest moral concern, though there is often very little evidence of such concern in statements about it. In fact, the reverse is true: the air offensive is singled out for the moral probity with which it was conducted. "Our air strikes," claimed President Bush, "were the most effective, yet humane, in the history of warfare" (1992, 576), and many agree with that verdict. Keegan's moral validation of the war owes much to the premise that "victory [was] achieved without the infliction of civilian casualties" (1993, 384), a view echoed by Hallion: "At the end of the Gulf War, the ability of Iraq to threaten its neighbors was no less incapacitated than that of Japan and Germany in 1945, but Baghdad was intact. Its civilian population was virtually untouched directly by the war. Humane values had, in fact, prevailed" (1992, 263–64).

In some respects the verdict is well founded. This was not area bombing in the World War II mode. Unlike their counterparts in that earlier conflict, coalition air forces in the Gulf War had both the capacity and the will to bomb targets precisely, and, though this was not the sole or even the main method of attack, it appears to have been the method employed against targets located in urban areas like Baghdad and Basra. The evidence suggests that, as a result, the number of civilians killed in the bombing itself was low, bearing in mind its intensity (one source suggests that less than 1,000 civilians died in the air campaign itself; see Heidenrich 1993, 119). Civilians were not directly targeted, and the number killed in the raids as a result of "collateral damage" was probably low enough not to seem disproportionate. In that sense the bombing appears to have upheld the requirements of just conduct. But is this the whole story? It seems that it is not.

The bombing strategy needs to be viewed in context. It was devised with the experience of Vietnam in mind. What the U.S. commanders, all of them veterans of the Vietnam War, feared most was a repeat of that debacle, another war of attrition leading to an ignominious political defeat.[9] The bombing strategy used in the Gulf War was designed to eliminate that possibility. As in the view of those British commanders in World War II whose military thinking was dominated by the experience of the trench warfare of World War I, strategic bombing was seen as the means of circumventing a war of attrition. In the Gulf War the strategy of a gradual process of escalated bombing adopted in Vietnam gave way to the strategy of the wholesale and instantaneous destruction of the infrastructure on which the Iraqi military machine depended for its effectiveness; "Rolling Thunder" was replaced by "Instant Thunder."[10]

The moral problems associated with this strategy were twofold. In the first place, the strategy seemed disproportionate by design. If there was to be any error, then it must be on the side of "overkill." Ensuring economy in the use of force—a basic requirement of *jus in bello*—was bound to prove difficult given the strategic concept of the bombing. Whereas a gradual escalation allows the proportionality of the bombing to be assessed and any necessary adjustments to be made, an immediate and total onslaught does not. The idea of "the more, the better" seems to have prevailed over the idea of the restrained and measured use of force.[11]

The second problem has to do with the question of discrimination. It is by no means clear that the air campaign upheld the principle of noncombatant immunity, as its defenders claim. Though civilians appear not to have been directly targeted (as they were in World War II), and though relatively few may have been killed in the raids themselves, the indirect foreseeable (and, perhaps, intended) effects of the bombing on the civilian population were devastating.

How devastating the effects of the bombing on the civilian population have been is another of those factual questions on which much moral criticism of the Gulf War turns and for which there is no agreed or certain answer. The subsequent deaths of many thousands of Iraqi citizens (especially children) have been attributed to the wholesale destruction of essential services effected by the bombing. That the deaths have occurred is not in any doubt. The problem is that they appear to have more than one cause, not only the bombing campaign but the effects of economic sanctions and of fierce persecution and deliberate neglect of large sections of the population, particularly the Kurdish and Shi'ite peoples, by the Iraqi regime itself. The relative weighting of these causes is uncertain. Apologists for the bombing claim that its impact has been secondary (see Heidenrich 1993, 119), while antagonists see it as the major factor. Whatever its relative weighting, there seems little doubt that the lethal (albeit indirect) effect of the bombing on the civilian population of Iraq was substantial, substantial enough to cast doubt on the moral image of the bombing campaign.

Defense of the bombing draws heavily on the distinction between "direct" and "indirect" killing—a distinction prominent in just war thinking. By just war standards, however, the use of that distinction in this case often appears suspect. To see why, it is necessary to distinguish between the two different senses of the word *indirect* that are at work in the moral analysis of the bombing. In the first sense the word describes the causal relation between an act and one of its effects: the causal connection between the bombing and the subsequent deaths of civilians is remote rather than proximate, mediate rather than immediate. The second usage focuses on the relation between one of the effects of an act and the intention of the agent: in the case of an act with dual or multiple effects, that effect is "indirect," which, though foreseen, does not form any part (not even a minor or subordinate part) of the agent's plan or design. In that sense the effect is "allowed" rather than "intended."

The defense of the bombing often seems, by implication at least, to rely too heavily on the fact that the harm to civilians was indirectly caused—that it was not high explosives that killed people but the epidemic that broke out (partly) as a result of the destruction of, or damage to, public utilities. Clearly, this is no defense. The fact that the effect is indirect in the causal sense does not, on its own, exonerate the agent or justify the act. The effect may be indirectly caused and yet directly intended. If the bombing was intended to have the indirect effect that it appears to have had on the health of the civilian population, then the moral claims made for it are bogus. This would constitute a clear violation of the principle of noncombatant immunity, a principle that the public defense of the bombing strongly invokes.

Were the indirect and harmful effects on noncombatants intended, or were they the unintended side effects of an attack on a legitimate military objective? That they were intended is certainly not beyond the bounds of credibility. Military leaders have long been persuaded of the military utility of attacks on civilian infrastructures. The degradation of civilian life that such attacks cause is intended to destroy enemy morale and the will to fight with a view to lessening or even eliminating the need for a more direct military confrontation with all its potential attendant losses (a key consideration in any war but one that applied with particular urgency to a "political" war like this one). Did such an objective form part of the bombing strategy in the Gulf War?

There is some evidence to suggest that it did. First, the plan for the strategic bombing, "Instant Thunder," was drawn up before a ground offensive was agreed on so that, in its original conception at least, the rationale of the bombing was not linked to the ground war (see Schwarzkopf and Petre 1992, 318–20). The original intention seems to have been to pursue the ends of war through the independent use of air power alone. The more independent the conception of the role of air power, the more total or comprehensive a bombing strategy is likely to be. The less the bombing was seen as preparation for a ground war, therefore, the more compelling, militarily speaking, the targeting of the civilian infrastructure (as such) would have become. Second, the subsequent record of the sanctions policy demonstrates a willingness on the part of the coalition leadership to pursue the kind of strategy that may have informed the bombing—that is, one that attempts to secure the compliance of the Iraqi government by the indirect (and therefore more politically acceptable) infliction of harm and suffering on the civilian population. Third, it is alleged that the bombing did attack the civilian infrastructure (as such), targeting not only key military objectives, like command and control centers, but public utilities, like sewage works and water purification plants, from the destruction of which no direct military benefit could have been expected to accrue (see, for example, McMahan and McKim 1993, 538; Simons 1998, 12). These allegations, if proven, would eliminate any ambiguity or room for doubt and would utterly destroy that moral defense of the bombing that argues that the harm to civilians, though foreseen, was not intended.

The status of so-called dual use targets is much more ambiguous and problematic. Let us suppose that the bombing was confined to utilities (like transport, communications, and power systems) from which coalition leaders could expect to derive an immediate and, potentially, decisive military advantage. The problem with attacks (even with precision attacks, which limit or exclude "collateral damage") on utilities that serve the needs of both the military and the civilian communities is the impossibility of achieving what may well be a key military objective without inflicting harm on the civilian population. The attacks disrupt vital civilian as well as military traffic, interrupt the supply of power to hospitals and water purification plants as well as military command and control centers. In the selection of such targets it is at least conceivable that the intention of the strategist is focused exclusively on the military effect of the bombing so that the civilian effect forms no part of the strategic plan. The very "mixed" nature of these targets means that right (or "indirect") intention cannot be ruled out (though it must not be taken for granted).

The existence or presence of right intention, however, does not bring the moral argument to an end (though critics of this analytical approach often assume that it does; e.g., Norman 1995, 107, 204). The reason why the moral permissibility of the act cannot be assumed—even when the evil effect is indirect in both a causal and an intentional sense—is clear: the agent may not intend the harmful side effect, yet it is his or her voluntary act that brings it about. Because the causal connection between the act of bombing and its indirect yet nonetheless lethal effect on civilians is both certain and foreseen, the agent or bomber must accept responsibility for the indirect effect. The question is whether the agent is justified in accepting that responsibility.

Though the agent must not *intend* the indirect effect, he or she must *attend* to it. The indirect harm to civilians must not be simply discounted or set aside as a matter of little consequence. For the bombing to be justified, the military benefit that it seems at least as likely to produce must be proportionate to the indirect or unintended harm that it seems likely to inflict. And because in this case what is at issue is the overall strategy of the war (and not just some specific military action), it may be necessary to appeal to the ends of the war as a whole rather than to some more limited military goal: Is the relief of Kuwait worth the sufferings likely to be inflicted on the undeserving people of Iraq by the strategy chosen for conducting the war?

Even if the overall strategy is thought to be justified, its execution requires further and continual moral scrutiny in the light of its foreseeable impact on the civilian population. Strategists must take pains not only to keep immediate "collateral damage" to a minimum (that seems to have been the case) but to limit subsequent indirect harm to the civilian population: for example, by careful scrutiny of the target list to ensure the military necessity or utility of the targets chosen; by continual review of the bombing campaign to ensure that it does not exceed the level required to produce the intended military effect; or by employing methods of attack that achieve the military objective while minimizing long-term damage to the civilian infrastructure.

It is not at all clear that the strategic bombing of Iraq was carried out in this restrained and economical manner. In fact, much of the evidence suggests the opposite. The overall conception of the bombing campaign ("Instant Thunder") militated against it. The length and inclusive nature of the target list, as well as the duration and intensity of the bombing, even took military experts by surprise (see Evans 1991; Schwarzkopf and Petre 1992, 430). There are strong grounds for thinking that coalition leaders and military planners, while morally (and politically) sensitive to the direct harming of civilians, were simply too ready to discount the indirect harm done to them by the bombing.

CONCLUSION

The manner in which the war was concluded and the events that have marked the uneasy "peace" to which it gave rise have done little to weaken the impression that the rights and interests of the civilian population (the real victims of Saddam Hussein) have been systematically ignored. The incitement to rebellion followed by acquiescence in its brutal suppression, together with the continuing and exclusive reliance on sanctions, despite their terrible consequences and apparent ineffectiveness, betray a willingness to pursue strategic objectives at whatever cost to the Iraqi people. For a war and a policy with such an avowed humanitarian purpose, that is a serious indictment.

All of this suggests that the moral assessment of the war is suitably complex and ambiguous. This was a war that in its conception and execution was, morally speaking, better than some and worse than others, but a "just war" in any pure or unqualified sense it was not. In that respect the Persian Gulf War seems like every other—real—war.

NOTES

1. For a full and systematic analysis of presidential war rhetoric, see Valls 1996.
2. In a report to the United Nations after the war, Pérez de Cuéllar wrote as follows

about the authorization of the use of force on a national and coalition basis: "In the circumstances and given the costs imposed and capabilities demanded by modern warfare, the arrangement seems unavoidable" (quoted in Heikal 1992, 354).

3. The qualification seems essential. There seems little doubt that the secretary general's approach to the crisis was rather more conciliatory than President Bush's. See the criticism within of U.S. diplomacy.

4. It has been argued that in the Gulf conflict the "worthy" and "sufficient" cause (the restoration of Kuwaiti sovereignty) was achievable without war and that what dictated war were strategic interests of dubious moral worth (see McMahan and McKim 1993, 540). If true, this is clearly very damaging. Even if the strategic interests were legitimate, they might qualify only as ancillary causes unable to carry the moral weight on their own, as they are being required to do by the terms of this criticism.

5. These dealings were, of course, often commercial rather than governmental (or, as in the case of some arms transfers, via a third-party state), but the commercial transactions did require governmental approval in the form of export licenses.

6. See Coates 1997, especially chapters 6–9, for a fuller treatment of just war principles and of their application to the Gulf War.

7. See Heikal 1992, 265 ff. Here, as elsewhere, the facts are uncertain and contested. Much of the evidence seems inconsistent with Heikal's claim that Iraq was looking for a way out. After a fruitless visit to Baghdad, Pérez de Cuéllar, the U.N. secretary general, observed, "You need two for tango. I wanted to dance but I didn't find any nice lady for dancing with" (*The Times*, 15 January 1991, 1B).

8. The moral complacency with which sanctions are often viewed, even (perhaps especially) by moral critics, is illustrated by the following: "The embargo on Iraq should have been allowed at least nine months or a year to work. Siege is an ancient and traditional language of judgement that the people of a country like Iraq and a leader like Saddam Hussein could understand" (Vaux 1992, 14).

9. Their fears were Iraq's best hope of success. A military victory was never anticipated by Iraq. Instead Iraq's strategy assumed a greater capacity to sustain losses, thereby enabling Iraq to outlast the United States.

10. "Instant Thunder" was expanded later to include attacks on Iraqi ground forces as the need for a ground war became accepted.

11. Evidence of "overkill" is not difficult to find. "After two weeks of war," General Schwarzkopf recalls,

my instincts and experience told me that we'd bombed most of our strategic targets enough to accomplish our campaign objectives; it was now time, I thought, to shift most of our air power onto the army we were about to face in battle. But our experts, a team of "battle damage assessment" specialists from the intelligence agencies in Washington who had been assigned to Central Command, disagreed. . . . They had us going in circles. They'd say things like, "You failed to destroy the power plant in Baghdad"; yet we knew that in Baghdad the lights were out. [Schwarzkopf and Petre 1992, 430]

4

The Just War Tradition and the Use of Nonlethal Chemical Weapons during the Vietnam War

Frances V. Harbour

During the Vietnam War, U.S. military forces almost certainly did not fight with intentionally lethal chemical weapons such as nerve agents, phosgene, or mustard gas (Ballingrud 1998; Bowen and Gard 1998; Priest 1998). The United States did use less toxic chemicals as adjuncts to more conventional weapons of war and chemical defoliants. The U.S. civilian government and the military objected to labeling either of these as chemical weapons (Harbour 1999, 47–51). Most other governments considered the harassing agents and defoliants the United States applied to be nonlethal chemical weapons, however, and they are included in the Chemical Weapons Convention of 1993.[1]

The United States itself routinely applied harassing agents, apparently first used in 1964 by South Vietnamese forces with American technology and materiel, by September 1968 (McCarthy 1969, 49). U.S. forces also applied chemical defoliants such as Agent Orange from January 1962 to January 1971. The former were part of the preparation for more conventional missions. The latter were aimed at disrupting or overwhelming North Vietnamese supply lines by destroying vegetation shielding key routes and by reducing food crops available to the Viet Minh and South Vietnamese National Liberation Front (Adams 1990, 75, 78).

Nonlethal chemical weapons were very controversial at the time. Supporters argued that nonlethal chemical weapons had important military benefits and therefore ought to be retained. Critics argued that using harassing agents and defoliants was a dangerous first step on a slippery slope to legitimizing the use of more lethal chemical weapons such as nerve and mustard gas (Finberg 1972, 17–19). They charged that the harassing agents were only a smoke screen for tactics that actually raised civilian casualties (McCarthy 1969, 47). Opponents said the defoliants caused too much harm to the ecosystem of Vietnam and possibly to the people exposed to them (Lewallen 1971).

The debate during the war caught important aspects of moral issues related to the use of nonlethal chemical weapons, concerns related to the justice in war principles of proportionality, discrimination, and double effect. Because there may be important differences of opinion about the implications of just war principles in specific cases, direct application of the just war tradition yields a more complex picture of the ethics of using nonlethal chemical weapons than either side would have accepted at the time. Use of the defoliants in an attempt to cut enemy supply lines and use of harassing agents as part of rescue missions would be acceptable under traditional just war thinking. Destroying crops with defoliants and a tactic that used harassing agents to drive people hidden in caves and dugouts out into the open where they could be more efficiently eliminated with conventional artillery would be impermissible. Let us take a closer look at the roots of these judgments in the Western just war tradition.

JUSTICE IN WAR AND NONLETHAL CHEMICAL WEAPONS IN VIETNAM

In the Western just war tradition, principles related to rightful conduct of war are known as justice in war or *jus in bello* principles. Once the war has begun, all the participants are supposed to be equally bound by justice in war principles. The two main principles are *proportionality* of means to ends and *discrimination* in targeting between combatants and noncombatants. The principle of double effect, which brings the two together, is intended to provide some additional protection to both combatants and noncombatants caught in the cross fire of war.

The just war tradition recognizes that consequences are important. The principle of proportionality means that harm from individual acts of war must not exceed what we are able to justify by the military and other benefits expected (Regan 1996, 95). I will argue below that the use of harassing agents as adjuncts to conventional barrages raised costs to noncombatants past the point at which the combined policy would be acceptable under the principle of proportionality. So, too, destruction of food crops, especially in this war for the hearts and minds of noncombatants, was very costly and, thus, also would have been impermissible under a thoughtful application of the principle of proportionality. On the other hand, rescuing downed airmen using harassing agents was beneficial in its military effects, yet had low costs to everyone—and hence would be permissible.

Jus in bello principles do not, however, simply brand a tactic or a class of weapons acceptable or unacceptable on the basis of consequences. Whatever the effects in terms of the war effort, each specific use of a weapon has to meet the strictures of the principle of discrimination. People applying the principle of discrimination may not *intentionally* target noncombatants under any circumstances, even as a means to other ends such as destruction of morale (Regan 1996, 87). I will argue below that destruction of food crops violated the principle of discrimination and that there are unresolved discrimination issues related to the harassing agents as well.

The just war tradition recognizes that combatants and noncombatants are intermingled in war zones and that it is impossible to fight even a just war with no harm at all to the innocent. The pacifist solution to this dilemma is to refrain from acts of war. The just war tradition's principle of double effect permits some but not all actions whose *unintended side effects* harm noncombatants. The principle of double effect's limits are quite strict.

Under the principle of double effect, we may only cause harm that we do not intend, that is, harm we do not desire for its ability to promote our goals; only such unsought harm can be considered a side effect, not a means or an end. Moreover, we may only use tactics and strategies whereby all the harm involved—intended as well as unintended—is balanced by the good expected from the permissible military action (Harbour 1999, 124–26). It is important to realize that hypocrisy and closing our eyes to unpleasant realities we would rather not think about do not change our real intentions (Yoder 1996).

Under the principle of double effect, then, we may not choose among "military" sites in order to pick the one that would simultaneously kill or harm the most noncombatants; hypocrisy does not change intentions. It would not be acceptable to destroy a whole country to bomb a munitions factory; the benefits are not proportionate to the moral costs, even if the target is otherwise acceptable. It would, however, be permissible to bomb an important munitions factory, even knowing that some civilians in the surrounding area would be killed. The harm to the noncombatants here is not intended to promote our goals, and the overall harm does not exceed the bounds of proportionality.

Thus, at least in the early years of the war, defoliation as part of the policy to try to cut off the supply and resupply of infiltrators and guerrillas from the north was arguably acceptable under the rubric of the principle of double effect. The target was not only military in character but nearly essential to the war effort. The most serious human costs of being exposed to defoliants were not yet knowable. It would have been almost impossible for an American military tactician of the era to argue that the known costs to the environment outweighed the military benefit or even the risks to the lives of U.S. soldiers and allies of *not* trying to close down the supply lines.

Before exploring the limitations of the just war tradition that the use of chemical weapons in the Vietnam War exposes and the wider implications of the application of the tradition for more contemporary military issues, let us turn to a closer examination of harassing agents and then defoliants.

HARASSING AGENTS, AIR RESCUE,
AND THE JUST WAR TRADITION

The just war tradition would almost certainly permit the use of harassing agents to rescue downed soldiers from hotly pursuing enemies, one of the documented uses of nonlethal chemical weapons in the Vietnam War. This tactic does not violate the principle of discrimination because the targets of the weapons are un-equivocally combatants. This is most straightforward if the pursuers wear uni-forms, but even if they do not, someone who fires on and pursues military forces is, by definition, a combatant and should expect return fire. The benefits of using nonlethal harassing agents were clear: Lethal danger to one's own soldiers was reduced both by taking the enemy out of commission and by the fact that not as much potentially lethal force has to be rained down on one's own men in the rescue attempt. Even the enemy—whose soldiers' lives matter to the just war practitioner—is better off being incapacitated with tear gas than with bullets.

From the perspective of the just war tradition, the only serious negative factor in using chemical agents to rescue men on the ground is the potential long-term cost of starting down the slippery slope of making gas more useable in war. Most just war thinkers would permit a military commander in the field to proceed on the basis of the immediate concerns if the potential costs are not very certain. A head of state or other high-level official could decide otherwise, however, and practitioners of the tradition would not object.

Both positions have been reflected in U.S. policy: In late 1974, when President Gerald Ford placed almost all other uses of nonlethal chemical weapons out of bounds as part of the agreement that unlocked ratification of the Geneva Protocol of 1925,[2] one of the half-dozen remaining applications was rescuing downed air-men.[3] In 1997, however, the Clinton administration forbade the use of harassing agents even as part of rescue missions. It took this position because of concerns over use of nonlethal chemical agents in war and because of relevant provisions of the Chemical Weapons Convention of 1993 (Gertz 1996).

HARASSING AGENTS AND BUNKERS

The moral questions surrounding the use of harassing agents to drive mixed groups of civilians and combatants out of protected bunkers and caves are consid-erably more complicated than those concerning rescue. If Viet Cong guerrillas and even sometimes the North Vietnamese regular army could find and keep se-cure shelter during the day, they could operate with greater ease at night. We know that this was their preferred pattern of operation. Many of their hiding places were simple caves and holes in the ground. Other hideouts, however, were elaborate permanent structures that extended for miles underground. The latter had air locks, stored food supplies, and reasonably comfortable sleeping quarters (Spiers 1989, 102).

From an American and South Vietnamese perspective, clearing protected hideouts of dangerous combatants was important to the counterinsurgency war. It also was a serious problem because caves and tunnels were often close to civilian homes and property. Even worse, hideouts might simply be shelters for civilians concerned about their safety from bombs and napalm in a war zone—or they could hide deadly combatants. Moreover, aside from the general moral desirability of trying to keep unintended or collateral harm to noncombatants low, in this war, winning the hearts and minds of local villagers was one of the essential goals of the war effort.

Nonlethal harassing agents seemed to offer the chance of controlling the level of collateral destruction while still having the potential to force enemy combatants out of hiding places. The U.S. government claimed that fewer civilians would be killed, especially because the close-up conventional attack that followed the gas at least theoretically could discriminate between combatants and noncombatants—whereas a general bombardment could not (see, for example, Westmoreland 1976, 366).

Other things being equal, controlled violence is morally preferable to wholesale violence under the just war principle of proportionality. The question, of course, is whether other things were equal in this case. From the perspective of the just war tradition, one must always begin the questioning with the issue of discrimination: Who is the real target of the weapon? Only if discrimination is satisfied is the just war thinker permitted to proceed to questions of proportionality. In the case of nonlethal weapons, the answer is sometimes ambiguous.

In the simplest account, the *intended* targets of the chemical weapons inside the hideouts were combatants, thus clearing the hurdle of the principle of discrimination. The tactic's potential protective value to noncombatants (as compared with blowing up the whole complex) would also help it with the issue of proportionality of harm to good. In this view, the relatively limited harm to noncombatants who also happened to be in hiding would be an unintended side effect and, thus, permissible under the principle of double effect.

Unfortunately, the situation was not quite so simple. If the expected presence of civilians in the caves and bunkers provides the *reason* for choosing nonlethal chemical weapons rather than conventional weapons, are civilians part of the *intended* target of the weapons? Under such circumstances, is the (limited) harm to noncombatants a means to the end of expelling the hidden enemy? If so, such harm is intended, not a mere side effect, and the principle of discrimination forbids intentionally harming noncombatants for *any* purpose.

But what if the real purpose of using highly potent forms of tear gas was not reducing harm to noncombatants? The historical evidence supports the contention that after some months of such use, the Americans and their allies increasingly used the harassing agents to drive all of those in caves or bunkers into the open so that they could be attacked more *efficiently* by conventional means (Spiers 1989, 105). The nonlethal chemical arms thus more and more became weapons used because of their effects on military forces not their protective effects on civilians. This goes a considerable way toward resolving the earlier problem raised under the principle of discrimination. If harassing agents were chosen for their military effects rather than to reduce the chances of civilian casualties, any discrimination issue disappears. This is ironic because civilian casualties also went up as lethal force was directed at everyone who came out of the hideouts.

Using nonlethal chemical weapons as adjuncts to more conventional weapons thus raises a problem with proportionality and double effect. To the extent that the tactic was effective in forcing people out of hiding places before a conventional attack, civilian casualties go up along with military ones. In the rush from a cave or bunker, the attackers might not *intend* to "target" civilians, per se, but many of them would be killed. The principles of proportionality and double effect do not require that military planners always choose the tactic with the smallest loss of civilian life, but they do demand that even unintended harm be proportionate to the military good expected. Although using harassing agents in order to be more discriminating in targeting might yield more military good than harm to noncombatants, it is hard to argue that the combined chemical/massive conventional attack could do so.

Using gas in conjunction with conventional attack was attractive to the military. The military benefits were clear, although hard to gauge precisely. The combination of gas and then artillery increased efficiency of each and was a step toward solving the difficult military problem of clearing tunnels and hideouts (Blumenfeld and Meselson 1971, 81–83). For these reasons, from 1967 to 1974 the Joint Chiefs of Staff withstood considerable civilian political pressure to include nonlethal chemical arms in the country's definition of prohibited chemical weapons. The chiefs continued to take this stand even after use of nonlethal chemicals on the battlefield stopped. Conceding the point would have pleased the Nixon administration's highest civilian officials and unlocked the deadlock in the Senate over ratifying the 1925 Geneva Protocol,[4] but it would also have precluded potentially useful military tactics at a later time and opened up the military to increased levels of criticism for having used chemical weapons in Vietnam.

There were, however, factors reducing the value of the tactic from both moral and political perspectives. Not least, it increased harm of noncombatants more than effectiveness in rooting out combatants. This is partly because gas was more effective in disgorging unprotected civilians; guerrillas or members of the North Vietnamese regular army were much more likely to have gas masks. Moreover, unprotected women, children, and the elderly are much more likely than even unprotected men to be seriously harmed by the high concentrations of harassing agents that would be experienced inside a cave or bunker. And, finally, how could attackers in the heat of battle judge whether someone emerging from a dugout was a civilian or a guerilla or, indeed, whether the whole hideout was a bomb shelter or a bunker? The military benefits and overall costs would be radically different in the two cases and not subject to reliable estimation in advance.

Precisely how high the actual costs were in terms of the principle of proportionality depends on how often mainly civilian hiding places were inadvertently targeted, how often civilians were intermingled with combatants in military or guerilla bunkers, and how often the hideouts were exclusively combatant territory. Unfortunately, these data are lost in time. At minimum, however, the dilemmas discussed here put into serious question the ethical advantages of choosing harassing agents to reduce civilian casualties.

We do know that many army officers came to believe that the tactic further alienated civilians during a war for their loyalty (see, for example, Lewallen 1971, 119). Furthermore, widespread international criticism of the use of harassing agents raised the political costs of the tactic even more. On balance, then, applying the principle of proportionality would have put the use of harassing agents as ancillary weapons out of bounds.

DEFOLIANTS AND THE VIETNAM WAR

In the case of defoliants, the proportionality and discrimination issues are even more complex than for harassing agents. Just war principles of discrimination and proportionality would almost certainly not support the use of chemical defoliants to destroy food crops. Destroying food crops with chemical defoliants not only fails to meet the standard of the principle of discrimination (and double effect) but could not even pass an independent evaluation under the principle of proportionality. Justice in war principles probably would, however, have permitted fairly extensive defoliation of supply trails because of the crucial military importance of these missions and the fact that the tradition does not provide the same protected status to the environment as it does to noncombatant humans. What is less clear is how to evaluate the meaning of widespread ecological damage to the region and how to weigh in probability of defeat or victory in the evaluation of benefits and costs.

In a very narrow sense, using defoliants for any purpose cannot violate the principle of discrimination. Military personnel do not use them directly to inflict intentional pain or death on people, civilian or otherwise. But there are other ways of harming people than simply blowing them up or causing injury or death with weapons. Destroying a person's means of life, livelihood, or property harms the person involved in a very real sense. Destroying plants can be intended to harm noncombatants in any or all of these ways. It seems, therefore, plausible to say that some uses of defoliants can be considered violations of the principle of discrimination because the plants involved are so closely tied to their human *owners*.

Not all plants connect so intimately with human life and physical well-being and so are not covered by *traditional* definitions of the principle of discrimination. Nevertheless, a full accounting of proportionality must include environmental damage as part of the consequentialist weighing of harm and good, even if the damage does not directly affect people and even though it is very difficult to know just how much weight to give.

DESTRUCTION OF FOOD CROPS AND
THE JUST WAR TRADITION

In just war terms, is destroying food crops with defoliants more like deliberately choosing to bomb a civilian neighborhood to affect the course of a war or more like bombing a munitions factory knowing some unintended harm to noncombatants will also result? One way of putting the ethical question involved is to ask whether the crops targeted were "civilian" foodstuffs, and hence presumably protected, or military materiel that happened to be of an edible variety. The issue is complicated because a food crop is a dual use item. It can belong to and be intended by its owners for noncombatants, or it can be an essential part of a war effort by feeding soldiers, or it can even be both at once.

Michael Walzer argues in his now classic *Just and Unjust Wars* (1992) that some of the activities of people in military forces are military in nature and some are more basically human and would have to be performed whether there was a war on or not. When engaging in these essentially human practices, according to Walzer, a person is more civilian than military. People in military forces need to be fed and clothed and their health must be cared for whether they are in uniform or not. Because they cater to these human activities, farms, clothing factories, and hospitals should not be military targets, even though the war could not be fought or won without them. Targeting such sites is, thus, a violation of the principle of discrimination, says Walzer (1992, 145–46).

Walzer's argument is controversial in the case of enemy farmers; and destruction of enemy food crops has certainly been a part of war in many eras. But it is equally true that destruction of one's own crops by the enemy is almost universally included on lists of enemy wrongs. In this framework, it would not matter whether farmers willingly or unwillingly gave up their crops to National Liberation front and North Vietnamese forces; food crops are protected because eating is essentially a civilian activity.

A less controversial reading of the principle of discrimination would still suggest that the policy of intentionally destroying food crops of South Vietnamese farmers was not acceptable. Although the initial decision to spray depended on an assurance that it was possible to distinguish between Viet Cong crops and civilian crops (Adams 1990, 75), the limitation steadily eroded. By 1967, the Joint Chiefs of Staff claimed that destroying the crops was needed to push the Viet Cong to divert manpower to farming and transport instead of combat (Buckingham 1982, 136). What this justification added up to, however, was the argument that if friendly or neutral civilians' crops could be destroyed, then enemy combatants would have to grow their own or expend more manpower in bringing food down from the north.

The new official justification thus strengthens an argument that the crops themselves were so closely tied to civilian life that harming the crops was in fact intentionally harming civilians. As the U.S. and the North Vietnamese governments acknowledged, these missions targeted crops in order to remove the foodstuffs they represented from the control of the farmers. *Because the farmers might be robbed or coerced,* their own government and its ally destroyed the farmers' property. Destroying farmers' crops without compensation or due process, thus, was harming those farmers, not a mere side effect of harm to enemy military materiel, much less an enemy war production plant. Under some traditional accounts of the principle of discrimination, it might have been permissible to target farms of those who were providing food more or less willingly to North Vietnamese regulars and Viet Cong guerrillas, as the original policy intended; but many of the problems in fighting the Vietnam War came precisely from the fact that it was impossible to judge such facts reliably. That the enemy sometimes took possession of the crops is relevant to consequentialist judgments, but it is not relevant to the principle of discrimination, which forbids *intentional* harm to noncombatants in and of itself. A legalistic quibble that the principle of discrimination is intended mainly to protect enemy noncombatants misses the point of the principle: preventing intentional harm to innocents.

The policy of destroying food crops in the Vietnam War would not pass muster under the principle of proportionality either. Destroying crops had many foreseeable side effects, not least harming civilians by reducing their food supply. And, as with the use of the pesticide DDT at about the same time in the United States, it is now widely believed that the herbicides used against crops and other vegetation in Vietnam had harmful secondary effects on the health of the people exposed to them. How much of this was known to the U.S. and South Vietnamese governments at the time is still under debate. What should have been clear to everyone, however, in a conflict in which one of the main war aims was winning the hearts and minds of the wary civilian population, destroying civilian property, livelihoods, and food supplies in order to inconvenience the enemy would almost certainly produce more harm than good over the long run on both military and humanitarian grounds. Even if we do not accept Walzer's segregation of basic human needs from other material supporting a war effort, or even the idea that harm to property is harm to its owners, these missions failed to meet the consequentialist strictures of the principle of proportionality.

TRAILS, PATHS, AND JUNGLE CANOPY

One of the most persistent military problems in the Vietnam War was the constant resupply of arms, materiel, and men from the North. Paths and trails that passed under triple-canopy rain forest in the northern part of South Vietnam could not be readily monitored, let alone shut down from the air. Further south, keeping the enemy out without destroying the countryside and the civilians they were supposed to protect and woo was a crucial problem for soldiers that was never fully solved. The trails offered another lethal danger as well: ambush. Small groups of guerrillas hiding along paths could attack squads of American and South Vietnamese soldiers from leafy hiding places.

Nonlethal chemical weapons seemed at least a partial solution to both problems. Herbicides could cut the canopy hiding northern trails, while placing (and re-placing) persistent harassing agents on known routes both north and south could at least force unprotected North Vietnamese resupply missions onto less easily traveled routes. And if trails traveled by Americans could be kept clear of vegetation, it was hoped that the ambushes could be reduced as well.

Evaluating these uses of nonlethal chemical weapons shows limits of the just war tradition's principle of discrimination. Although the trails, paths, and roads being used by guerrillas, infiltrators, and their suppliers often had noncombatant traffic as well, these were not owned by noncombatants or as tightly connected to civilian purposes as were the food crops discussed above. Neither paths nor forest canopies are protected in and of themselves, at least in a traditional account of noncombatant immunity, and therefore they do not raise the principle of discrimination. The justice in war issues here are related to proportionality.

The proportionality principle applied in the justice in war side of the just war tradition is different from the utilitarian's maximum happiness. Proportionality does not require soldiers, sailors, or air personnel to maximize the happiness of all concerned or even to choose the best of all solutions. In the *jus in bello* equation, proportionality, required of both sides, allows each to assign utility to its own winning and to judge benefits on that basis.

Did the use of chemical harassing agents to deny the use of trails and herbicides for deforestation and defoliation fall within these rather permissive guidelines? Using a traditional just war standard, it was almost certainly permissible to destroy trees and other plants to cut off supply lines and to reduce ambush, absent promises not to do so. Jungle habitats, inconvenience in transport for local civilians, and even hypothetical future danger to American soldiers and bystanders from exposure to the chemicals would be weighed against the iron reality that if resupply could not be cut off, the war was all but lost. The military utility in this case is so high that it ranks close to true military necessity. The initial decision to try the tactic was, thus, justifiable in *traditional* just war terms. It is still worth asking questions about the tradition itself: whether the rather cavalier treatment of nonhuman life is morally justifiable—and whether both sides in a war really should be able to assign the same utility to their own victory.

CONCLUSION

Traditional interpretations of Western just war principles shed considerable light on the use of nonlethal chemical weapons in the Vietnam War. The principle of discrimination sharpens and clarifies the vague intuition that there is something wrong with poisoning food supplies. And the principle of proportionality directs us to cast the net of consequences wider than simply evaluation of military benefits and costs. Using these principles, it is clear that the fact that a technology does not by itself kill is not enough to make it acceptable under all circumstances. Novel technology does not free us from asking traditional but difficult questions about intentions and moral value.

Looking at traditional justice in war principles in light of the use of nonlethal chemical weapons in Vietnam leaves us, however, with some equally troubling questions about the tradition itself. For example, although the principle of proportionality allows some consideration of environmental harm in adding up costs of a tactic or strategy, the principle of discrimination does not give the ecosystem of a target area any special moral standing. During the Vietnam War, the jungles and downstream habitats of Vietnam and surrounding areas suffered significant long-term damage. John Lewallen, writing in 1971, calls the extensive use of herbicides in the Vietnam War "ecocide." While Lewallen's conclusion may or may not be too extreme, at minimum, giving more weight to nonhuman life in a proportionality balance does seem increasingly important as the technical capacity for long-term and permanent destruction of the environment grows. As our sense of the interconnectedness of life grows, specific protection of nonhuman life might also be considered under the principle of discrimination.

Another issue that is increasingly important as technology changes is the question of risking unknown future harm. In the case of the herbicide Agent Orange, the full extent of the unintended costs to American soldiers, their families and allies, Vietnamese civilians, and even the enemy were to a large extent unforeseen. The risks were not completely unknown, however. By the late 1960s there was considerable information on the harmful effects of using the pesticide DDT, for example. Authorities knew an ingredient of Agent Orange could cause cancer in laboratory animals (see, for example, Hersh 1968, 153–54, 157–58). Spraying large quantities of a chemical strong enough to pierce and tame triple-canopy jungle was bound to have significant harmful effects on humans and other creatures exposed to it.

Closing our eyes or not finding out about risks does not take away their moral weight or our duty to exercise due caution. Given the near necessity of cutting supply lines in Vietnam, decision makers applying the just war tradition probably would have decided to take the risks anyhow. The apparent ease with which leaders proceeded, apparently without considering possible future costs carefully, should warn us, however, of how easy it is to ignore uncomfortable future dangers.

Even within the rule-oriented just war tradition, the principle of proportionality requires consequentialist thinking. Making consequentialist decisions requires guessing about the future: future costs, future benefits. That the future dangers are so often mere possibilities makes them hard to weigh against the wished-for benefits, but the need to try does not disappear. The rapid expansion in use of both herbicides and harassing agents from arguably acceptable beginning points to policies that the just war tradition would reject shows that evaluating proportionality or even discrimination is not a one-time decision. So, too, the potential for taking the first steps down a slippery slope should have been a real ethical issue, given the seductiveness of escalation and the human love of precedents. Did nonlethal chemical weapons in Vietnam lay part of the groundwork for use of lethal chemical weapons in the Iran–Iraq war?

And, finally, there is the question of what impending defeat—or even receding potential for success—should imply. Here, too, the just war tradition is silent, at least in its modern incarnation. Certainly the temptation as defeat gets closer is to take more and more desperate action to keep it at bay. It is to the credit of the U.S. government that it did not use lethal chemical weapons or nuclear arms in the Vietnam War. But it is worth asking whether planners should evaluate the actual probability of success in decisions about what to do in war, as well as in the initial decision to enter the conflict.

As probability of victory recedes, it is hard to see how missions with only a slender chance of actually promoting the expected benefits of victory could have the same moral weight in justifying costs. This dilemma was especially important in Vietnam in the case of trying to keep trails clear by the use of herbicides. At what point should military decision makers stop asking risks and sacrifices of their own people and, indeed, of others as well? The psychology of defeat may be such that it is nearly useless to counsel increased moderation of means. Nevertheless, a tactic incurring widespread ecological damage, and unknown future risks to one's own soldiers as well as others, surely was only one of the tactics whose consequences became even more problematic under such conditions.

In some ways, the arguments over whether American forces should have used nonlethal chemical weapons in the Vietnam War seem mainly of historical interest. The United States is very unlikely to use nonlethal chemical weapons in such a way again. For one thing, the political and legal climate of the 1960s and 1970s was quite different from that of today. Saddam Hussein had not yet used chemical weapons on the Iranian army or on his own Kurdish citizens. The Chemical Weapons Convention of 1993—which expressly forbids the use of harassing agents and herbicides as weapons—was not even on the international horizon in the late 1960s. Indeed, the United States did not become a party to the Geneva Protocol of 1925 until January 1975. The change in perception of the dangers of chemical weapons together with the new legal and political commitments make it much less likely that moral questions about harassing agents and herbicides as weapons of war will arise again for the United States (Price 1997).

Nevertheless, the morality of harassing agents and defoliants is relevant to the future of warfare in the twenty-first century. Chemical warfare is almost certainly not over. The weapons' relative simplicity of manufacture, together with a reputation as "the poor man's nuclear weapon," will probably continue to make them attractive to countries that either perceive dire security dilemmas or whose ambitions to be treated as serious players in the international arena is higher than their distaste for chemical arms. The study of the ethics of chemical weapons, thus, remains relevant to the future of warfare.

Equally important, several of the questions that came up in connection with the chemical weapons of the Vietnam War are related to their nonlethal characteristics. Today militaries around the world are exploring new technologies hailed as nonlethal contributions to conventional warfare such as "super glues" and "super lubricants" to halt forward motion on a battlefield. The use of harassing agents and herbicides in the Vietnam War raises the issue of possibly hidden costs of using weapons not intended in themselves to kill people.

And, finally, in an era of changing technology it is important to continue to hold up new technologies to traditional moral questions and criteria. Tradition may not have the last word, and only a living and sometimes evolving tradition can help us with actual decisions. Bringing enduring wisdom to bear on new issues can, however, only help us in our continuing quest to devise military tactics and strategies that are both effective and morally sound.

NOTES

1. The treaty is known formally as the Convention on the Prohibition of the Development, Production, Stockpiling and Use of Chemical Weapons, and on Their Destruction.

2. The treaty is known formally as the Protocol for the Prohibition of Use in War of Asphyxiating, Poisonous or Other Gases and of Bacteriological Methods of Warfare.

3. The Ford administration declared that there would be no use of herbicides except around the defensive perimeter of bases; the harassing agents would be limited to "defensive military modes to save lives, such as controlling rioting prisoners of war, protecting civilians being used to mask or screen attacks, rescue of personnel such as downed air crews in remotely isolated areas, and protection of convoys in rear echelon areas" (*New York Times*, 11 December 1974, 9).

4. Virtually alone among governments around the world, the Kennedy, Johnson, and Nixon administrations maintained that harassing agents and defoliants were not "chemical weapons," as defined by the treaty. They added that the United States was not a party to the Geneva Protocol in any event. When, under pressure, President Richard Nixon did submit the Geneva Protocol for ratification in August 1970, at the insistence of the Joint Chiefs of Staff he explicitly exempted nonlethal weapons from the U.S. definition (Smith 1970, 1). The joint chiefs continued to maintain this position until late 1974.

PART III

TERRORISM AND POLITICAL VIOLENCE

5

Can Terrorism Be Justified?

Andrew Valls

As the chapters in the previous section amply demonstrate, just war theory, despite its ambiguities, provides a rich framework with which to assess the morality of war. But interstate war is only the most conventional form of political violence. The question arises, Is it the only form of political violence that may ever be justified? If not, how are we to assess the morality of other cases of political violence, particularly those involving nonstate actors? In short, does just war theory apply to terrorism, and, if so, can terrorism satisfy its criteria?

In the public and scholarly reactions to political violence, a double standard often is at work. When violence is committed by states, our assessment tends to be quite permissive, giving states a great benefit of the doubt about the propriety of their violent acts. However, when the violence is committed by nonstate actors, we often react with horror, and the condemnations cannot come fast enough. Hence, terrorism is almost universally condemned, whereas violence by states, even when war has not been declared, is seen as legitimate, if not always fully justified. This difference in assessments remains when innocent civilians are killed in both cases and sometimes when such killing is deliberate. Even as thoughtful a commentator as Michael Walzer, for example, seems to employ this double standard. In his *Just and Unjust Wars*, Walzer considers whether "soldiers and statesmen [can] override the rights of innocent people for the sake of their own political community" and answers "affirmatively, though not without hesitation and worry" (1992, 254). Walzer goes on to discuss a case in point, the Allied bombing of German cities during World War II, arguing that, despite the many civilians who deliberately were killed, the bombing was justified. However, later in the book, Walzer rejects out of hand the possibility that terrorism might sometimes be justified, on the grounds that it involves the deliberate killing of innocents (1992, chapter 12). He never considers the possibility that stateless communities might confront the same "supreme emergency" that justified, in his view, the bombing of innocent German civilians. I will have more to say about Walzer's position below, but for now I wish to point out that, on the face of it at least, his position seems quite inconsistent.

From a philosophical point of view, this double standard cannot be sustained. As Coady (1985) argues, consistency requires that we apply the same standards to both kinds of political violence, state and nonstate. Of course, it may turn out that there are simply some criteria that states can satisfy that nonstate actors cannot, so that the same standard applied to both inevitably leads to different conclusions. There may be morally relevant features of states that make their use of violence legitimate and its use by others illegitimate. However, I will argue that this is not the case. I argue that, on the most plausible account of just war theory, taking into account the ultimate moral basis of its criteria, violence undertaken by nonstate actors can, in principle, satisfy the requirements of a just war.

To advance this view, I examine each criterion of just war theory in turn, arguing in each case that terrorism committed by nonstate actors can satisfy the criterion. The most controversial parts of my argument will no doubt be those regarding just cause, legitimate authority, and discrimination, so I devote more attention to these than to the others. I argue that, once we properly understand the moral basis for each of these criteria, it is clear that some nonstate groups may have the same right as states to commit violence and that they are just as capable of committing that violence within the constraints imposed by just war theory. My conclusion, then, is that if just war theory can justify violence committed by states, then terrorism committed by nonstate actors can also, under certain circumstances, be justified by it as well. But before commencing the substantive argument, I must attend to some preliminary matters concerning the definition of *terrorism*.

DEFINITIONAL ISSUES

There is little agreement on the question of how *terrorism* is best defined. In the political arena, of course, the word is used by political actors for political purposes, usually to paint their opponents as monsters. Scholars, on the other hand, have at least attempted to arrive at a more detached position, seeking a definition that captures the essence of terrorism. However, there is reason, in addition to the lack of consensus, to doubt whether much progress has been made.

Most definitions of terrorism suffer from at least one of two difficulties. First, they often define terrorism as murder or otherwise characterize it as intrinsically wrong and unjustifiable. The trouble with this approach is that it prejudges the substantive moral issue by a definitional consideration. I agree with Teichman, who writes that "we ought not to begin by *defining* terrorism as a bad thing"

(1989, 507). Moral conclusions should follow from moral reasoning, grappling with the moral issues themselves. To decide a normative issue by definitional considerations, then, ends the discussion before it begins.

The second shortcoming that many definitions of terrorism exhibit is being too revisionist of its meaning in ordinary language. As I have noted, the word is often used as a political weapon, so ordinary language will not settle the issue. Teichman (1989, 505) again is correct that any definition will necessarily be stipulative to some extent. But ordinary language does, nevertheless, impose some constraints on the stipulative definition that we can accept. For example, Carl Wellman defines *terrorism* as "the use or attempted use of terror as a means of coercion" (1979, 251) and draws the conclusion that when he instills terror in his students with threats of grade penalties on late papers, he commits terrorism. Clearly this is not what most of us have in mind when we speak of terrorism, so Wellman's definition, even if taken as stipulative, is difficult to accept.

Some definitions of terrorism suffer from both of these shortcomings to some degree. For example, those that maintain that terrorism is necessarily random or indiscriminate seem both to depart markedly from ordinary usage—there are lots of acts we call terrorist that specifically target military facilities and personnel—and thereby to prejudge the moral issue. (I will argue below that terrorism need not be indiscriminate at all.) The same can be said of definitions that insist that the aim of terrorism must be to terrorize, that it targets some to threaten many more (see, for example, Khatchadourian 1998). As Virginia Held has argued, "We should probably not construe either the intention to spread fear or the intention to kill noncombatants as necessary for an act of political violence to be an act of terrorism" (1991, 64). Annette Baier adds that "the terrorist may be ill named" because what she sometimes wants is not to terrorize but "the shocked attention of her audience population" (1994, 205).

With all of this disagreement, it would perhaps be desirable to avoid the use of the term *terrorism* altogether and simply to speak instead of political violence. I would be sympathetic to this position were it not for the fact that *terrorism* is already too much a part of our political vocabulary to be avoided. Still, we can with great plausibility simply define *terrorism* as a form of political violence, as Held does: "I [see] terrorism as a form of violence to achieve political goals, where creating fear is usually high among the intended effects" (1991, 64). This is a promising approach, though I would drop as nonessential the stipulation that terrorism is usually intended to spread fear. In addition, I would make two stipulations of my own. First, "violence" can include damage to property as well as harm to people. Blowing up a power plant can surely be an act of terrorism, even if no one is injured. Second, for the purposes of this chapter, I am interested in violence committed by nonstate actors. I do not thereby deny the existence of state terrorism. Indeed, I endorse Gordon and Lopez's discussion of it in their chapter in this volume. However, for the purposes of my present argument, I assume that when a state commits terrorism against its own citizens, this is a matter for domestic justice, and that when it commits violence outside of its own borders, just war theory can, fairly easily, be extended to cover these cases. The problem for international ethics that I wish to address here is whether just war theory can be extended to nonstate actors. So my stipulative definition of *terrorism* in this chapter is simply that it is violence committed by nonstate actors against persons or property for political purposes. This definition appears to leave open the normative issues involved and to be reasonably consistent with ordinary language.

JUS AD BELLUM

It is somewhat misleading to speak of just war *theory*, for it is not a single theory but, rather, a tradition within which there is a range of interpretation. That is, just war theory is best thought of as providing a framework for discussion about whether a war is just, rather than as providing a set of unambiguous criteria that are easily applied. In what follows I rely on what I believe is the most plausible and normatively appealing version of just war theory, one that is essentially the same as the one articulated and developed by the preceding chapters. I begin with the *jus ad bellum* criteria, concerning the justice of going to war, and then turn to *jus in bello* criteria, which apply to the conduct of the war.

Just Cause

A just cause for a war is usually a defensive one. That is, a state is taken to have a just cause when it defends itself against aggression, where *aggression* means the violation or the imminent threat of the violation of its territorial integrity or political independence (Walzer 1992). So the just cause provision of just war theory holds, roughly, that the state has a right to defend itself against the aggression of other states.

But on what is this right of the state based? Most students of international ethics maintain that any right that a state enjoys is ultimately based on the rights of its citizens. States in and of themselves have value only to the extent that they serve some good for the latter. The moral status of the state is therefore derivative, not foundational, and it is derivative of the rights of the individuals within it. This, it seems, is the dominant (liberal) view, and only an exceedingly statist perspective would dispute it (Beitz 1979b; Walzer 1992).

The right that is usually cited as being the ground for the state's right to defend itself is the right of self-determination. The state is the manifestation of, as well as the arena for, the right of a people to determine itself. It is because aggression threatens the common life of the people within a state, as well as threatening other goods they hold dear, that the state can defend its territory and independence. This is clear, for example, from Walzer's (1992, chapter 6) discussion of intervention. Drawing on John Stuart Mill (1984), Walzer argues that states generally ought not to intervene in the affairs of other states because to do so would be to violate the right of self-determination of the community within the state. However, once the right of self-determination is recognized, its implications go beyond a right against intervention or a right of defense. Walzer makes this clear as well, as his discussion of Mill's argument for nonintervention is followed immediately by exceptions to the rule, one of which is secession. When a secessionist movement has demonstrated that it represents the will of its people, other states may intervene to aid the secession because, in this case, secession reflects the self-determination of that people.

In the twenty years since Walzer presented this argument, a great deal of work has been done on nationalism, self-determination, and secession. Despite the range of views that has developed, it is fair to say that something of an overlapping consensus has formed, namely, that under certain circumstances, certain kinds of groups enjoy a right of self-determination that entitles them to their own state or at least to some autonomy in a federal arrangement within an existing state. The debate is mostly over what these circumstances are and what kinds of groups enjoy the right. For example, Allen Buchanan, in his important book *Secession* (1991), argues that the circumstances must include a historical injustice before a group is entitled to secede. Others are more permissive. Christopher Wellman (1995) and Daniel Philpott (1995) argue that past injustice is not required to entitle a group to secession and, indeed, that any group within a territory may secede, even if it is not plausibly seen as constituting a nation.

The modal position in the debate is, perhaps, somewhere between these positions, holding that certain groups, even absent a history of injustice, have a right to self-determination but that this applies not to just any group but only to "peoples" or "nations." This is essentially the position taken by Kymlicka (1995), Tamir (1993), Miller (1995), and Margalit and Raz (1990). There are, of course, important differences among these authors. Kymlicka argues that groups with "societal cultures" have a right to self-government but not necessarily secession. Margalit and Raz advance a similar argument, and their notion of an "encompassing group" is very close to Kymlicka's "societal culture." Tamir emphasizes that, in her view, the right to self-determination is a cultural right, not a political one, and does not necessarily support a right to political independence. Miller does interpret the right of self-determination as a right to a state, but he hesitates to call it a right, for it may not always be achievable due to the legitimate claims of others. (His concern would perhaps be alleviated by following Philpott in speaking of a "prima facie" right.)

For the purposes of my present argument, I need not enter this important debate but only point out that any one of these views can support the weak claim I wish to make. The claim is that under some circumstances, some groups enjoy a right to self-determination. The circumstances may include—or, following Buchanan, even be limited to—cases of injustice toward the group, or, in a more permissive view, it may not. This right may be enjoyed only by nations or by any group within a territory. It may be that the right of self-determination does not automatically ground a right to political independence, but if some form of self-determination cannot be realized within an existing state, then it can, under these circumstances, ground such a right. For the sake of simplicity, in the discussion that follows I refer to nations or peoples as having a right of self-determination, but this does not commit me to the view that other kinds of groups do not enjoy this right. Similarly, I will sometimes fail to distinguish between a right of self-determination and a right to a state, despite realizing that the former does not necessarily entail the latter. I will assume that in some cases—say, when a federal arrangement cannot be worked out—one can ground the right to a state on the right to self-determination.

My conclusion about the just cause requirement is obvious. Groups other than those constituted by the state in which they live can have a just cause to defend their right of self-determination. While just war theory relies on the rights of the citizens to ground the right of a state to defend itself, other communities within a state may have that same right. When the communal life of a nation is seriously threatened by a state, that nation has a just cause to defend itself. In the case in which the whole nation is within a single state, this can justify secession. In a case in which the community is stateless, as with colonial rule, it is probably less accurate to speak of secession than national liberation.

This is not a radical conclusion. Indeed, it is recognized and endorsed by the United Nations, as Khatchadourian points out: "The UN definition of 'just cause' recognizes the rights of peoples as well as states," and in Article 7 of the definition of *aggression*, the United Nations refers to "the right to self-determination, freedom, and independence, as derived from the Charter, of *peoples* forcibly deprived of that right" (1998, 41). So both morally and legally, "peoples" or "nations" enjoy a right to self-determination. When that right is frustrated, such peoples, I have argued, have the same just cause that states have when the self-determination of their citizens is threatened.

Legitimate Authority

The legitimate authority requirement is usually interpreted to mean that only states can go to war justly. It rules out private groups waging private wars and claiming them to be just. The state has a monopoly on the legitimate use of force, so it is a necessary condition for a just war that it be undertaken by the entity that is uniquely authorized to wield the sword. To allow other entities, groups, or agencies to undertake violence would be to invite chaos. Such violence is seen as merely private violence, crime.

The equation of legitimate authority with states has, however, been criticized by a number of philosophers—and with good reason. Gilbert has argued that "the equation of proper authority with a lawful claim to it should be resisted" (1994,

29). Tony Coates (1997, chapter 5) has argued at some length and quite persuasively that to equate legitimate authority with state sovereignty is to rob the requirement of the moral force that it historically has had. The result is that the principle has become too permissive by assuming that any de facto state may wage war. This requirement, then, is too easily and quickly "checked off": If a war is waged by a state, this requirement is satisfied. This interpretation has meant that "the criterion of legitimate authority has become the most neglected of all the criteria that have been traditionally employed in the moral assessment of war" (Coates 1997, 123). Contrary to this tendency in recent just war thinking, Coates argues that we must subject to close scrutiny a given state's claim to represent the interests and rights of its people.

When we reject the view that all states are legitimate authorities, we may also ask if some nonstates may be legitimate authorities. The considerations just adduced suggest that being a state is not sufficient for being a legitimate authority. Perhaps it is not necessary either. What matters is the plausibility of the claim to represent the interests and rights of a people. I would like to argue that some nonstate entities or organizations may present a very plausible case for being a people's representative. Surely it is sufficient for this that the organization is widely seen as their representative by the members of the nation itself. If an organization claims to act on behalf of a people and is widely seen by that people as legitimately doing so, then the rest of us should look on that organization as the legitimate authority of the people for the purposes of assessing its entitlement to engage in violence on their behalf.

The alternative view, that only states may be legitimate authorities, "leads to political quietism [and is] conservative and uncritical" (Coates 1997, 128). Once we acknowledge that stateless peoples may have the right to self-determination, it would render that right otiose to deny that the right could be defended and vindicated by some nonstate entity. As Dugard (1982, 83) has pointed out, in the case of colonial domination, there is no victim state, though there is a victim people. If we are to grant that a colonized people has a right to self-determination, it seems that we must grant that a nonstate organization—a would-be state, perhaps—can act as a legitimate authority and justly engage in violence on behalf of the people. Examples are not difficult to find. Coates cites the Kurds and the Marsh Arabs in Iraq and asks, "Must such persecuted communities be denied the right of collective self-defense simply because, through some historical accident, they lack the formal character of states?" (1997, 128).

It must be emphasized that the position advocated here requires that the organization not only claim representative status but be perceived to enjoy that status by the people it claims to represent. This is a rather conservative requirement because it rules out "vanguard" organizations that claim representative status despite lack of support among the people themselves. The position defended here is also more stringent than that suggested by Wilkins, who writes that it might "be enough for a terrorist movement simply to claim to represent the aspirations or the moral rights of a people" (1992, 71). While I agree that "moral authority may be all that matters" (Wilkins 1992, 72), I would argue that moral authority requires not merely claiming to represent a people but also being seen by the people themselves as their representative.

How do we know whether this is the case? No single answer can be given here. Certainly the standard should not be higher than that used for states. In the case of states, for example, elections are not required for legitimacy, as understood in just war theory. There are many members of the international community in good standing that are not democratic regimes, authorized by elections. In the case of nonstate entities, no doubt a number of factors will weigh in, either for or against the claim to representativeness, and, in the absence of legal procedures (or public opinion polls), we may have to make an all-things-considered judgment. No doubt there will be some disagreement in particular cases, but all that is required for the present argument is that, in principle, nonstate organizations may enjoy the moral status of legitimate authorities.

Right Intention

If a national group can have a just cause, and if a nonstate entity can be a legitimate authority to engage in violence on behalf of that group, it seems unproblematic that those engaging in violence can be rightly motivated by that just cause. Hence, if just cause and legitimate authority can be satisfied, there seems to be no reason to think that the requirement of right intention cannot be satisfied. This is not to say, of course, that if the first two are satisfied, the latter is as well, but only that if the first two requirements are met, the latter can be. All that it requires is that the relevant actors be motivated by the just cause and not some other end.

Last Resort

Can terrorist violence, undertaken by the representatives of a stateless nation to vindicate their right of self-determination, be a last resort? Some have doubted that it can. For example, Walzer refers to the claim of last resort as one of the "excuses" sometimes offered for terrorism. He suggests that terrorism is usually a first resort, not a last one, and that to truly be a last resort, "one must indeed try everything (which is a lot of things), and not just once. . . . Politics is an art of repetition" (1988, 239). Terrorists, according to Walzer, often claim that their resort to violence is a last resort but in fact it never is and never can be.

Two problems arise concerning Walzer's position. First, related to the definitional issues discussed above and taken up again below when discrimination is treated, Walzer takes terrorism to be "an attack upon the innocent," and he "take[s] the principle for granted: that every act of terrorism is a wrongful act" (1988, 238). Given the understanding of terrorism as murder, it can never be a justified last resort. But as Fullinwider (1988) argues in his response to Walzer, it is puzzling both that Walzer construes terrorism this way, for not all terrorism is random murder, and that Walzer simply takes it for granted that nothing can justify terrorism. Walzer's position is undermined by a prejudicial definition of *terrorism* that begs the substantive moral questions, reflected in the fact that he characterizes arguments in defense of terrorism as mere "excuses."

The second problem is that again Walzer appears to use a double standard. While he does not say so explicitly in the paper under discussion, Walzer elsewhere clearly endorses the resort to war by states. Here, however, he argues that, because "politics is an art of repetition," the last resort is never arrived at for nonstate actors contemplating violence. But why is it that the territorial integrity and political independence of, say, Britain, justify the resort to violence—even violence that targets civilians—but the right of self-determination of a stateless nation never does? Why can states arrive at last resort, while stateless nations cannot? Walzer never provides an answer to this question.

The fact is that judgment is called for by all political actors contemplating violence, and among the judgments that must be made is whether last resort has been. This is a judgment about whether all reasonable nonviolent measures have been tried, been tried a reasonable number of times, and been given a reasonable amount of time to work. There will always be room for argument about what *reasonable* means here, what it requires in a particular case, but I see no justification for employing a double standard for what it means, one for states, another for nonstate actors. If states may reach the point of deciding that all nonviolent measures have failed, then so too can nonstate actors.

Probability of Success

Whether terrorism ever has any probability of success, or enough probability of success to justify embarking on a terrorist campaign, depends on a number of factors, including the time horizon one has in mind. Whether one considers the case of state actors deciding to embark on a war or nonstate actors embarking on terrorism, a prospective judgment is required, and prospective judgments are liable to miscalculations and incorrect estimations of many factors. Still, one must make a judgment, and if one judges that the end has little chance of being achieved through violence, the probability of success criterion requires that the violence not be commenced.

Does terrorism ever have any probability of success? There are differing views of the historical record on this question. For example, Walzer thinks not. He writes, "No nation that I know of owes its freedom to a campaign of random murder" (1988, 240). Again, we find that Walzer's analysis is hindered by his conception of what terrorism is, and so it is of little help to us here. To those who have a less loaded notion of terrorism, the evidence appears more ambiguous. Held provides a brief, well-balanced discussion of the issue. She cites authors who have argued on both sides of the question, including one who uses the bombing of the U.S. Marines' barracks in Beirut in 1982 (which prompted an American withdrawal) as an example of a successful terrorist attack. Held concludes that "it may be impossible to predict whether an act of terrorism will in fact have its intended effect" but notes that in this it is no different from other prospective judgments (1991, 71). Similarly, Teichman concludes that the historical evidence on the effectiveness of terrorism is "both ambiguous and incomplete" (1989, 517). And Baier suggests that, at the least, "the prospects for the success of a cause do not seem in the past to have been reduced by resort to unauthorized force, by violent demonstrations that cost some innocent lives" (1994, 208). Finally, Wilkins (1992, 39) believes that some terrorist campaigns have indeed accomplished their goal of national independence and cites Algeria and Kenya as examples.

I am not in a position to judge all of the historical evidence that may be relevant to this issue. However, it seems clear that we cannot say that it is never the case that terrorism has some prospect of success. Perhaps in most cases—the vast majority of them, even—there is little hope of success. Still, we cannot rule out that terrorism can satisfy the probability of success criterion.

Proportionality

The proportionality criterion within *jus ad bellum* also requires a prospective judgment—whether the overall costs of the violent conflict will be outweighed by the overall benefits. In addition to the difficulties inherent in prospective judgments, this criterion is problematic in that it seems to require us to measure the value of costs and benefits that may not be amenable to measurement and seems to assume that all goods are commensurable, that their value can be compared. As a result, there is probably no way to make these kinds of judgments with any great degree of precision.

Still, it seems clear that terrorism can satisfy this criterion at least as well as conventional war. Given the large scale of destruction that often characterizes modern warfare, and given that some very destructive wars are almost universally considered just, it appears that just war theory can countenance a great deal of violence if the end is of sufficient value. If modern warfare is sometimes justified, terrorism, in which the violence is usually on a far smaller scale, can be justified as well. This is especially clear if the end of the violence is the same or similar in both cases, such as when a nation wishes to vindicate its right to self-determination.

JUS IN BELLO

Even if terrorism can meet all the criteria of *jus ad bellum,* it may not be able to meet those of *jus in bello,* for terrorism is often condemned, not so much for who carries it out and why but for how it is carried out. Arguing that it can satisfy the requirements of *jus in bello,* then, may be the greatest challenge facing my argument.

Proportionality

The challenge, however, does not come from the proportionality requirement of *jus in bello.* Like its counterpart in *jus ad bellum,* the criterion requires proportionality between the costs of an action and the benefits to be achieved, but now the requirement is applied to particular acts within the war. It forbids, then, conducting the war in such a way that it involves inordinate costs, costs that are disproportionate to the gains.

Again, there seems to be no reason to believe that terrorist acts could not satisfy this requirement. Given that the scale of the death and destruction usually involved in terrorist acts pales in comparison with that involved in wars commonly thought to be just, it would seem that terrorism would satisfy this requirement more easily than war (assuming that the goods to be achieved are not dissimilar). So if the means of terrorism is what places it beyond the moral pale for many people, it is probably not because of its disproportionality.

Discrimination

The principle of discrimination holds that in waging a war we must distinguish between legitimate and illegitimate targets of attack. The usual way of making this distinction is to classify persons according to their status as combatants and noncombatants and to maintain that only combatants may be attacked. However, there is some disagreement as to the moral basis of this distinction, which creates disagreement as to where exactly this line should be drawn. While usually based on the notion of moral innocence, noncombatant status, it can be argued, has little to do with innocence, for often combatants are conscripts, while those truly responsible for aggression are usually not liable (practically, not morally) to attack. Moreover, many who provide essential support to the war effort are not combatants.

For the moment, though, let us accept the conventional view that discrimination requires that violence be directed at military targets. Assuming the line can be clearly drawn, two points can be made about terrorism and discrimination. The first is that, a priori, it is possible for terrorism to discriminate and still be terrorism. This follows from the argument presented above that, as a matter of definition, it is implausible to define terrorism as intrinsically indiscriminate. Those who define terrorism as random or indiscriminate will disagree and maintain that "discriminate terrorism" is an oxymoron, a conceptual impossibility. Here I can only repeat that this position departs substantially from ordinary language and does so in a way that prejudges the moral issues involved. However, if my argument above does not convince on this question, there is little more to be said here.

Luckily, the issue is not a purely a priori one. The fact is that terrorists, or at least those called terrorists by almost everyone, in fact do often discriminate. One example, cited above, is the bombing of the barracks in Beirut, which killed some 240 American soldiers. Whatever one wants to say to condemn the attack, one cannot say that it was indiscriminate. Fullinwider cites the example of the kidnapping, trail, and killing of Aldo Moro by the Italian Red Brigades in 1978 and argues that, whatever else one might want to say about it, "there was nothing indiscriminate about the taking of Aldo Moro" (1988, 250). Coady (1985, 63) cites another example, that of an American diplomat in Uruguay who was targeted and killed in 1970 because of the assistance he was providing to the authoritarian regime. These may be the exceptions rather than the rule, but it clearly is not accurate to say that terrorists—and there was never any doubt that these were acts of terrorism—never discriminate.

It might be useful to look, one last time, at Walzer's position on this issue because, from the point of view I have developed, he errs on both the conceptual and the empirical question. Walzer maintains that "terrorism in the strict sense, the random murder of innocent people, emerged . . . only in the period after World War II" (1992, 198). Previously, nonstate actors, especially revolutionaries, who committed violence did discriminate. Walzer gives several examples of this in which Russian revolutionaries, the Irish Republican Army, and the Stern Gang in the Middle East went to great lengths to not kill civilians. He also notes that these people were called terrorists. Yet he refuses to say that they *were* terrorists, insisting instead that they were not, really, and using scare quotes when he himself calls them terrorists. This is tortured analysis indeed. Why not simply acknowledge that these earlier terrorists were indeed terrorists while also maintaining, if evidence supports it, that today more terrorists are more indiscriminate than in the past? I suspect that Walzer and I would agree in our moral assessment of particular acts. Our main difference is that he believes that calling an act terrorism (without the scare quotes) settles the question.

All of this is consistent with the assumption that a clear line can be drawn between combatants and noncombatants. However, the more reasonable view may be that combatancy status, and therefore liability to attack, are matters of degree. This is suggested by Holmes (1989, 187), and though Holmes writes as a pacifist critic of just war theory, his suggestion is one that just war theorists may nevertheless want to endorse. Holmes conceives of a spectrum along which we can place classes of individuals, according to their degree of responsibility for an aggressive war. At one end he would place political leaders who undertake the aggression, followed by soldiers, contributors to the war, supporters, and, finally, at the other end of the spectrum, noncontributors and nonsupporters. This view does indeed better capture our moral intuitions about liability to attack and avoids debates (which are probably not resolvable) about where the absolute line between combatants and noncombatants is to be drawn.

If correct, this view further complicates the question of whether and when terrorism discriminates. It means we must speak of more and less discriminate violence, and it forces us to ask questions like, To what *extent* were the targets of violence implicated in unjust aggression? Children, for example, would be clearly off-limits, but nonmilitary adults who actively take part in frustrating a people's right to self-determination may not be. With terrorism, as with war, the question to ask may not be, Was the act discriminate, yes or no? but, rather, How discriminate was the violence? Our judgment on this matter, and hence our moral appraisal of the violence, is likely to be more nuanced if we ask the latter question than if we assume that a simple yes or no settles the matter. After all, is our judgment really the same—and ought it be—when a school bus is attacked as when gun-toting citizens are attacked? Terrorism, it seems, can be more discriminate or less so, and our judgments ought to reflect the important matters of degree involved.

One final issue is worth mentioning, if only briefly. Even if one were to grant that terrorism necessarily involves the killing of innocents, this alone does not place it beyond the scope of just war theory, for innocents may be killed in a just war. All that just war theory requires is that innocents not be *targeted*. The basis for this position is the principle of double effect, which holds, roughly, that innocents may be killed as long as their deaths are not the intended effects of violence but, rather, the unintended (though perhaps fully foreseen) side effects of violence. So the most that can be said against my position, even granting that terrorism involves the killing of innocents, is that the difference between (just) war and terrorism is that in the former innocents are not targeted but (routinely) killed while in the latter they are targeted and killed. Whether this is a crucial distinction is a question that would require us to go too far afield at this point. Perhaps it is enough to say that if there are reasons to reject the principle of double effect, such as those offered by Holmes (1989, 193–200), there is all the more basis to think that terrorism and war are not so morally different from each other.

CONCLUSION

I have argued that terrorism, understood as political violence committed by nonstate actors, can be assessed from the point of view of just war theory and that terrorist acts can indeed satisfy the theory's criteria. Though stateless, some groups can nevertheless have a just cause when their right to self-determination is frustrated. Under such circumstances, a representative organization can be a morally legitimate authority to carry out violence as a last resort to defend the group's rights. Such violence must conform to the other criteria, especially discrimination, but terrorism, I have argued, can do so.

The argument has taken place entirely within the just war tradition but can be endorsed from other perspectives as well. For example, Annette Baier, though no just war theorist, comes to a very similar conclusion:

> It is fairly easy to say that the clearer it is that the terrorist's group's case is *not* being listened to in decision making affecting it and that the less violent ways to get attention have been tried in vain, the more excuse the terrorist has; that his case is better the more plausible his claim to represent his group's sense of injustice or wrong, not just his own; that the more limited, the less indiscriminate, his violence, the less outrage will we feel for his inhumanity. Those are not daring conclusions. [1994, 217]

Indeed they are not daring conclusions, and mine certainly are not. I have avoided consequentialist arguments that might, on utilitarian grounds, justify violence for the greater good to be achieved. I have not endorsed the notion of collective guilt, which, in my view, goes too far in eroding the distinction between combatants and noncombatants (see Wilkins 1992). My argument would not support the violence of a vanguard party, committing violence in the hope of winning the support of those it claims to already represent. Hence, the argument presented here places real, stringent moral limits on violence committed by nonstate actors.

Indeed, placing limits on violence is what just war theory is all about. As Coates argues in his contribution to this volume, the main purpose of just war theory is to constrain violence. Coates emphasizes that just war theory should not convince perpetrators of violence of their own righteousness but, rather, is meant to instill a sense of limits and restraint. If we assume that terrorism is beyond the pale, however, we deprive ourselves of the capacity to impose some moral limits. If terrorists are monsters, then there is no reasoning with them. However, if we take their claims seriously, if we assess their violence by the same standards used to assess the violence of states, we at least have a chance that just war theory will impose some restraint on them, as it does (or at least is supposed to) with states.

It is important to be clear about what I have not argued here. I have not defended terrorism in general, nor certainly have I defended any particular act of violence. It follows from my argument not that terrorism can be justified but that if war can be justified, then terrorism can be as well. I wish to emphasize the conditional nature of the conclusion. I have not established just war theory as the best or the only framework within which to think about the moral issues raised by political violence. Instead I have relied on it because it is the most developed and widely used in thinking about violence carried out by states. I have done so because the double standard that is often used in assessing violence committed by states and nonstate actors seems indefensible. Applying just war theory to both, I believe, is a plausible way to bring both kinds of violence under one standard.

I have little doubt that most terrorist acts do not satisfy all of the criteria of just war theory and that many of them fall far short. In such cases we are well justified in condemning them. But the condemnation must follow, not precede, examination of the case and is not settled by calling the act terrorism and its perpetrators terrorists. I agree with Fullinwider that, while terrorism often fails to be morally justified, "this failure is contingent, not necessary. We cannot define terrorism into a moral corner where we do not have to worry any more about justification" (1988, 257). Furthermore, failure to satisfy the requirements of just war theory is not unique to acts of terrorism. The same could be said of wars themselves. How many wars, after all, are undertaken and waged within the constraints imposed by the theory?

The conditional nature of the conclusion, if the above argument is sound, forces a choice. Either both interstate war and terrorism can be justified or neither can be. For my part, I must confess to being sorely tempted by the latter position, that neither war nor terrorism can be justified. This temptation is bolstered by pacifist arguments, such as that presented by Holmes (1989, chapter 6), that the killing of innocents is a perfectly predictable effect of modern warfare, the implication of which is that no modern war can be just. That is, even if we can imagine a modern just war, it is not a realistic possibility. Though the pacifist position is tempting, it also seems clear that some evils are great enough to require a response, even a violent response. And once we grant that states may respond violently, there seems no principled reason to deny that same right to certain nonstate groups that enjoy a right to self-determination.

6

The Ethics of IRA Terrorism

David A. George

The title "Irish Republican Army" (IRA) applies to militant Irish republicans whose aim is to end United Kingdom jurisdiction in Ireland by force of arms against the persons and property of civilians, police officers, and military personnel and through exploiting the fear that this violence creates. Such armed attacks by the IRA were directed against other citizens of the United Kingdom of Great Britain and Ireland between 1919 and 1921. They continued to be internal or noninternational after the Irish Free State was formed from twenty-six of the thirty-two Irish counties in 1922. A majority faction of the IRA then fought against the Free State army, which included the minority IRA faction. It was only after the Irish civil war ended in 1923 that the IRA and its armed violence acquired an international dimension.

The rump IRA was now a Dublin-based organization, the members of which lived in both the Irish Free State and the United Kingdom. Until 1950, it carried out sporadic attacks on Free State police officers, jailers, jurors, witnesses, and other civilians while intermittently pursuing irredentist terrorist campaigns to eliminate U.K. jurisdiction over Northern Ireland. In 1939, after first issuing an ultimatum, then a formal declaration of war against the government of the United Kingdom of Great Britain and Northern Ireland, it embarked on an ill-conceived and abortive random bombing campaign in mainland Britain, which effectively came to an end in the following year. It launched a series of futile cross-border raids into Northern Ireland between 1956 and 1962, principally to attack police stations, and it renewed its current terrorist campaign there when major civil disorder in 1968–1969 following civil rights marches provided a suitable situation for it to exploit (Bell 1972, 175–211, 341–97; Coogan 1987, 150–73, 377–418). Factional divisions within the IRA in this latest campaign led to the organization splintering into six militant republican groups between 1970 and 1997, each claiming to be the genuine Irish Republican Army. In each case, the violence employed by the group was terrorist.

Terrorism is sometimes defined by moral philosophers in terms of violence against innocent individuals (e.g., Coady 1985, 52; Primoratz 1990, 135; Smith 1991, 25; Walzer 1992, 198), but when this happens it no longer makes sense to ask whether terrorist violence might, in some circumstances, be morally justified. That possibility has been ruled out by the way in which acts of terrorism have been defined; if it is morally wrong to harm the innocent, it follows that terrorism is immoral by definition. It can only be justified by ignoring whether those attacked are innocent, nocent, or both indiscriminately and can only be assessed simply in terms of its consequences. At issue will be whether or not the benefits achieved by terrorism outweigh the costs of their attainment, for example, in terms of suffering and death, and for this calculation the benefits and costs must be commensurable (Hare 1979b, 245–46). And if it is said that the moral arithmetic of so aggregating the costs and benefits of harming people is morally repugnant and that the conclusions that follow are no less morally repellent (Wallace 1995, 308), such arithmetic may be unnecessary if terrorist acts prove inefficacious, that is, if they fail to achieve their political ends.

This utilitarian approach is, however, unnecessary, for terrorism can be adequately defined without reference to the moral status of the targets attacked. It need not be intrinsically immoral by definitional fiat, and a nonconsequentialist justification of it is therefore possible. Terrorism may be characterized as a special tripartite form of armed violence, namely, as the use, or the threatened use, of lethal armed force against persons and the destructive violence against property in order to coerce a third party (like a government or the general public), by the psychological impact of the violence, into meeting the wishes or satisfying the demands of its perpetrators. Thus defining terrorism, this chapter addresses the problem, When, if ever, is it morally justified for the IRA to resort to terrorist violence in order to end U.K. jurisdiction over Northern Ireland and incorporate the province into an authentic Irish republic?

From this deontological perspective, it is always morally wrong to kill, injure, or otherwise harm innocents, that is, those individuals who are not responsible for some particular legal or moral wrongdoing. It is assumed that a class of the morally and legally guilty exists, in which case terrorist violence against its members might be morally justified. They might, for instance, be legitimately punished or justifiably attacked as nocent combatants in a just war. Punishment will, however, be excluded here, for it is an internal or noninternational use of force. Although recent attempts have been made to justify some IRA terrorism as punishment for antisocial behavior (Families Against Intimidation and Terror [FAIT], personal communication, 18 July 1998), those subjected to its savage "punishment" beatings, shootings, and "executions" have been, like the perpetrators, residents of the predominantly Roman Catholic neighborhoods of Northern Ireland, which the IRA strives to control. So, instead of examining the validity of the IRA's claim to dispense justice through the punishment of alleged wrongdoers, this chapter will concentrate on the IRA's other claim to a just resort to, and use of, arms, namely, in its putative international war against the United Kingdom. What follows, then, is a moral interpretation or analysis of IRA terrorism from within the just war tradition of international ethics (see Johnson 1981, xxi–xxiv; 1984, 12).

TERRORISM IN THE JUST WAR TRADITION

Because terrorism could be morally justified when it is not directed against the innocent, three just war principles in particular will be of decisive importance in its moral appraisal. Each is directly connected to the innocent/nocent moral dichotomy.

Terrorist violence must first satisfy the *jus in bello* (justice in war) principle of discrimination, which prohibits intentional attacks on morally innocent noncombatants, if it is to count as a justly waged war. This moral distinction between noncombatants and combatants (or between illegitimate and legitimate targets of attack) is derived from the logically prior *jus ad bellum* (justice of war) principle of just cause. In classic just war thought, the generic just cause for resort to war is that a wrong had been done to the community. Consequently, it was just to draw the sword against those individuals who had wronged the community but unjust to do so against those who had done the community no wrong (Vitoria 1991, 303–04). Just cause, therefore, determines not only when war may be a legitimate recourse but also those persons against whom it may be justly waged (combatants) and those who are morally exempted from attack (noncombatants) (Finnis 1998, 284–85). But not every harm or injury done to the community gives sufficient ground for going to war: they must be of considerable gravity to warrant hostilities against the wrongdoers. Whether a particular wrong is sufficiently grave to constitute a just cause has to be authoritatively determined, and this is the function of the legitimate authority in the community, traditionally, its sovereign ruler. Also, the sovereign ruler must weigh the probable good expected from securing redress of the wrong against the probable evil anticipated from waging a war; it must, that is, address proportionality (Johnson 1984, 61–62; Suarez 1944, 805–06, 817–18; Vitoria 1991, 304). The principle of legitimate authority also directly determines when terrorist violence is morally justified. If the intentionally lethal or destructive violence of the terrorist is a public not a private act, that is, if it is perpetrated by a public body acting with legitimate authority and not by private individuals devoid of this authority, then war that could be just is waged (see Anscombe 1970, 45; Gilbert 1994, 28).

Strictly, this principle applies only to offensive just war, whereby redress of a wrong done or right infringed is initiated through force of arms because it cannot be remedied in any other way. Offensive war involves a first use of armed force, as does a war of aggression; but in the former case this is to remedy the infringement of a right, whereas in the latter there is no such just cause. When people react to an unjust lethal attack by repelling it with armed force, any private individual is entitled to wage this defensive kind of just war "without any other person's authority" (Vitoria 1991, 299). Nor is a special justifying ground needed for the response of defensive war, for it is an involuntary act that just and peaceful people are forced to take against unjust aggression. Or, as Vitoria quotes from the *Digest*, "force is [always] lawful to repel force *[vim vi repellere licit]*" (1991, 297). In this kind of just war, not only is the principle of legitimate authority inapplicable, then, but so too is the principle of just cause; offensive wars alone require a just cause (Finnis 1996, 19, 21; Suarez 1944, 815–16; Vitoria 1991, 303).

Before I consider whether its goals constitute a just cause for resort to offensive war, the prior issue of whether IRA acts of terrorism should be regarded as public acts of war—and hence morally justifiable in just war terms—or as prima facie private acts of violence—and, thus, devoid of legitimate authority and justice—will be analyzed. The IRA's goals of terminating U.K. jurisdiction and re-uniting Ireland are nevertheless relevant here, for they are public ends, not private purposes. To that extent, at least, the IRA's armed struggle against the United Kingdom is closer to war, with its public purpose, than it is to crime, which is normally committed for the criminal's personal benefit.

IRA CLAIMS TO LEGITIMATE AUTHORITY

The original IRA of 1919–1921, though claiming to be the "National Army" or the "Army of Ireland" in defense of "the newborn Republic," carried out its violent campaign against the United Kingdom for two years independently of the body that had declared Irish independence in January 1919, the self-styled Irish Assembly and de jure government of the Irish Republic proclaimed in 1916. The IRA refused to swear the new oath of allegiance to the Irish National Assembly introduced in August 1920, and it was not until March 1921 that the IRA acknowledged that it acted under the assembly's (revolutionary) authority.

In December 1938, the new IRA claimed that the legitimate government of the Republic of Ireland, now said to be the second National Assembly of 1921–1922, had transferred its de jure authority to the Army Council of the IRA. A month later, this body formally declared war on the U.K. government as the "Government of the Irish Republic." Among contemporary IRA factions, the Provisional IRA (PIRA) has adopted a position that combines elements from the IRA stance of March 1921 and that of December 1938. In other words, like the new IRA of 1922–1970, it claims to be the de jure government of the Irish Republic as well as its army, but, like the old IRA of 1919–1921, it purports to derive its authority to wage war from the first National Assembly, as "its direct representatives [*sic*]." The Provisional IRA further claims to be "the legal representatives [*sic*] of the Irish people," although not as a result of any recent election. It has claimed an electoral mandate for its actions from the results of the Irish constituencies in the United Kingdom's general election of 1918 (Bell 1972, 186–88; Bishop and Mallie 1988, 31; Coogan 1987, 43–44, 159, 164–67; Hepburn 1980, 112–13; B. O'Brien 1993, 289–90).

If any one of its three claims to rightful authority is valid, the IRA meets the first test of a just resort to war. In what follows, those claims based on an Irish Republic and National Assembly will be examined first, then the claim of the PIRA to be the representative of the Irish people will be considered.

LEGITIMATE AUTHORITY AS SOVEREIGNTY

Over the past three hundred years, the just war principle of legitimate authority has been subordinated to, and even identified with, the legal and political principle of state sovereignty. Any sovereign state with a government in effective control of the territory over which it claims jurisdiction has a right to wage war in the prevailing interpretation (Coates 1997, 125; Johnson 1984, 23), although some theorists (e.g., Regan 1996, 20–47) add the U.N. Security Council as a sovereign body with legitimate authority. In this interpretation of the principle, the IRA's claim to rightful authority depends on it fulfilling three conditions: that a sovereign Irish Republic existed from 1916; that between January 1919 and July 1922, the self-styled Irish National Assembly (Dáil Éireann) was its government; and that this all-Ireland government controlled the national territory—the island of Ireland—over which jurisdiction was claimed. It is a simple matter to show that none of these three formal criteria of legitimate authority has ever been met.

The first modern Irish state, the Irish Free State, was created by legislation enacted by the U.K. Parliament in the Government of Ireland Act (1920), the Irish Free State [Constitution] Act (1922), and the Irish Free State [Agreement] Act (1922), which incorporated the "Articles of Agreement" concluded in 1921 between the U.K. government and the Sinn Féin Party, and by the subsequent international recognition of the state. Its constitutional status, however, was not that of an independent republic: it had Dominion status within the British Commonwealth, like Canada, thereby owing supreme allegiance to the British monarch as head of state (Hepburn 1980, 119, 135). Nor was the Irish state a republic, in the IRA's sense of the term, even when it finally severed its British link to become the Irish Republic in 1949. The territory controlled by its government still comprised only twenty-six of the thirty-two counties of Ireland, and its conservative social and economic policies meant it was nothing like "an Irish Socialist Republic based on the 1916 Proclamation" to which the IRA aspired and for which it continues to strive (Dillon 1994, 266). It may be concluded, then, that the authen-

tic Irish Republic proclaimed in 1916, reaffirmed in 1919 by the first Dáil Éireann
and the object of allegiance of militant Irish republicans ever since, was, and is,
a legal nonentity.

But if it was a fictive state, its government—Dáil Éireann—was no less of a
fiction. The first and second National Assemblies were said by their advocates to
be de jure bodies: they were never the de facto government of Ireland, despite
the temporary existence of Sinn Féin Party kangaroo courts and IRA gunmen
ostensibly performing police functions in parts of Ireland during the summer
months of 1920 (Kotsonouris 1994, 17–50; Mitchell 1995, 236–40). In the U.K.
general election of 1918, the republican party (Sinn Féin) won seventy-three of
the one hundred and five Irish seats in the Westminster Parliament. Six seats were
won by the Irish Party (constitutional nationalists), and the Unionists won the
remaining twenty-six seats. In January 1919, twenty-six of the Sinn Féin Members of Parliament (MPs) met in Dublin and called themselves and the absent
MPs elected for Irish constituencies the Assembly of Ireland (Dáil Éireann). This
private gathering of Westminster MPs had neither legal standing nor constitutional significance, for it was the meeting of a revolutionary body. Later in the
month, the Sinn Féin MPs, now thirty-seven in number, declared Irish independence, affirmed their allegiance to the 1916 Irish Republic, announced that a state
of war between Britain and Ireland existed, produced a policy program, elected
an executive, and appointed three delegates to the peace conference at Versailles.
The representatives of the international community at Versailles, however, continued to recognize the United Kingdom of Great Britain and Ireland as a sovereign state and its government as the lawful government of this state. Consequently, they treated the self-styled Irish delegates as private individuals, not as
government emissaries, and dismissed their pleas.

Following the establishment of two parliaments for Ireland by the United
Kingdom in 1920, a fifty-two-seat northern one based in Belfast and a 128-seat
southern one based in Dublin, separate elections were held for each in May 1921.
However, the first Dáil ignored the separate elections and treated all 180 candi-
dates elected in May as though they were elected to a single all-Ireland Assembly,
the second Dáil Éireann (Macardle 1968, 251–55, 414, 453, 851). (All Irish parliaments since Dáil Éireann 1919–22 are treated as illegitimate by IRA factions
to the present day because they are based on the partition of Ireland into a southern Irish state and the Northern Ireland province of the United Kingdom.) Yet
again, make-believe—an Irish National Assembly—was substituted for the legal
reality of two parliaments: once more it was supposed that the revolutionary will
of private individuals overrode constitutional law.

Because the Irish Republic proclaimed in 1916 was never a sovereign state
and the self-styled all-Ireland parliaments of 1919–22 were never governments
exercising control over the territory of Ireland, neither is capable of providing
the IRA and its factions with a legitimate authority to wage war, either at the time
or since. This summary dismissal of the IRA claims is easy because sovereignty

is an attribute of the state and, perhaps, of the U.N. Security Council too, and so it is inevitably absent from any insurgent terrorist group like the IRA.

Lack of sovereignty, however, may result in a more relaxed view of the formal requirements of legitimate authority, whereby sovereignty is treated as inessential to a legitimate authority to wage war and is replaced by a substitute. James Turner Johnson's observation is pertinent here: "Perhaps more than any other just war concept, that of right authority may seem irrelevant to an age when such cynicism exists about state power and in which, by contrast, popular revolutionary movements have for some persons taken on the presumption of legitimacy that formerly attached to the state" (1984, 53). Johnson goes on to argue that by 1982 the PLO "had certainly reached the stage of de facto legitimacy," that is, "enjoying right authority or having *compétence de guerre*" through being well consolidated politically and by virtue of possessing extensive military forces that were increasingly engaged in conventional military actions (1984, 54). How these attributes are supposed to confer moral legitimacy, as distinct from power and force, is unclear, for legitimacy is a de jure, not a mere de facto, concept. What appears to have happened is that the moral concept of right authority has been replaced by the conception of *compétence de guerre* as a technical capability for conducting conventional military operations. Similarly, legal facts about insurgents, such as their having a public purpose, a degree of organization, and a modicum of success, in addition to their readiness to adhere to the laws of war, neither constitute legitimate (moral) authority nor confer that moral status on the revolutionary group (pace O'Brien 1981, 19, 158–62). So long as IRA claims to legitimate authority depend on the formal criterion of sovereignty, or on a factual or legal substitute for sovereignty, they will not succeed. Legitimate authority is primarily a moral not a legal concept, however, and in terms of this moral dimension the third IRA claim to rightful authority, as the representative of the Irish people, seems much more promising.

LEGITIMATE AUTHORITY AS A MORAL CONCEPT

According to the best recent statement of this just war principle, states derive their right to war not from the fact of their sovereignty but from their membership in a moral community, the values of which they share and the law of which they uphold and implement—to which they are also subject, namely, the law and values of international society. Thus, states will have legitimate authority to wage war only insofar as they act in a public capacity as agents of this entire community by upholding its law, defending its order, and promoting its common good (Coates 1997, 126–28). Because terrorist groups are not members of international society, even if, like the IRA, they have an international dimension by operating across state borders, this formulation of the principle clearly restricts its application to states and their governments.

But the international community is not the only moral community. It is therefore possible, in principle, that another body has legitimate authority insofar as it acts in a public capacity as the agent of a moral community other than international society, by upholding its law, defending its order, and promoting its common good. If this other moral community is identified as the state, the body that acts in a public capacity as its agent is normally its government. It will have legitimate authority to employ coercive force within the state (punishment) as the agent of the state, in addition to the legitimate authority it possesses when it acts on behalf of the international community to wield coercive force outside the state (war). Right authority to wage war and to administer punishment thus derive from essentially different moral communities, although not completely so. For states may act as agents of the international community by trying, convicting, and punishing international criminals, like pirates, rather than waging war on them. Matters are more complex, however, when the state (and even more so the nation) is the moral community and at issue is whether or not it can confer legitimate authority to wage war on an agent other than the government. In other words, can some substate body, other than a government, act in a public capacity as agent of the state or nation, and if so, could this body have rightful authority to wage war? and against what enemy?

Although the United Kingdom, as a state, counts as a moral community, the IRA has never claimed to act on behalf of its citizens in armed opposition to the government: on the contrary, its (third) claim is to act against the British government as the representative of the Irish people or nation. That nations are ethical communities, in the sense that members are bound together by a nexus of significant rights and duties to one another that they do not have toward others, is argued by David Miller (1995, 67–73), and his argument will be adopted here. The Irish people, as well as the Irish state, counts as a moral community, then. The problem that immediately arises, however, is, Who are members of the Irish nation? Are they restricted to that part of the population of the island of Ireland whose religion is Roman Catholicism and who were originally of Gaelic culture? Or do they include the Protestant population of Northern Ireland, despite the fact they identify themselves as British and, therefore, as part of a different moral community? Are only the present-day inhabitants of Ireland qualified as members of the Irish people, or may those of Irish descent, living in, say, the United Kingdom, Canada, the United States, and Australia, be added to the membership list? And if included, is the list restricted to the first generation, or do second, third, and later generations also count? And is descent qualified by religion? Does it apply only to those who identify themselves as of Irish ancestry, and so on? Regrettably, there is no solution to this problem, for membership in the Irish nation, unlike citizenship in the Irish state, is a wholly indeterminate matter. Any claim to represent the Irish people and act as its agent thus founders on the fact that the particular group of individuals in question is, unavoidably, chosen in an arbitrary way; the members of the moral community of the Irish people are whomever someone decides they are, though, in this respect, they are no different from other nations. But if the Irish "people" is an indeterminate group, it is difficult to see how the IRA could act in a public capacity as its agent by upholding its values, defending its order, and promoting its common good, for the particular group for which it acts will never be one that everyone recognizes as the Irish nation.

A second problem is that there are rival claimants for the IRA as the representative agent of the Irish people. Between 1970 and 1999 there were six rival IRA factions, all claiming to be the authentic IRA and, thus, representative agent of the Irish people while denying the claims of their rivals. In addition, the constitution of the Irish Republic that was actually established in 1949 claims jurisdiction over the entire territory and population of Ireland, and so the Irish government also has a claim to be the representative of the Irish people. As it is possible for the Irish population to choose who does and does not represent it, the obvious way to settle the matter is by democratic votes. The fact that Provisional Sinn Féin, the political wing of the largest of the present-day IRA factions (PIRA), polls approximately 2 percent of the total vote in the general elections in the Irish Republic and between 10 and 15 percent in recent general elections in Northern Ireland means that it is difficult to see how this IRA faction represents the Irish people, in whatever way that body is defined. It is true that the PIRA enjoys wider public support in material, political, and moral terms than, say, the left-wing Italian Red Brigades, and in this sense, as Tony Coates argues, it "does have roots in the community which it claims to represent" (1997, 144). But all this falls far short of the popular support for the constitutional political parties in the Irish Republic or in Northern Ireland. As far back as 1922, the IRA and its factions have enjoyed only minority support from the Irish population, and even before then it may have only had the support of the majority of the population between March 1921, when it acknowledged the authority of Dáil Éireann, and the adoption of the Anglo-Irish Articles of Agreement in December 1921.

A third difficulty with the notion that the IRA represents the Irish people when it engages in armed struggle against the U.K. government is its inveterate sectarianism (Burton 1978). Instead of acting on behalf, and with the legitimate authority, of the Irish people in its terrorist campaigns, it has (allegedly) acted for Roman Catholics against the Protestant members of the Irish population. In short, their terrorism-as-war has had a distinctively sectarian, and hence private, character. The pattern was set between 1920 and 1923, when the IRA reduced the Protestant population of southern Ireland by more than a quarter through a process that today is termed "ethnic cleansing." In a single county (Cork) during this period, seventy of the 200 civilians shot by the IRA were Protestants, which is five times the percentage of Protestants in the civilian population. Attacks on property were even more sectarian in character. Of the twenty-four farms expropriated by the IRA in the county, none was owned by Catholics, and of the 130 homes destroyed by the IRA, only seventeen were not owned by Protestants (Hart 1996, 81–98).

More recently, in the context of intercommunal (sectarian) rioting between 1969 and 1972 and of police and army searches for terrorist suspects and weapons, the official IRA and PIRA "defended" Roman Catholic neighborhoods in Belfast and Londonderry by bombs, bullets, and barricades (Barzilay 1973, 44–49). Later on, Protestants and their property were targeted for attack. During the mid-1980s, for example, PIRA carried out a campaign of ethnic cleansing of Protestants, especially farmers, in the counties bordering the Irish Republic (*Sunday Times*, 29 March 1998). In the early 1990s, it launched its "economic war" by bombing predominantly Protestant towns in Northern Ireland, destroying the business property of the mainly Protestant owners and flattening the town centers. IRA bombing of Protestant housing estates in the same period was also unmistakably sectarian in character (Bruce 1997, 66–67). Such examples can easily be multiplied because the pattern of targeting by the PIRA and by the other IRA factions shows a consistently sectarian character. What is disputed is only the extent of its sectarianism relative to the sectarianism of the loyalist terrorists (Bruce 1997; Burton 1978, 37–67; Dingley 1998, 107–14; Drake 1998; White 1997a, 22–55; 1997b; 1998, 168–70;). Anecdotal evidence supports these data. Sinn Féin president and member of the PIRA's ruling Army Council, Gerry Adams, publicly condemns sectarianism but has privately boasted, "[I] would wade up to my knees in Protestant blood" to achieve a united Ireland (Bennett 1998, 25).

In these examples, the PIRA, like its predecessors, has acted in a purely sectarian fashion and not in a public capacity as agents of the Irish people—which, by its own definition, includes Protestants—by upholding its norms and values, defending its order, and promoting its common good. For this reason, and for reasons discussed above, it has failed to exercise the legitimate authority of the Irish people as a moral community.

RIGHT INTENTION

A further implication of its sectarian violence is that it violates the *jus ad bellum* principle of right intention. Right intention in a just war means an overall concern to achieve peace and well-being while restraining evil. It, thus, excludes what St. Augustine calls "the desire for harming, the cruelty of avenging, an unruly and implacable animosity, the rage of rebellion, the lust of domination and the like" (quoted in Aquinas 1974, 161). That rage and implacable sectarian animosity added to the absence of the overall end of just war, namely, a just peace, mean the IRA's intention was wrong or unjust, in addition to its hostile acts being devoid of legitimate authority. Right intention may also imply a commitment not to harm or kill innocents by design (Finnis 1998, 285). Be that as it may, for present purposes it will be assumed that, despite having a wrong intention, IRA attacks could be contingently directed against nocent combatants, as defined by its just cause, and so intentionally avoid innocent noncombatants. In that event, the just war principle of discrimination is applicable to IRA terrorism.

JUST CAUSE AND IRA GOALS

The just cause for resort to an offensive just war is an injustice or wrong done to the political community. Defensive just war, as previously noted, needs no just cause, though this does not entail that every defensive war is just (Coates 1997, 157). If an attack is initiated by the state to secure retribution or reparation for a wrong (other than an unjust attack) done to it or to another member of the international society of states, and the guilty party has refused or failed to redress this injustice, it has a transparently verifiable just cause for resort to war. What counts as a wrong to the political community is indicated by Suarez. He lists the seizure of property by a foreign sovereign and refusal to restore it; a denial, without reasonable cause, of the common rights of nations, such as the rights of transit and trading; and "any grave injury to one's reputation or honor" (1944, 817), although comparable lists by other writers in the classic just war tradition inevitably vary. As Grotius observes, "it is evident that the sources from which wars arise are as numerous as those from which lawsuits spring; for where judicial settlements fail, war begins" (1925, 171). All the wrongs that could be listed, however, have two crucial common features: first, they are all justiciable, that is, they are analogous to a "cause of action" in Anglo-American law, for which a remedy (redress) may be sought before a court of law (Finnis 1998, 284). Grotius (1925, 555) holds that claims not actionable in law cannot be prosecuted in war; just war is legal action carried on by other means. In the absence of an international court for sovereigns to secure the redress denied them, resort to war to secure it is just. Second, redressing the specific wrongs listed (and the just repulsion of an aggressive attack) will have the conservative function of restoring the moral status quo disrupted by the injustices done to the political community. Just war is the remedy of *restitutio in integrum,* a restoration of legal relations to their former, unimpaired (or just) condition (see Rachel 1916, 183). It is quite different from a holy war, which is fought to promote "some political structure or course of political events in this world" held to be God's providential will for the human race (Riley-Smith 1992, 8), and from its contemporary counterpart, ideological warfare, which is fought to promote a revolutionary polity or to advance a revolutionary course of sociopolitical events in accordance with the laws of history or some other secular substitute for the will of God.

A contemporary restatement of the conception of just cause in the classic just war tradition is provided by Terry Nardin. He writes,

> Although the criteria of justice in war have traditionally allowed the pursuit of certain ends as a lawful ground for using force, it is a misconception to think that force

is justified if it is used for a good end. An act of war, like any other act, is just or unjust in relation to the considerations of a moral practice, not in relation to its instrumental utility for the realization of desired ends. [1983, 278]

So, for example, while it might be morally desirable to end the suffering of animals subject to vivisection, this good end is not a just cause for armed terrorist attacks on animal laboratories or against scientists who conduct such animal experiments. It is extrinsic to the moral practice; it has nothing to do with the rights that exist under the rules and norms that constitute the international society of states (or any other moral community) and the shared practice of securing redress for their infringement by states (or by other moral communities). The counterpart to such extrinsic, ideological goals in the early period of the just war tradition were religious objectives, pursuit of which converted the limited warfare permitted by just war principles into the unrestricted and gratuitous violence of a crusade or holy war (Johnson 1973, 220). Resort to war must be for transparently verifiable reasons or on nonmetaphysical grounds, that is, "in principle open to judgment by third parties standing outside the conflict" (Johnson 1984, 61, 194). Justiciable wrongs arising from a breach of international rules and norms appear to pass this test; religious and ideological goals, it would seem, do not.

The cause for which the IRA has traditionally fought and for which its factions still fight today is the nationalist goal of an authentic, all-Ireland Republic. A precondition for achieving this goal of Irish national self-determination is that U.K. jurisdiction in any part of Ireland ends, and this is the immediate, irredentist purpose of IRA terrorists. On the face of it, the IRA pursuit of national self-determination is an instrumental use of violence to realize a desired and, maybe, a desirable end rather than the attempt to redress a justiciable wrong arising from breach of the constitutive rules and norms of international society. If so, it cannot be a just cause. But against this it may be urged that the rules and norms of the contemporary international society of states make national self-determination or independent nation-statehood a right of all peoples. Indeed, the two *International Covenants on Rights* of 1966 declare in their common Article 1, "All peoples have the right of self-determination" (Brownlie 1992, 114, 125). From this point, it is a short step to take to suppose that a denial of this right to a people is a wrong that justifies a resort to arms against the state that forcibly deprives it of that right. U.N. General Assembly resolution 3314 on aggression (1974) "converts aggression into just war" when the "certified good cause" is national self-determination, according to Claude (1980, 95).

Against this position it should be observed that, despite the universalist language of the 1966 *International Covenants* and similar U.N. documents, it is a contingent fact that there is no agreed legal definition of a "people," and so there is no universal criterion of nationality or any agreed procedure for determining the "national territory" on which an independent nation-state is to be established. Indeterminacy is the result. It is therefore unsurprising that in practice the United

Nations has, on the one hand, restricted the application of the right to colonies, where a single and separate nation or people rarely exists, and, on the other, has extended it to those citizens of independent states who are deemed to be subject to "racist" regimes or to "alien occupation and domination" (often supposed to be nonwhites in apartheid South Africa and Palestinians in the territories of Gaza and the West Bank, occupied by Israel since 1967). In effect, the United Nations overcame the problem of indeterminacy by stipulating the meaning of *peoples* for the purpose of application of the right. This arbitrary restriction of the right is inapplicable in the case of Northern Ireland, however, for despite PIRA claims to the contrary, it is not a colony of the United Kingdom in international law; nor are its resident U.K. citizens subject either to a racist regime or to alien occupation and domination. We are left, therefore, with an indeterminate Irish "people," which necessarily cannot be the bearer of a determinate right, of which it cannot therefore be forcibly deprived.

Be that as it may, the right of self-determination of peoples is part of international law and consequently has little or no bearing on the moral issue of justice in a just war. If it were a universally applicable moral right, it would run into precisely the same problem as the universal legal right of self-determination, that is, it would be incapable of universal implementation. Given the indeterminacy of "peoples," implementation of the right in some cases is only possible by not implementing or denying it others. For example, if the people of Northern Ireland exercise their right of self-determination by choosing to remain citizens of the United Kingdom, as they did most recently in the referendum of 1998, this can only be achieved at the expense of the Irish people (deemed to include the people of Northern Ireland) exercising its right of self-determination in a single independent state over the whole of Ireland, and, of course, vice versa.

In summary, the IRA's end of Irish national self-determination is either an ideological goal, an international legal right, or an international moral right. If it is either of the latter two, it appears to meet the justiciable criterion, and its achievement against a forcible denial restores the legal and moral status quo ante. Implementation of both rights, however, is inherently discriminatory and contrary to their universal character, a feature that, it might be supposed, disqualifies their infringement from constituting a just cause for the first use of force in a just war. Irish national self-determination, therefore, seems to be an ideological objective, and, as such, it cannot be a just cause because it is not, in principle, justiciable. And if there is no just cause, the *jus in bello* principle of discrimination is impossible, for there now is no way of distinguishing wrongdoers who deserve to be attacked (combatants) from innocents who do not (noncombatants). All individuals must now be presumed morally innocent. Consequently, in a resort to arms in pursuit of Irish national self-determination, those who are intentionally attacked and killed, whether civilians, service personnel, or police officers, are not war casualties but innocents and, therefore, murder victims. This hard conclusion might be avoided, however, if IRA terrorism were essentially reactive to unjust aggression, for as previously argued, neither legitimate authority nor just cause is required in a defensive just war.

DEFENSIVE JUST WAR: THE IRA AND ARMED RESISTANCE TO TYRANNY

When a government wields power in a private capacity, not as agent of the moral community of the state, such an unconstitutional, private appropriation of the public power constitutes tyranny. Tyranny occurs through either a private individual or a group usurping the office of government by forcibly seizing power, or else it results from a government with legitimate authority exceeding its constitutionally limited, public powers and, thus, acting unlawfully and, necessarily, oppressively. Instead of upholding the very basis of the political community—its bonds of law—tyrants subvert and destroy this law by their lawless rule and, thus, undermine the state. Rather than promoting the communal good, they abuse power to pursue their private interests; and instead of defending the order of the state by public coercive force, tyrants attack it by arbitrary, private acts of violence directed against the lives, liberties, and properties of its citizens. Within the just war tradition of thought, such lawless, violent rulers are deemed to be at war with those over whom they ruled—and not only with them; they were held to be enemies of God and of the human race (Buchanan 1579, 51–53; Locke 1960, 319–20, 467). Should the U.K. government be a tyranny, either by usurping or abusing power, its exercise of power would constitute an unjust aggression against which a right of armed resistance may be legitimately exercised, that is, a defensive war will be a just resort.

So it makes sense to ask, Has Britain usurped power in Ireland? Or, if it exercises lawful power, has it abused that power to the extent that armed resistance to the attack is legitimate? The title to rule Ireland as its feudal lord was granted to the English Crown in 1155 by Pope Adrian IV, and the grant gave explicit authority to subdue the inhabitants, making them law-abiding Christians (Curtis 1961, 56–57; Martin 1993, 57–58). That lawful title was not invalidated by the need to reconquer Ireland in the sixteenth and seventeenth centuries. Later, the Irish Parliament voted to enter into a full union with Britain, and the United Kingdom of Great Britain and Ireland was created as a result by the Act of Union of 1800. The democratically elected parliament of this state set up two parliaments in Ireland in 1920 and partitioned the island in 1921–22. The case for the British Crown and its ministers constituting a tyranny by usurpation is, pace Simpson (1986, 80–84), not a strong one then.

It is true, however, that there were some abuses of power in Northern Ireland during the lifetime of its provincial government and parliament at Stormont (1920–74). There was limited but real discrimination against Roman Catholics in public housing and in the allocation of jobs in local government (as in private sector employment); in some areas, there was electoral discrimination too. Sometimes the claims of discrimination may have been largely bogus, and in others the actual extent of the discrimination might have been exaggerated (*Sunday Tribune*, 18 October 1998). It is arguable whether or not it was as widespread and severe as the discrimination suffered by blacks in the United States over the same period. Nonetheless, such abuses of power can be, and have been, removed by normal democratic procedures in both cases, so IRA terrorism hardly qualifies as a last resort. But even if these abuses of power were still in place, a resort to arms to secure redress for the resulting injustices would be a completely disproportionate response to the nature and extent of the wrong done. Abuses of power that are remediable by the democratic process are not equivalent to armed aggression, the repulsion of which in a defensive war would be just.

For a war to count as just, it must meet a stringent condition, namely, it must satisfy all the criteria of just war. If it should be unjust in only one respect, whether the just war principle violated is one that determines when resort to war is justified (*jus ad bellum*) or whether the principle that is infringed assesses if war is being justly waged (*jus in bello*), that single injustice undermines the case for it being counted as a just war (see Aquinas 1974, 161; Finnis 1996, 18). Possible exceptions to the general moral injunction to preserve human life should be allowed if, and only if, they can be fully morally justified. IRA terrorism, it has been argued, violates three *jus ad bellum* principles—legitimate authority, just cause, and right intention—and the *jus in bello* principle of discrimination. Accordingly, it is not a just war.

One final line of argument in the moral assessment of IRA terrorism remains, however. This political violence might be justified from a utilitarian perspective.

THE COSTS AND BENEFITS OF IRA TERRORISM

On a utilitarian argument, there is nothing intrinsically evil about IRA terrorism. However cruel or savage it may be, it will be morally justified if the benefits gained outweigh its costs to the immediate victims and to the wider society.

Data on the costs of IRA terrorism exist but are incomplete, especially for early campaigns. Taylor calculates that in the first campaign (1919–21) more than 500 (26 percent) military and police officers were killed and that there were over 700 IRA (37 percent) and over 700 civilian (37 percent) fatalities (1997, 12). There were seven civilian fatalities in the 1938–40 mainland campaign (Dillon 1994, 16, 36, 39), and six police officers were killed in the cross-border campaign of 1956–62 (Bishop and Mallie 1988, 45); but the total number of injuries is unknown, as is the value of property destroyed or damaged, in all three campaigns. The effects on civil liberties and quality of life are unquantified costs. Data for another IRA campaign, 1969–94, show that of the 3,593 fatalities—the equivalent in percentages to 100,000 deaths in the United Kingdom or 500,000 fatalities in the U.S.A.—1,900 or 54 percent were civilian. Nearly half (1,684) the fatalities were the direct result of IRA terrorism. Injuries totaling 37,451 were reported for 1971–96, or roughly ten for every fatality, and 68 percent of these were injuries to civilians (Fay, Morrissey, and Smyth 1999, 168–69, 178).

The benefits of IRA terrorism are easy to calculate. After some eighty years of terrorism, the IRA has failed to achieve its goal of a united Ireland within the socialist Republic proclaimed in 1916 or its precondition, the end of U.K. jurisdiction in Ireland. A decision to end jurisdiction over twenty-six Irish counties and grant them independent self-government but to exclude the six northern counties from this new Irish regime was made by the U.K. government in 1916, that is, well before the IRA began its terrorist campaign in 1919 (Lyons 1973, 385). Government policy was implemented between 1920 and 1922. Since then, IRA terrorism has not achieved its goals, and it is arguable that the Belfast Agreement, concluded on Good Friday, 1998, and to which PIRA's political wing, Sinn Féin, was party, has copper-fastened the partition of Ireland for the foreseeable future. Thus, the benefits of a united Ireland to date amount to nil. IRA terrorism is inefficacious in relation to the kind of outcomes needed to achieve those benefits that might exceed the huge costs of its terrorism, namely, the realization of its ultimate ends.

In contrast, it is moderately effective in achieving its proximate ends, such as securing the release of imprisoned comrades; building morale within the group and among sympathizers; advertising the group and its grievances to the public; provoking severe countermeasures by government in order to attenuate its public support; discrediting, and in other ways neutralizing, effective opposition; winning a seat at the negotiating table; and so on. But the benefits from achieving these subordinate ends accrue to the terrorists not to the wider society, and, at best, the value to them is slight when compared with the severe harm inflicted on the victims of their terrorism. The moral arithmetic of the cost of harming Mrs. Jean McConville, a Belfast widow and mother of ten children, who was covertly murdered by PIRA and secretly buried over twenty years ago for cradling a fatally wounded soldier in her arms, and whose remains have yet to be returned to her next of kin for Christian burial, when set against the benefits to PIRA of this act assisting its campaign of alienating Catholics from U.K. troops, is easy. It does not favor the terrorists.

CONCLUSION

Terrorist violence by the IRA, when alternative democratic opportunities to pursue its aims exist in the United Kingdom, is unjustified on utilitarian grounds. Its violent methods are inefficacious in relation to its ultimate political ends that *might* produce benefits of the magnitude needed to offset the very high costs of the terrorism. Their relative effectiveness as means to lesser IRA ends is insufficient, for the resulting benefits are only to the IRA and so relatively slight that they do not outweigh the costs. Because the costs outweigh the benefits, IRA terrorism is unjustified from a utilitarian standpoint. When it is analyzed as offensive war, it lacks a just cause, and, hence, the principle of discrimination is inapplicable to IRA attacks. These must therefore be against presumed innocents. The IRA also lacks legitimate authority, so its terrorism is not offensive public warfare but, rather, private violence. When evaluated in terms of defensive war, IRA terrorism is not found to be justified armed resistance to an unjust aggression because U.K. jurisdiction over Northern Ireland is not a usurped power, and admitted past abuses do not amount to it waging an unjust war on its Roman Catholic citizens. Neither offensively nor defensively, then, is IRA terrorism a just war. Yet the arguments adduced here go further. If they are valid, they show that IRA terrorism does not morally count as war at all but merely as murder and other violent crimes.

Terrorism in the Arab–Israeli Conflict

Neve Gordon and George A. Lopez

The peace rally was coming to an end, and the extraordinary turnout seemed to reassure Prime Minister Yitzhak Rabin that he had enough public support to carry on with the Oslo Peace Accords. Surrounded by bodyguards, he left the podium walking leisurely toward his car. Suddenly four shots were heard; Rabin fell to the ground as the bullets penetrated his body. The assassin, a Jewish extremist associated with a small group called Eyal (Fighting Jewish Organization) told the investigators that he murdered the prime minister in order to destroy the peace process.

Following the 4 November 1995 assassination, Shimon Peres became Israel's prime minister. A secure 20 percent lead over his rival, Binyamin Netanyahu, motivated Peres to call for early elections, moving the date forward from the fall to 29 May 1996. A public opinion poll taken on 9 February 1996, four months after he entered office, indicated that the gap between the two politicians had not changed (Gallup Opinion Poll 1998). On February 25, two suicide terrorists, members of Izzadin el-Kassam, the military wing of the Islamic fundamentalist group Hamas (Islamic Resistance Movement), detonated pipe bombs that were attached to their bodies; one on a commuter bus in Jerusalem, killing twenty-six people, including three U.S. citizens, and wounding eighty others; the other at a bus station near Ashkelon, killing two Israeli soldiers. Messages received by news agencies said the attacks were perpetrated by the Hamas as an act of reprisal for the death of Yahya Ayyash. Ayyash, also known as "the Engineer," had masterminded several attacks against Israel and was murdered on January 5 by a booby-trapped mobile telephone planted by Israel's secret service.

Reporting from Israel on the day of the two suicide attacks, *New York Times* correspondent Serge Schmemann wrote that "while Prime Minister Shimon

Peres and his Labor Party have held a sizable lead in public-opinion polls over the conservative Likud opposition since the assassination of Prime Minister Yitz-hak Rabin in November, all political pundits have said that [the differential] could change sharply and rapidly if Palestinian terrorists struck again" (*New York Times*, 26 February 1996). As if to fulfill Schmemann's prediction, six days later, on March 3, a suicide bomber detonated a bomb on a Jerusalem bus, killing nine-teen people and injuring six others. The next day yet another Izzadin el-Kassam terrorist exploded himself outside Dizingoff Center, Tel-Aviv's largest shopping mall, killing twenty people and wounding seventy-five, including two U.S. citi-zens.[1] A Gallup poll from March 15 indicates that Peres's lead decreased dramat-ically as a result of these attacks and that the gap between the two contenders was no longer significant, 44 percent for Peres as opposed to Netanyahu's 41 percent. Two and a half months later, Peres lost the elections by a margin of 1 percent, and Netanyahu, the newly elected prime minister, abandoned the peace process specified in the Oslo Accords.

These events seem to confirm that political terrorism is firmly linked to an existing political order in the sense that the objectives of the terrorists are to un-dermine (or uphold) a system of government or a specific policy promoted by the government. Both Rabin's assassin and the Hamas committed violent acts in order to cripple the peace process between the Israeli government and the Pales-tinian Authority. Moreover, history teaches that in this region it is not uncommon for terrorism to be employed as a political tool. Even before World War II the Middle East was infested with domestic terrorism, while in the 1960s it became the center for several prominent organizations that have employed terrorism in the international arena (Alexander and Sinai 1989, xi). Currently, five out of the seven states considered by the United States to be sponsors of international ter-rorism are located in the Middle East (U.S. Department of State 1998, 23).

Using terrorist attacks perpetrated in the context of the Arab–Israeli conflict as a point of reference, this chapter underscores the significance of the controversies regarding terrorism's definition. After depicting a number of incidents of Pales-tinian terrorism, we turn to examine the definition of terrorism used by the U.S. Department of State. We inquire whether the definition captures the particular nature of these terrorist acts, examining whether it improves our understanding of the unique strategy employed by terrorists, while discussing the significance of including the perpetrator's identity in the definition. Next, we offer an alternative definition of terrorism that accentuates only the nature of the act and introduces another set of cases, this time focusing on violent acts perpetrated by the State of Israel in Lebanon, the West Bank, and the Gaza Strip. This new definition and these cases enable us to problematize two components that are often associated with terrorism: the actor's identity and the methods employed. By way of conclu-sion, we argue for the establishment of international institutions that can help arrest terrorism.

PALESTINIAN TERRORISM

In 1948, following the partition of the country by the United Nations and after the British mandatory power pulled out, five Arab armies invaded Palestine—those of Egypt, Jordan, Iraq, Syria, and Lebanon—in support of the Palestinians. The ensuing war transformed the Arab–Jewish struggle in and over Palestine into an Arab–Israeli conflict. Indeed, the war's political consequences were momentous. On the one hand, the establishment of the State of Israel in an area larger than the one allotted to it by the U.N. partition resolution was consolidated. On the other hand, the Arab Palestinian state envisaged by that resolution did not come into being, and the area allocated to it was divided by Jordan, Egypt, and Israel (Rabinovich 1991, 38). In addition, the refugee problem was created, and today there are an estimated three million Palestinian refugees, of which over half live outside the West Bank and Gaza Strip (Boutwell and Mendelson 1995, 72).

Eleven years after the war, while living in Kuwait, Yasser Arafat founded Fatah, an organization whose major objective was to create a Palestinian state and, by extension, to annihilate Israel. It was only in 1965, however, that Fatah's military arm, al-Asifa (the Storm), began carrying out guerrilla operations inside Israel (Alexander and Sinai 1989, 7; Cobban 1984, 23). A year earlier the Palestinian Liberation Organization (PLO), which would become the umbrella organization for most Palestinian groups, was founded by Ahmad al Shuqairy, who declared that the purpose of the organization was to "drive the Jews into the sea" (Anderson and Sloan 1995, 268).[2] While these were the initial signs of the Palestinian liberation movement's reawakening, the question of Palestine reemerged in the international arena in full force only after Israel's occupation of the West Bank and Gaza Strip during the Six Day War; this was the first time that one authority controlled all of pre-1948 Palestine.[3]

The Popular Front for the Liberation of Palestine (PFLP) was founded a few months after the 1967 war, and, similar to the existing organizations, its objective was to establish a homeland for the Palestinians in what had become Israel. Already in mid-1968 its members hijacked an El Al (Israeli) airliner en route from Rome to Tel-Aviv, and in December, PFLP terrorists raided an El Al Boeing at the Athens airport, killing one Israeli (Alexander and Sinai 1989, 11). Despite the fact that it was a very small organization, during the late 1960s and in 1970 the PFLP was the major perpetrator of Palestinian terrorism. Its leaders realized not only that the assaults imposed the Palestinian question on the international agenda but that by committing terrorist acts the group broadened its support among Palestinians, thus strengthening its prospect of becoming a viable alternative to Fatah.

In September 1970, PFLP terrorists hijacked four planes (a fifth attempt to hijack an El Al airliner was prevented by Israeli security personnel on board). Three of the four were forced to fly to Zarqa airfield in Jordan, and the fourth was flown to Cairo. While the 400 hostages were ultimately set free in exchange for the release of terrorists being held in West European jails, all four planes were blown up in order to draw public attention. The Zarqa hijacking brought to a showdown the mounting tension between the Palestinian refugees and King Hussein of Jordan, who felt that his sovereignty was being eroded as a result of Palestinian activity in the country. After a few months of fighting between the Jordanian army and the PLO, an estimated 3,000 PLO combatants and civilians were killed, and about 150,000 Palestinians were expelled to Syria; most of them sought refuge in Lebanon (Alexander and Sinai 1989, 13; Cobban 1984, 52).

These incidents lead to the creation of the notorious organization Black September, which, in its first four years of existence, functioned under the supervision of Fatah. By 1971 the clandestine group had assassinated Jordanian Prime Minister Wasfi al Tall in Cairo. Its most infamous terrorist act was, however, the Munich massacre. On 5 September 1972, eight masked gunmen raided the compound of the Israeli team in the Olympic Village, murdering an Israeli athlete and his coach outright and taking the remaining athletes hostage. In the skirmish between the terrorists and the German police, the former killed all nine hostages, while the police killed five terrorists, capturing the remaining three (Alexander and Sinai 1989, 14; Anderson and Sloan 1995, 231; Nasr 1997, 59–62).[4] To be sure, the Palestinian question did enter the international public domain because of the Munich carnage, yet the actual act led to widespread moral indignation. Palestinians had violated, it appeared to many, an area that was safe and "beyond politics."

Terrorism was utilized by the different Palestinian groups not only in the international arena but inside Israel as well. In 1974, for example, three members of the Democratic Front for the Liberation of Palestine—a splinter group born out of an ideological division within the PFLP—took over a school in Ma'alot, an Israeli town located near the Lebanese border. When the negotiations broke down and the Israeli troops stormed the dormitory, the terrorists machine-gunned the children, killing twenty-seven and wounding an additional seventy (Alexander and Sinai 1989, 209; Anderson and Sloan 1995, 90). Also during that year, three Fatah members penetrated the Israeli town Naharia via boat, murdering four Israelis and wounding eight others, while three members of the Popular Front for the Liberation of Palestine–General Command, another PFLP splinter group, attacked the Israeli town Qiryat Shemona, killing twenty people and wounding sixteen, before committing suicide by setting off explosive charges (Alexander and Sinai 1989, 210–214; Anderson and Sloan 1995, 285).

Over the years, Western countries, Arab states, and moderate Palestinians also became targets of Palestinian terrorism. Perhaps the most notorious terrorist group was Abu Nidal's organization, which in the mid-1980s lit "a bonfire of violence" in the region (Seale 1992, 228). Abu Nidal conceived the Middle East conflict to be a zero-sum game, and anyone willing to compromise in order to reach a peaceful resolution was consequently considered to be an enemy of the Palestinian cause.[5] A few incidents from 1985 exemplify the scope of Abu Nidal's activities. In May, Egyptian police arrested an Abu Nidal agent who was planning to detonate a truckload of explosives outside the U.S. embassy in Cairo, while in August, an explosion at a hotel resort near Athens injured thirteen, including six British citizens. A grenade attack on the Café de Paris in Rome injured forty in September, and in November an Egyptian airliner was hijacked by Abu Nidal terrorists and forced to land in Malta; six passengers were killed before Egyptian commandos stormed the plane. In December, Abu Nidal gunmen simultaneously attacked El Al ticket counters at both Rome and Vienna airports, hurling grenades and opening fire on the crowd; some twenty people were killed, and 120 were wounded in this foray (Alexander and Sinai 1989, 208; Seale 1992, 234–37; U.S. Department of State 1987, 3).

DEFINING TERRORISM

With this generalized portrayal of Palestinian terrorism in mind, we can turn to examine the common characteristics of all these acts, whether it be the Munich massacre, the assassination of Jordan's prime minister, or the bombing of a restaurant in Rome. This inquiry is intimately related to terrorism's definition, for it is precisely the definition that is supposed to capture both the common and unique attributes of the phenomenon signified by the word *terrorism*. Although no single definition of terrorism has gained universal acceptance, we chose to explore the one employed by the U.S. Department of State because it is predominant and has immediate implications for policy. The definition is divided into three clauses, of which the first reads, "The term 'terrorism' means premeditated, politically motivated violence perpetrated against noncombatant targets by subnational groups or clandestine agents, usually intended to influence an audience" (U.S. Department of State 1998, vi).[6] The activities described above correspond with this clause of the definition, for they were violent, premeditated, and usually perpetrated against noncombatant targets. In addition, the acts were politically motivated. Nonetheless, the clause, or for that matter the definition itself, does not capture a certain dimension that we tend to associate with terrorism and that appears to be integral to all the acts just mentioned: namely, that the political objective is not encapsulated in the act itself. As with Rabin's assassin who slew the prime minister in order to arrest the peace process, the purpose of Palestinian terrorism is not to kill innocent people but to advance certain political goals. While acts committed during guerrilla warfare or a military assault may be an end in themselves (like capturing a disputed territory), a terrorist act is always a means, and, therefore, its political objective always transcends the act itself. Leila Khaled, a well-known terrorist who was captured during a failed El Al hijacking in 1970, made a similar point when she stated that "the hijackings were used as a kind of struggle to put the question—who are the Palestinians?—before the world. Before we were dealt with as refugees. We yelled and screamed, but the whole world answered with more tents and did nothing" (quoted in Nasr 1997, 57).

This dimension of political terrorism is hinted at by the definition's affirmation that terrorism is "usually intended to influence an audience." One should keep in mind, however, that the Palestinian terrorist acts were meant to affect three distinct audiences, albeit in different ways. First, the terrorists intended to intimidate and create fear in the Jewish and Israeli public and, thus, undermine the Israeli government, which is responsible for guaranteeing the population's security (clearly some groups had similar objectives regarding Jordan and perhaps other countries). The logic underlying this objective is based on the denial of Israel's right to exist. Later, the abandonment of terrorism became a card in the negotiation process; U.S. and Israeli recognition of the PLO was contingent on its renunciation of terrorism.[7]

Second, the terrorists strove to gain widespread exposure through the media in order to present the plight of the Palestinians to the public (this is the idea conveyed by Khaled). The Palestinians wanted recognition from the international community that they had been dispossessed and that they too deserve a homeland. It was not a question of more tents for the refugees but, rather, of self-determination. Third, in the competition over Palestinian support each group recognized that terrorist acts were usually very advantageous. Generally speaking, the Palestinian population supported the groups that it believed were fighting for the Palestinian cause. Consequently, when the PFLP embarked on a campaign of international terrorism in the late 1960s, it won public support. Today, however, things are quite different. Support for Abu Nidal declined in the late 1980s, and even Hamas suicide bombings are criticized by the majority of the Palestinian population.

Returning to the State Department's definition, one also notices that this clause includes the identity of the actor. Insofar as only "subnational groups or clandestine agents" are the perpetrators of terrorism, a state, as such, cannot practice terrorism. Accordingly, terrorism is confined to nonstate actors. While the methods of terrorism are not mentioned in the definition itself, the exclusion of state actors from the definition implicitly delimits the methods employed by terrorists to those available to nonstate actors. Tanks and warplanes, for instance, are not used by terrorists, and systematic interrogation, which might include torture, is not considered to be terrorist. Conversely, if tanks and warplanes are employed, then the act is not terrorism. While the acts we described correspond with this aspect of the definition, the question we intend to ask in the next section is whether the identity of the actor and the methods used should be integral to terrorism's definition.

The second clause of the U.S. Department of State's definition is based on what appears to be a tautological idea: the difference between terrorism and international terrorism is the international dimension—"The term 'international terrorism' means terrorism involving citizens or the territory of more than one country" (1998, vi). In other words, two categories are introduced—citizenship and territory—in order to affirm the international component: any terrorist act that involves a plurality of at least one of these categories is considered to be international. Clearly the acts described above satisfy this clause.

The third and final clause intends to capture not only the term *terrorist group* but the notion of state-sponsored terrorism, which was officially introduced by the U.S. Department of State in 1979: "The term 'terrorist group' means any group practicing, or that has significant subgroups that practice, international terrorism" (1998, vi). This clause is complex because it attempts to corroborate the notion that only nonstate actors can practice terrorism while simultaneously granting a role to the state. By distinguishing between a group that actually practices terrorism and a group that does not employ terrorism but has "significant subgroups" that practice terrorism, the State Department makes room for the idea of state-sponsored terrorism without having to entertain the notion that states are actually perpetrators of terrorism.[8] This clause is also in tune with the predominant assumptions of the realist school because it reinforces the notion that states are the major actors in the international arena.

State sponsorship is an important aspect of terrorism, for it is well known that most terrorist groups cannot function or even survive for an extended period of time without the support of states. As the State Department suggests, states tolerate and support terrorist groups by allowing them to open offices within their territories that are used for recruitment of personnel and planning of terrorist acts. States provide funding for terrorist groups, supply safe havens for terrorists, help train agents, and even use their diplomatic leverage in order to facilitate communication between, and transfer explosives into, other countries. In this manner, states enhance the terrorist's capabilities and make law enforcement efforts to counter terrorism more difficult (U.S. Department of State 1998, 23).

Although we have not yet mentioned this aspect of Palestinian terrorism, some of the aforementioned violent acts were sponsored by states. As indicated, according to the U.S. Department of State, five—Iran, Iraq, Libya, Sudan, and Syria—out of the seven states that are considered to be sponsors of international terrorism are located in the Middle East (1998, 23). Consider, for a moment, Syria's role as a sponsor. While Syria has not been directly involved in terrorist attacks for some time now, in the early 1980s it was considered to be a haven for terrorist groups. A 1987 U.S. Department of State report discussing Syria's complicity in terrorism states that

> Syria prefers to support groups whose activities are generally in line with Syrian objectives rather than to select targets or control operations itself. Damascus utilizes these groups to attack or intimidate enemies and opponents and to exert its influence in the region. Yet at the same time, it can disavow knowledge of their operations. Such Syrian-supported groups have carried out scores of attacks against Palestinian and other Arab, Turkish, Israeli, and Western targets during the past 3 years. [1987, 1]

The State Department suggests that 500 people were either killed or wounded by Syrian-supported groups during the period 1983–86. In the report one finds testimony provided by Nizar Hindawi, an Abu Nidal operative who was caught while trying, by means of a pregnant Irish girlfriend, to place a bomb on an El Al plane leaving London's Heathrow Airport for Tel-Aviv. During the investigation, Hindawi revealed that he was recruited by an aide to Major General al-Khuli, chief of Syrian Air Force intelligence. From the evidence presented during his trial, we learn that

> al-Khuli's operatives: (1) supplied Hindawi, a Jordanian, with a Syrian passport; (2) gave him $12,000 and promised him more money when he completed the mission to plant a bomb aboard an El Al civilian airliner; (3) provided him with the bomb which he carried into London aboard the Syrian Arab Airlines [SAA], which also gave him SAA crew member hotel accommodations; and (4) trained him in the bomb's use. [U.S. Department of State 1987, 1]

Hindawi's case exemplifies how closely a state can work with a terrorist group, so much so that it is hard to determine who is the actual initiator of the terrorist act—Abu Nidal or Syria.

The U.S. Department of State also asserts that "when King Hussein launched his February 1985 peace initiative [with Israel], Jordan became a major target [of terrorism]. But when Jordanian–Syrian relations warmed in mid-1985, attacks on Jordanians at home and abroad diminished" (1987, 2). This trend not only lends considerable support to the claim of Syrian control of terrorist groups but also attests that it is using these groups to advance its own political goals. Terrorism becomes the tool of a state without the state actually having to practice it. Sponsorship shifts the power from the terrorist group back to the state, in the sense that if Jordan is interested in stopping the terrorist activities, it needs to appease Syria and not the actual perpetrators.

Terrorist groups, one should note, have complex relationships with their state sponsors. On the one hand, terrorists usually have their own agenda and do not want to be co-opted by states. Concerned that his autonomy was in jeopardy, Abu Nidal moved from Iraq to Syria and then to Libya. On the other hand, the state supports and protects the terrorist group. Other than Abu Nidal, Syria is said to have supported a variety of Palestinian terrorist organizations including Saiqa, Abu Musa's group, the PFLP, and the PFLP–General Command. Non-Palestinian groups like the Japanese Red Army and the Pakistani al Zulfikar received Syrian assistance as well.

The manner in which the State Department defines terrorism is crucial because it determines the data incorporated into its "terrorism databank." Not only the State Department but the Central Intelligence Agency and even RAND conceive terrorism to be the illegitimate use of force by nonstate actors and "rogue regimes" like Libya and Syria. This definition has immediate, and at times far-reaching, political implications. The inclusion of the "state-sponsored terrorism" category, for example, plays a significant role in U.S. politics, for U.S. law imposes trade and other restrictions on countries that sponsor terrorism. On a deeper level, the integration of the actor's identity in terrorism's definition opens the door for a double standard. If the actor's identity, not solely the act itself, determines whether it falls under the term *terrorism*, then, at least theoretically, terrorism can always be attributed to the state's official enemies and never to the state itself or its allies. Keeping this in mind, we now turn to examine Israel's actions.

ISRAELI STATE TERRORISM

Before the State of Israel was established, the Jewish population living in Palestine formed different political organizations, some of which had military arms. Irgun and Lehi were two relatively small groups that adopted terrorism as a strategy of political action.[9] Lehi terrorized the British forces in Palestine during the 1940s and murdered at least fifteen moderate Jews. In 1944, Lehi operatives working in Cairo assassinated Lord Moyne, the British minister for Middle East affairs. Lehi and Irgun members collaborated in 1946, bombing the British civil administration offices located at the King David Hotel in Jerusalem. Over ninety people, many of whom were Jewish, were killed in that operation. One month before the British forces pulled out of Palestine, the two groups attacked the Palestinian village Deir Yassin, killing some 250 men, women, and children; "there were also cases of mutilation and rape" (Morris 1987, 113). The news of the massacre and threats that more was to come prompted many Palestinians living in nearby villages to flee their homes when, a month later, the fighting between the Jews and Arabs began (Anderson and Sloan 1995, 194; McGowan and Ellis 1998).

These actions, while not adding to our understanding of terrorism, indicate that Palestinians were not necessarily the first perpetrators of terrorism in the Middle East. But the question that interests us here is whether Israel, as a state, employs terrorism and not whether certain Jewish groups practiced terrorism prior to the state's establishment. Because the State Department restricts the actual practice of terrorism to nonstate actors, we cannot use its definition of terrorism in the following discussion. Accordingly, we have formulated a different definition of political terrorism:

> Terrorism is a form of political violence that by design violates some of the society's accepted moral and legal codes, is often ruthlessly destructive, and is somewhat unpredictable in who will be its instrumental targets. Terrorism hardly constitutes mindless violence. Instead, it reflects a detailed strategy that uses horrific violence to make people feel weak and vulnerable, often disproportionate to either the terror-

ist acts or to the terrorists' long-term power. This fear seeks to promote concrete
political objectives.

This definition captures all the incidents of Palestinian terrorism described
above. Yet it does not identify the perpetrator of the act and, therefore, does not
determine in advance that nonstate actors are the sole agents of terrorism. Once
the actor is considered to be an insignificant variable, it becomes easier to judge
the act according to its nature. Terrorism can no longer be consigned only to the
competing sources of power—that is, official enemies—but may be attributed to
any actor. Consequently, some of the major aspects that allowed for the emergence of a double standard are overcome. The definition also does not indicate
the means by which terrorism is carried out, entailing that the perpetrators can
use handguns and small bombs or tanks and warplanes. As a result, it enables us
to treat Israel and the Palestinians, at least initially, as having an equal capacity
to employ terrorism.

Examining Israel's actions in Lebanon, one notices that it has often used methods of terror. Notable examples are two fairly recent operations: Accountability
(July 1993) and Grapes of Wrath (April 1996). Israel's stated political objective
in these operations was to foment a refugee flow from southern Lebanon to the
north in order to put pressure on the Lebanese government so that it, in turn,
would curb guerrilla actions perpetrated by the Hezbollah. In a report on Operation Accountability, Human Rights Watch (HRW) asserts,

> While Israel has claimed that broadcast warnings to the civilian population in south-
> ern Lebanon were made with a view to protecting civilians from collateral injury in
> attacks on strictly military objectives, a number of factors make it reasonable to as-
> sume that the intention was in fact to sow terror among the civilian population. The
> SLA [South Lebanon Army] radio station broadcast threats of a general nature,
> warning anyone remaining in certain areas that they would be in danger of being hit.
> As the pattern of physical damage showed, the IDF [Israel Defense Force]/SLA then
> subjected entire villages to area bombardment. The threats and the nature of the at-
> tacks make it clear that in significant areas in southern Lebanon whole populations—
> indeed anyone who failed to flee by a certain time—were targeted as if they were
> combatants. [1996, 9][10]

HRW notes that in addition to subjecting villages to a massive shelling bar-
rage, "the IDF also executed what appear to have been calculated direct attacks
on purely civilian targets. One such series of attacks was carried out against Si-
don's wholesale vegetable market, far from the front line in south Lebanon"
(1996, 9). HRW estimates that some 120 civilians were killed and close to 500
injured during the operation. In addition, the bombing led to the immediate displacement of an estimated 150,000 to 200,000 people, and four months after the
attack some 32,000 to 40,000 civilians were still displaced (1996, 83). Furthermore, "by the end of Operation Accountability, conservative damage estimates

suggested that some 1,000 houses had been destroyed, and 15,000 houses had sustained light damage. Israeli forces cut civilian water and electricity supplies, damaged schools, mosques and churches, and targeted a number of cemeteries with shell fire" (HRW 1996, 8).

Less than three years later, Israel launched a similar attack, this time calling it Grapes of Wrath. According to Israel's prestigious paper, *Ha'aretz* (21 April 1996), internal reports of the northern border's military command indicate that in the first few days of the operation Israeli Air Force planes bombed 300 sites in Lebanon, resulting in the displacement of approximately 400,000 civilians and demolition of over 200 houses. Moreover, some 198 civilians were killed— including the 97 refugees in the village of Kana killed as a result of the miscalculated firing of a rocket.

To be sure, these operations correspond with the definition of terrorism, for they violate some of society's accepted moral and legal codes, are ruthlessly destructive, and unpredictable in who will be targeted. As with Palestinian terrorism described earlier, the objective of Israel's operations in Lebanon was not to kill civilians. Yet the Israeli generals who planned the action knew in advance that innocent people would surely die as a result of the bombing, and in line with the definition these generals contrived a detailed strategy that used horrific violence in order to make people feel weak and vulnerable. The engendered fear seeks to promote concrete political objectives that exceed the violent act, for, as mentioned, Israel terrorized the population of southern Lebanon so that it, in turn, would pressure the Lebanese government to clamp down on the Hezbollah. Considering that Operation Grapes of Wrath was launched a few weeks before the 1996 Israeli elections, it is also conceivable that Prime Minister Shimon Peres wanted to influence the Israeli public as well by showing that he was not weak and indecisive on matters of security.

Other activities in Lebanon correspond with this definition of terrorism. For instance, Israeli commando units kidnapped Sheik Abd al-Karim Obeid and Mustafa al-Dirani from their homes in 1989 and 1994 respectively. Both Shi'a leaders have since been held incommunicado; they have never been charged or tried, and Israel has declared that they will be released only in exchange for Israeli service persons missing in action (MIAs) in Lebanon or for concrete information about these Israelis. According to HRW, Israeli officials have also indicated more generally that the release of other Lebanese detainees is linked to the issue of Israeli MIAs. HRW points out that insofar as Israel conditions the release of Lebanese detainees on securing information from third parties about Israeli MIAs, "those detainees are being held as hostages." Hostage taking is indefensible, HRW contends, and cannot be justified by the actions of other parties to a conflict (1997, appendix 1).

Israel has employed terrorism not only in the international arena but also in the territories it occupied in 1967, the West Bank and Gaza Strip. During the Intifada (the Palestinian uprising that began in December 1987), Israeli undercover units penetrated Palestinian settlements, killing Palestinians by means of summary executions; the unit would locate the victim and, without attempting arrest, would shoot in order to kill. These units, according to HRW, killed more than 110 Palestinians from the beginning of the Intifada until November 1992.[11] Interestingly, the Israeli government acknowledged its responsibility for many of these killings, even though they "constitute violations of international law and of the law that Israel professes to apply in the occupied territories" (HRW 1993, 1). Aside from the fact that the State of Israel was the perpetrator of these killings, the actions and methods used by the undercover units and the objectives Israel wanted to achieve by these killings conform to the definition of terrorism used here.

Israel's practice of state-sanctioned torture also qualifies as an act of political terrorism. It is well known that torture is not only used to extract information or to control the victim; it is also used to control the population as a whole. As an imminent threat, torture is used to intimidate groups or individuals who oppose the existing order within the country in which they reside. When one analyzes the history of the use of torture, where it was practiced, and why, one will see that torture is not simply about inducing a person to speak; rather, it is about silence—ensuring that particular activists are broken and popular opposition remains suppressed (B'Tzelem 1997; Gordon and Marton 1995; HRW 1994; Physicians for Human Rights 1995).

CONCLUSION

Once one accepts the above definition of terrorism, it becomes obvious that states can terrorize and can use soldiers, airplanes, and tanks to do so. The means applied are irrelevant; a plane bombing in southern Lebanon or a suicide bomber can achieve similar objectives. Again and again states utilize methods of terror against their enemies in order to accomplish a particular premeditated political goal. Israel's violence, and that used by states as diverse as Nigeria and the United States, suggests that terror should not be reduced to the difference between nonstate and state action. The character of the perpetrator does not determine the nature of the act, or, conversely, the character of one act does not necessarily predict the type of perpetrator.

By way of conclusion we would like to raise two issues that may be conducive to the reduction of terrorism. First, we believe that the significance of excluding the actor's identity from terrorism's definition cannot be overemphasized. Such an exclusion exposes some of the problems inherent in the Weberian hypothesis that the state has monopoly over the legitimate use of force. This hypothesis, it appears, is based on the presupposition that legitimacy is determined with respect to the state. For if the state has monopoly over the use of legitimate force, it must first be able to determine legitimacy, indicating that the state precedes legitimacy or, more precisely, justice. But if one conceives the state as having the capability to practice terrorism, which we believe to be by definition illegitimate and unjust, then justice must precede the state. Once one agrees that the state is not above justice, one will be able to accept that it can employ illegitimate violence and practice terrorism.

Disrupting the dichotomy between, on the one hand, the state that holds the monopoly over the legitimate uses of violence and, on the other, nonstate actors that do not mitigates the double standard mentioned earlier. We believe that the way terrorism is currently constructed has more to do with who the actor is, and what its specific relation to the existing hegemonic system is, and not so much with the type of actor (state or nonstate). The actor's exclusion from the definition will surely help eliminate some of the double-speak that surrounds the discourse on terrorism. Once the definition of terrorism focuses solely on the nature of the act, it will be harder to persevere in the common practice of referring to terrorism perpetrated by the state or an ally as "maintaining order," "ensuring security," or "upholding democracy." Exposing terrorism for what it is is a necessary first step toward arresting it.

Second, one needs to go beyond the debate pertaining to terrorism's definition and recast the discourse surrounding the violent acts. One way to begin is by confronting, where appropriate and relevant, the all-too-linear view taken by social science in analyzing political violence. More precisely, we contend that the cause-effect assumptions about insurgent terrorism need to be challenged. Consider the effort of mainstream scholars and policy makers to trace the causes of terrorism to either the presence of technology, transnationalism and telecommunications, or ideology—usually Marxist (Lopez 1995, 264).[12] We, by contrast, do not believe that an examination of ideology or technological development will disclose terrorism's causes; moreover, it is time to probe the issue from a fresh standpoint. This entails asking new questions, such as, How does the absence of certain rules and institutions in the international order create conditions whereby groups and states with grievances find little recourse, save resorting to terrorist violence?

With questions like this, one could, for example, stimulate an investigation of how, in countries where terrorism is prevalent, the development of global institutions such as an international criminal court or mediation agency—which would hear and judge the grievances of both state and nonstate actors—could prevent terrorism by providing nonviolent alternatives. Investigations like this are fundamental, and they might even lead to the establishment of such institutions.

Rethinking international terrorism along these lines helps *resist* the tendency to conceive terrorism positively, as induced from an internal character or disposition that compels the actor toward violence. Paraphrasing Simone De Beauvoir, people are not born but, rather, become terrorists (1989). Accordingly, terrorism should be considered as predominantly negative, namely, that it arises because of social injustice accompanied by a lack of meaningful alternatives by which disempowered political groups or even states might have their grievances re-dressed. Such an outlook is essential to any effort striving to curb terrorism. It is clear to us that as part of the peace process the different parties must acknowl-edge the historical use of terrorism by both actors, for only the delegitimation and renunciation of such terrorism will prevent violence from derailing the proc-ess and destroying the promised comprehensive peace. And only a just peace can deal a deathblow to Middle East terrorism.

NOTES

1. According to Harvey Kushner, from the signing of the Oslo Accords in September 1993 and until 1996, almost 200 Israelis died as a result of suicide attacks (1996, 330).

2. In 1969, Arafat became the chairman of the PLO and retained this position until the signing of the Oslo Accords. He is currently the president of the Palestinian Authority in the Gaza Strip and West Bank.

3. U.N. Resolution 242 was adopted following the 1967 war. The idea of land in ex-change for peace, which became the basis for the peace negotiations, was first articulated in this resolution.

4. A few months later Black September hijacked a Lufthansa plane, and Chancellor Willy Brandt decided to release the three terrorists who had been captured in exchange for the hostages on the plane. In a three-year period, from 1971 to 1974, Black September carried out at least thirty-four noteworthy actions: sixteen bombings, eleven assassina-tions, three hijackings and another three hostage seizures, and one rocket attack on the U.S. embassy in Beirut (Anderson and Sloan 1995, 61).

5. In April 1983, for instance, Abu Nidal operatives assassinated Issam Sartawi, a PLO leader who publicly advocated dialogue with Israeli peace activists.

6. For the purpose of this definition, the term *noncombatant* is interpreted to include, in addition to civilians, military personnel who at the time of the incident are unarmed or not on duty (U.S. Department of State 1998, vi).

7. In 1988, Yasser Arafat declared publicly that the PLO renounces terrorism; this led to Washington's recognition of the organization and opening of diplomatic talks.

8. The analysis of "state terrorism" or "the state and terrorism" does have a long-standing literature and meaning, as well as rhetoric, in the study of political terrorism. A decade ago, scholars (Duvall and Stohl 1988; Stohl 1988; Stohl and Lopez 1988) provided the demarcations among important categories, for example, distinctions between state-supported and surrogate terrorism.

9. Today's prominent political party Likud is a direct extension of these two groups. Former Prime Ministers Menachem Begin and Yitzhak Shamir were the leaders of Irgun and Lehi, respectively.

10. The SLA is Israel's mercenary army in southern Lebanon.

11. The victims of these executions are of two kinds: "wanted" and masked people. Of the 110 people killed by the undercover units, forty-two were wanted. "Wanted" people are "Palestinians named on a security force's list of militants who are suspected of being armed, highly dangerous, and responsible for politically motivated violence" (HRW 1993, 3). Note that they are merely suspected. Masked people are "youths who mask their faces,

whose identities are not known to the security forces when they encounter one another, who generally are unarmed, or carry at most 'cold weapons' such as axes and chains, and who are routinely shot while imposing no imminent mortal danger to security agents" (HRW 1993, 3).

12. Technology refers to the availability of arms and related tools for carrying out terror. Transnationalism involves the movement of peoples with relative ease across borders such that terrorists could be trained in one state, perpetrate their deed in another, and move to a safe haven in yet another. Telecommunications is considered to promote terrorism because it guarantees a wider audience and helps make terrorism into a form of political theater.

PART IV

HUMANITARIAN INTERVENTION

8

Humanitarian Intervention and State Sovereignty

Simon Caney

Is state sovereignty inviolable? Embedded in the international system is a commitment on the part of states to respect state sovereignty. In addition, the United Nations affirms in Article 2(7) a principle of nonintervention, and in Article 2(4) it proscribes the use of force. Is this, however, morally justifiable? May a state or international institution (like the United Nations) intervene in the affairs of another state? Is there, for example, a case for intervention on humanitarian grounds when a state is harming its own citizens? In such cases, is there a right to intervene, or do we have an obligation to intervene? It is important to examine these questions because situations frequently arise in which external agencies (like states or international institutions) have engaged in intervention. The United Nations, for example, sought to create "safe havens" in northern Iraq in April 1991 and to create "an aerial exclusion zone" in southern Iraq during the summer of 1992 to protect Shiite Muslims (Griffiths, Levine, and Weller 1995, 48–50). In addition, it intervened in Somalia, adopting an arms embargo in January 1992 and then sending in troops to enforce the peace and to defend those supplying aid (Morphet 1995, 222–23).[1] Similarly, in the former Yugoslavia it adopted several measures including applying an arms embargo in 1991, granting the U.N. Protection Force permission to deploy force to defend itself in 1992, and creating safe havens in a number of places including Srebrenica and Sarajevo in 1993 (Griffiths, Levine, and Weller 1995, 53–55).[2] Such activity has not been confined to the United Nations, and single countries have also engaged in acts of intervention: thus, India intervened in what was then East Pakistan in 1971 and America intervened in Grenada in 1983.[3]

This chapter will address the ethical question of whether we should endorse humanitarian intervention. To do this it will begin by analyzing how we should define humanitarian intervention. It will next examine the main argument for humanitarian intervention before then examining counterarguments. Having argued that there is a case for intervention on humanitarian grounds, the chapter will then analyze the conditions that must be satisfied before intervention is attempted and finally will conclude by arguing that even if intervention is morally justified, this does not entail that international law should affirm a right to humanitarian intervention.

DEFINING HUMANITARIAN INTERVENTION

It is important to start by addressing the question, "What is humanitarian intervention?" To answer this we must first provide a definition of *intervention* before then analyzing the nature of a *humanitarian* intervention. Much has been written on the issue of how to define *intervention*, and a number of different definitions have been proposed.

A good place to start is the definition given by the international relations scholar Hedley Bull. Intervention, Bull maintains, is "dictatorial or coercive interference, by an outside party or parties, in the sphere of jurisdiction of a sovereign state, or more broadly of an independent political community" (1984, 1). While this definition has several virtues, it does, however, need to be modified. In particular, its use of the pejorative words *dictatorial* and *interference* is unhelpful, suggesting, before any normative considerations have been adduced, that intervention is wrong.[4] What is required, therefore, is a definition that abjures the use of such value-laden words (Caney 1997, 28). In line with this, we can revise Bull's definition as follows: an intervention is a coercive action "by an outside party or parties, in the sphere of jurisdiction of a sovereign state, or more broadly of an independent political community." This is, I believe, a plausible and accurate definition.

Two features of this definition should be stressed. First, it is important to note that intervention necessarily involves coercion, and, thus, not all action that alters a state's behavior counts as intervention. Noncoercive forms of action (like persuasion or diplomacy), on this definition, do not count as interventionary (Brown 1992, 112).[5] Second, as Bull's definition recognizes, and as others have also stressed, the agents engaging in intervention may be bodies other than states (Hoffmann 1984, 10; McMahan 1986, 25–26; Vincent 1974, 4–5). Intervention can be conducted by a number of different bodies—including, for example, states, associations of states, international institutions, social institutions like churches, or even economic enterprises.

Several scholars have proposed narrower definitions, and it is worth addressing some of these proposals. First, some argue that intervention must necessarily employ force or military power. Jack Donnelly, for example, defines *intervention* in terms of coercion and then identifies coercion with force (1993, 608–10).[6] As several writers have pointed out, however, this is an unduly narrow definition (McMahan 1986, 25; Smith 1989, 4; Vincent 1974, 7–8).[7] It neglects nonmilitary ways of determining another state's behavior like economic sanctions or trade embargoes. As Mark Wicclair points out, the misgivings some people have about intervention apply not just to military modes of intervention but also to nonmilitary modes (1979, 143). What is sometimes objected to is the use of coercion—for one state to be determining what happens in another country—but coercion can take different forms, and we therefore have no reason to limit intervention to military modes of coercion alone.

A second restriction should also be considered. Some, for example, argue that intervention, by definition, is an action against the interests or wishes of another state (see, for example, Wicclair 1979, 143–44). Thus, for A to engage in intervention in state B, A must be acting against B's wishes. While this is often so, we have no reason to narrow intervention solely to such cases (McMahan 1986, 26–27; Smith 1989, 2, n. 3). In some cases, for example, a state invites outside agencies to come to its assistance (perhaps to overcome some internal revolutionaries), and it is natural to describe those outside agencies as intervening in that country's affairs. In addition, sometimes an external body is invited in by two parties to a conflict to help resolve the disagreement. In April 1990, for example, the government in El Salvador and the rebels invited the United Nations to intervene to help resolve the conflict (Munck and Kumar 1995, 169–79, especially 170).

A more general point about defining intervention should also be made. As Charles Beitz notes, there is a good case for adopting a wide definition of intervention (1979b, 72–74). A wide definition enables us, when considering the moral legitimacy of intervention, to bear in mind the variety of different methods available and to distinguish between the advantages of different modes of intervention. The wider the definition, the more types of action are considered and the fuller the picture one gets as to what should be done.

Having defined intervention, we can now analyze what is meant by terming an intervention a "humanitarian intervention." In this chapter, I shall define an intervention as a humanitarian intervention if one of its central aims is to protect the welfare of the members of another state. Some might demur from this definition, arguing that humanitarian interventions are interventions undertaken for no reason other than to protect the welfare of members of another state. As Mason and Wheeler plausibly argue, however, in such a definition there are no humanitarian interventions and there is little point in proposing to define a phenomenon in such a way that it has no application to our world (1996, 95). Thus, a humanitarian intervention, as I define it, is an intervention that is undertaken in part for humanitarian reasons. Interventions that are undertaken simply in order to increase the intervener's prestige or security interests are, therefore, not included as humanitarian interventions. In addition, and perhaps more controversially, on this definition interventions designed to protect one's own nationals residing in a foreign state are also not included as humanitarian interventions (Akehurst 1984, 99–104).

Now, combining this account of humanitarianism with the earlier definition of intervention, it follows that humanitarian intervention should be defined as

> coercive action "by an outside party or parties, in the sphere of jurisdiction of a sovereign state, or more broadly of an independent political community" (Bull 1984, 1), which is undertaken, partly or exclusively, to protect the welfare of the members of that political community.

Two further points should be made before appraising the justifiability of humanitarian intervention. First, when judging these arguments we should bear in mind whether they address the (weaker) claim that outside agencies have a right to intervene or the (stronger) claim that they have an obligation to intervene. The latter is, clearly, more difficult to establish because it claims not just that they are permitted to intervene but that they ought to do so. In what follows, I shall concentrate on this stronger claim but will draw attention to the weaker claim when it is relevant. Second, it is important to stress that a sound appreciation of the case for and against intervention should note the many forms that intervention can take. Military interventions, for example, can involve the creation of safe havens, the deployment of troops, or the provision of training and weapons. Alternatively, it might involve weapon inspections and the destruction of weapons. Furthermore, as was mentioned earlier, intervention may involve nonmilitary types of coercion including embargoes, sanctions, or monitoring elections. All of these are acts that coerce another state or the members of another state. It is important, however, to note their diversity because some objections to intervention may have force against some types of interventionary behaviors but not others.

THE CASE FOR HUMANITARIAN INTERVENTION

Let us now, therefore, address the normative question of whether humanitarian intervention is justifiable and in particular whether external agencies have an obligation to intervene. Many do believe that humanitarian intervention is sometimes justified. Many, for example, think it right for external agencies to intervene to prevent a state engaging in genocidal policies against some of its own people or if there is widespread human rights abuse. On what grounds, however, can we justify intervention?

The standard case for humanitarian intervention rests on four important claims.[8] First, proponents of humanitarian intervention affirm the cosmopolitan claim (made by, among others, Barry, Beitz, and Pogge)[9] that individuals have moral interests or a moral status that is worthy of respect. Some would employ the concept of rights and emphasize people's human rights, say, not to be killed or imprisoned without trial. Others eschew the concept of rights and might emphasize people's needs or interests, arguing that there is a humanitarian case for intervening when people are in great need. Whichever approach is adopted, however, both are united in their commitment to the claim that individuals have a moral worth that should be respected and moral interests that should be protected.

Second, and relatedly, proponents of humanitarian intervention make the further claim that states have value only to the extent that they respect people's moral interests or moral standing. States do not have a right to rule regardless of their citizens' welfare. Thus, not only do individuals have moral standing (assumption 1): states have moral value only insofar as they further people's interests (Barry 1999, 35–40; Beitz 1988b, 192; 1994). Those who endorse a set of human rights, therefore, argue that states have value only insofar as they act in a just fashion and respect people's rights: if they violate them, then external intervention may be justified to rectify this situation (Barry 1998, 153, 160; 1999, 40; Beitz 1979b, 69–92; Doppelt 1980; Pogge 1992; Smith 1998, 76–78). In addition, some develop the idea of rights further, arguing that states have legitimacy if their members agree or would agree to them. In this "contractarian" approach, therefore, states are not legitimate when they do not command the consent of their people (Luban 1980a, 167; Teson 1988, 112–13; Wicclair 1980, 293–302).[10] The case for humanitarian intervention, however, does not rest on a commitment to contractarianism: it assumes, simply, that state sovereignty is justified only when it furthers human interests.

These first two assumptions, however, do not establish an obligation to intervene on humanitarian grounds. This requires a third assumption, namely, that people's rights or interests generate obligations on others (Pogge 1994, 89).[11] That is, external agencies have a duty not just not to violate people's rights but also to ensure that other people's rights are respected.[12] Without this further assumption, one can show at most that humanitarian intervention is permissible: that is, that people have a right to intervene.[13] To show that people have an obligation to intervene, this further third assumption is required.

Fourth and finally, the case for humanitarian intervention rests on the further assumption that acts of humanitarian intervention can work. Clearly this assumption is crucial, and if it proved to be the case that humanitarian interventions never succeeded in meeting the appropriate humanitarian ends, there could be no case for such policies. Here, it is appropriate to note that many who are deeply committed to the protection of human rights are wary of humanitarian intervention precisely because they are skeptical of the success of humanitarian interventions. Distinguished cosmopolitan thinkers like Beitz (1980, 390–91) and Booth (1994, 65–70; 1995, 120–21), for example, are critical of military intervention for precisely this reason.

To sum up, therefore, the case for humanitarian intervention claims that all persons have fundamental interests (assumption 1) and that states do not have value except insofar as they respect these interests (assumption 2). It claims further that external agents have duties to protect people's fundamental interests (assumption 3) and that this obligation sometimes requires external intervention because it is an effective way of protecting such interests (assumption 4).

ARGUMENTS AGAINST HUMANITARIAN INTERVENTION

Many, however, have deep misgivings about humanitarian intervention, and this section seeks to explore some of the most commonly expressed counterarguments.[14] Attention will be focused, in particular, on three types of counterargument, namely, the arguments that humanitarian intervention is illegitimate because (a) it fails to respect a people's right to self-government, (b) it destroys international stability, and (c) it rarely succeeds.[15]

Self-Government

Let us consider those who affirm a community's right to be self-governing to oppose intervention. A number of distinct arguments have been given that make this claim.

The Rights of States

Some, like Christian Wolff, affirm the intrinsic right of states to be independent in order to defend nonintervention. In *Jus Gentium Methodo Scientifica Pertractatum*, Wolff maintains that "the law of nations is originally nothing else than the law of nature applied to nations, which are considered as individual persons living in a state of nature" (1934, 84). Throughout, states are assumed to be analogous to persons, and given that the latter should be respected as independent, it follows that states should be as well (1934, 9). As Wolff writes, "Since by nature nations are bound to each other in the same way as individuals are bound to individuals, every nation also ought to allow to another nation its right" (1934, 135). Hence, "no ruler of a state has the right to interfere in the government of another" (1934, 131, see also 130–33).

As critics of this argument have pointed out, however, it is not plausible to claim that states are analogous to persons (Beitz 1979b, 69–71, 74–76, 81; McMahan 1986, 28–30, especially 29). They lack the moral properties we attribute to human beings. We thus have no reason to think that states should be given intrinsic value, and Wolff's view that, like persons, states possess independent value—value, that is, regardless of how they affect humans—is highly implausible. The cornerstone of this traditional argument is, thus, deeply counterintuitive.

The Rights of Communities

More recently an argument against intervention has been developed by Michael Walzer. Like the preceding argument it affirms the right of a collectivity in order to oppose intervention, but unlike the preceding argument it does not attribute independent moral value to states. Walzer's argument makes two essential claims. First, he defends what he terms "communal integrity," reasoning that "the idea of communal integrity derives its moral and political force from the rights of contemporary men and women to live as members of a historic community and to express their inherited culture through political forms worked out among themselves" (1980, 211). In short, communal self-government is desirable (see also Walzer 1980, 225–26). Walzer then argues that those outside a state are unable to judge whether that state represents a form of communal self-government. And because they are ignorant about the internal affairs of another state, they should adopt a "morally necessary presumption[, namely,] that there exists a certain 'fit' between the community and its government and that the state is 'legitimate.' It is not a gang of rulers acting in its own interests, but a people governed in accordance with its own traditions" (Walzer 1980, 212). Thus, given that communal integrity is valuable and given that external bodies must (because of their ignorance) assume that a state embodies the norms of the community, external bodies should eschew intervention. They do not have a right (let alone an obligation) to intervene.[16]

Walzer's argument has received a great deal of discussion. One serious problem with his argument concerns his second claim that external agents are too ill-informed to be able to assess whether there is a "fit" between a people and a state (and should therefore simply assume that there is). As many have noted, this claim is simply implausible (Beitz 1980, 386; Doppelt 1980, 400; Luban 1980b, 395; McMahan 1986, 42–43). External bodies, like the United Nations, can surely draw on research of another country, survey its infrastructure, socioeconomic base, traditions, history, and so on, and thereby reach an informed opinion on whether there is "fit." Furthermore, in many cases there is no match between a state and a community, most states being multinational, multiethnic, and multicultural (Brown 1993, 517–18). And there are many glaring cases in which the political elite does not represent the values of the entire population but, rather, only a subsection (Beitz 1980, 385–86). In such cases, to respect the state is to grant protection of one community but in doing so to enable it to persecute other communities (McMahan 1986, 33). Thus, the ideal of "communal integrity" provides very little support for state sovereignty and nonintervention.[17]

International Order

A second argument against humanitarian intervention affirms the importance of a stable international order. It then argues that permitting (or defending) humanitarian intervention encourages other interventions and thereby destroys international order. Intervention should, therefore, be rejected because to permit it would engender instability. This argument has been stressed by a number of writers including Bull (on which see Nardin 1983, 5, 18–19; Slater and Nardin 1986, 87; Vincent 1974, 328–33; Wheeler 1992, 463–77).[18]

It is, however, unpersuasive. First, the argument's empirical assumption that defending intervention will encourage further interventions and thus destabilize the global order is implausible. As Beitz (1988a, 187) and McMahan (1986, 44) note, many interventions have taken place that have not triggered other interventions or in any other way destabilized global politics. As McMahan further adds (1986, 43–44), it is hard to see why reaching a moral conclusion about the justifiability of intervention will affect the conduct of states.

In addition, even if humanitarian intervention did generate instability, this alone does not establish that it is wrong. It would do so only if we attributed supreme importance to preserving the international status quo. We therefore need to know whether the current international system is worth preserving and whether a more attractive alternative is attainable. The value of stability (including international stability) is a function of the value of the current arrangements. Appeals to international order are, therefore, incomplete and need to be supplemented by an argument showing that the international system is fair and morally legitimate (Beitz 1988a, 187–88; Wicclair 1979, 150). Furthermore, and relatedly, to prioritize stability is to reward the most powerful who—if they cannot get their way—will generate instability. It appeases the most powerful and disenfranchises the weak who are unable to threaten instability (Caney 1997, 30). As Rawls expresses the point, "to each according to his threat advantage is not a principle of justice" (1971, 141). Arguments invoking the importance of order are, thus, incomplete and rest on the dubious assumption that intervention engenders instability.

The Ineffectiveness of Intervention

For many, however, the problem with humanitarian intervention lies not with its disregard for the rights of states or its alleged propensity to cause disorder. Rather, the problem is that, for a number of reasons, intervention does not succeed in its objectives. Someone might, therefore, accept assumptions 1, 2, and 3 of the argument for humanitarian intervention but have deep misgivings about the efficacy of humanitarian intervention (i.e., assumption 4). Those who oppose intervention are, thus, not necessarily indifferent to the plight of others. Caroline Thomas, for instance, affirms a pragmatic argument, drawing on examples like Tanzania's intervention in Uganda in 1978–79 and the Vietnamese intervention into Cambodia, to argue that interventions rarely work (1993, 91–103, especially 93–95). In addition, a recent analysis of U.N. peacemaking activities concludes that these have standardly proved to be unsuccessful (Diehl, Reifschneider, and Hensel 1996). These empirical examples cast doubt on the case for humanitarian intervention, but before we accept them, they need to be supplemented with theoretical explanations, showing why no intervention will further humanitarian ends. A number of reasons have been suggested as to why intervention will not work.[19]

Knowledge

First, some argue that external agencies are insufficiently well informed about another state and its population to make good decisions (Donnelly 1993, 640). The experiences of a number of interventions lend support to this argument. Ioan Lewis and James Mayall record, for example, that the U.N. intervention in Somalia (UNOSOM) was ill-informed. They argue that

> very few adequately representative Somali advisors were recruited, and UN officials generally could hardly have been more inadequately briefed about Somali society and culture. The huge gap between traditional Somali methods of dealing with foreigners and American high-tech put most of the UN staff at a great disadvantage in their local dealings. This is perhaps most graphically illustrated by U.S. helicopters dropping leaflets on a population with a primarily oral tradition whose sensitivity to radio broadcasting is famous in Africa. [1996, 121][20]

Similarly, the U.N. intervention in Cambodia (UNTAC) was afflicted by poor information. Mats Berdal and Michael Leifer, for instance, draw attention to the failure to have an intelligence unit tracking the movements of the Khmer Rouge and Vietnamese troops present in Cambodia (1996, 48–49). They argue, further, that UNTAC's success "required intimate knowledge of and sensitivity to the host culture. Yet both were in short supply and UNTAC's attempts to control the administration with any effect were wholly unsuccessful" (1996, 43–44).

Nonetheless, as a number of scholars have pointed out, the assumption that external agencies are always insufficiently informed is too sweeping (Adelman 1992, 71; Wicclair 1979, 153). States and international institutions can finance thorough and comprehensive analyses of the socioeconomic structure of another society, its political system, and its political culture. Moreover, all the examples above point to technical problems that can be rectified rather than to any deep or fundamental obstacle to one group of people understanding the nature of another society.

Improper Motives

A second reason for doubting whether interventions will further humanitarian objectives is voiced by Stanley Benn and R. S. Peters (1959, 361). They argue that states rarely act out of altruism and contend that they will usually intervene to further their national interests rather than the fundamental rights of people abroad. Similarly, realists are skeptical of the motives of states and, thus, are skeptical of the likelihood of genuinely humanitarian intervention (Morgenthau 1967, 430).

Three points, however, should be made about this argument. First, as Wicclair points out, this argument does not show that interventions will not further humanitarian ends. This would be the case only if we assume that a state's pursuit of its interests never includes policies that also further humanitarian aims (like the observance of human rights or the prevention of starvation). Policies motivated to some extent by the national interest may also have beneficial outcomes for others. Furthermore, states might acquire prestige and standing through humanitarian acts. A political leader might, for example, seek to enhance his or her reputation through securing a foreign policy success (such as facilitating peace in the Middle East) (Wicclair 1979, 152).

A second problem with this argument lies in its rather crude understanding of the motivations of states. It would be utopian and idealistic to think that states do not seek to further their national interests, but it is also unrealistic to think that they are never motivated by other concerns, including ideological commitments (Jervis 1988, 342–43; Waltz 1979, 91–92, 205). Furthermore, it is artificial to characterize a state's national interest independently of the moral beliefs of its leaders. For many, a state's national interest affirms and embodies certain moral principles and ideals.[21] Consequently, a state's pursuit of the national interest can include a commitment to humanitarian ideals.

A third limitation of this argument is that it fails to take into account the motives of a state toward its own citizens. External agencies, it is true, may seek to further their own interests and, therefore, not have the interests of those abroad at heart, but we should also note that many political elites, too, are not greatly concerned about the welfare of their own people (Teson 1988, 105). This is particularly likely to be true in nondemocratic states where the political leaders have no incentive to respect the rights of their subjects. In addition, it is likely to be the case in countries containing ethnic or cultural minorities (like Kurds in Iraq). In such circumstances it is simply utopian to think that the leaders of a state will always care more for the interests of all of their people than will external agencies. Benn and Peter's point is, thus, a salutary one, but it does not show humanitarian intervention to be inherently unsuccessful.

Resistance to Intervention

Even if external agencies are suitably well informed and motivated by the right considerations, humanitarian intervention might not succeed for other reasons. Interventions sometimes flounder simply because they encounter resistance from some of the members of the country that is subject to intervention. UNOSOM, for example, encountered resistance from Somalis once Admiral Howe began to hunt down General Aideed (Lewis and Mayall 1996, 116–18). Furthermore, in Cambodia, "SOC [State of Cambodia] ministries and officials deliberately obstructed UNTAC. It was made impossible, for example, for it to 'work as a partner with all existing administrative structures charged with public security' as stipulated in the implementation plan" (Berdal and Leifer 1996, 44).

Like the preceding points, this third consideration has a great deal of force and should not be dismissed lightly. Like the others, however, it does not represent an insuperable obstacle to humanitarian intervention. First, we should note that sometimes external agencies are invited in to help resolve a problem, and hence there is little resistance to intervention. The U.N. intervention in El Salvador is perhaps a good example of this: both participants in the civil war agreed to U.N. intervention (Munck and Kumar 1995, 170). Second, even where there is local resistance to intervention (say by a tyrannical state), it will not necessarily be more powerful than the intervening authority. Clearly, small local forces have often humbled interventionary forces, and external agencies have notoriously underestimated the potency of resistance. Nonetheless, we have no reason to assume that those who resist will in all cases prove to be more powerful than those intervening.[22] In short, then, interventions will not always encounter opposition, and when they do, those who oppose them are not always powerful enough to thwart the intervention's success. The third consideration, thus, does not establish that intervention will always prove futile.

Millian Considerations

A further reason for being skeptical about the success of humanitarian intervention has been suggested by John Stuart Mill. Mill argues that external interventions will rarely secure long-term success. He argues that a political system will prove viable only if the people are committed to it, and, he adds, a people will be committed only if they (and not some outside body) have fought for it. Thus, external agency will not secure long-term stability. As Mill writes, "If a people . . . does not value it [their freedom] sufficiently to fight for it, and maintain it against any force which can be mustered *within* the country, even by those who have the command of the public revenue, it is only a question in how few years or months that people will be enslaved" (1984, 122). He continues, "The evil is, that if they have not sufficient love of liberty to be *able to wrest it* from merely domestic oppressors, the liberty which is bestowed on them by other hands than their own, will have nothing real, nothing permanent" (1984, 122, emphasis added). So, even where external bodies have the requisite *knowledge, motivation,* and *capability* to overcome resistance, intervention will not work.

Now Mill is right to argue that a political system will thrive only if the people endorse it. This, however, does not justify a blanket repudiation of intervention. The central flaw in the argument is that it is simply incorrect to stipulate that only those able to conquer their oppressors (without outside aid) are committed to their political vision. Put another way, people may be wholly committed to their political ideal (they have "love of liberty") but are too weak because of a lack of resources and force to be able to overcome a despotic ruler (they are not "able to

wrest" power "from merely domestic oppressors"). An inability to fight should
not be confused with an unwillingness to fight. Mill's argument overlooks the
possibility that a people may be willing to fight for a state but be unable to overthrow the current tyranny without external aid (Mason and Wheeler 1996, 105;
Wicclair 1979, 151). One can, therefore, endorse Mill's central point—that people must be committed enough to their political vision to fight for it—and yet also
support humanitarian intervention. A people might, for example, be committed to
their political vision and also be aided by outside bodies to achieve their political
objectives.

In general, then, each of the three considerations raised against humanitarian
intervention does have force. But none of them—either alone or combined with
others—shows that intervention will never succeed. Accordingly, we require a
cautious and nuanced approach that, rather than rejecting intervention outright,
bears these weighty factors in mind and analyzes the circumstances in which interventions succeed.

Two further general points are also worth bearing in mind. First, when assessing the success of an intervention in meeting humanitarian goals, it is important
to compare it with other options (including noninterventionism) in meeting those
same goals. Consider, for example, a military intervention that does not eliminate
military conflict but does lessen the loss of human life more than a policy of
noninterventionism. Now, in such circumstances it is implausible to criticize humanitarian intervention as "unsuccessful" when it is more "successful" in meeting the humanitarian objectives than any of the other courses of action. In "absolute" terms, it does not meet its objectives, but "relative" to the other options
available it is the most successful, and, if our concern is to further humanitarian
ends, the latter (i.e., "relative") criterion is the one that we should adopt.

Second, when considering whether interventionism (or noninterventionism)
best furthers humanitarian ideals, we should take into account *not just* those cases
in which intervention did not promote the desired objectives as well as other options *but also* cases in which a policy of nonintervention was adopted but in
which, as a consequence, people suffered or lost their lives. People tend to focus
on interventions that do not succeed (either in absolute or relative terms) in furthering humanitarian goals. But they should also consider cases in which no intervention takes place and in which such noninterventionism is in relative (or
absolute) terms a failure in promoting humanitarian ends. They should, in other
words, consider the good sacrificed (in terms of meeting humanitarian objectives)
by nonintervention. Both of these factors, thus, point to ways in which our judgment of the success of humanitarian intervention may be distorted and in which
we may wrongly reject intervention when it represents the most successful of all
the options available.

WHEN IS HUMANITARIAN INTERVENTION JUSTIFIED?

Having analyzed both the justification and criticisms of humanitarian intervention and found that none of the objections to humanitarian intervention justifies

a blanket rejection, it is important to analyze when intervention is morally defensible.[23] If, as was argued earlier, there is a case for humanitarian intervention, we need to know what circumstances would justify intervention. A number of different proposals have been made.

Given the prominence of Michael Walzer's discussion of intervention, it is appropriate to begin with his account of when intervention is legitimate. According to Walzer, intervention is justifiable in three circumstances:

1. "when a particular state includes more than one political community, when it is an empire or a multinational state, and when one of its communities or nations is in active revolt, foreign powers can come to the assistance of the rebels";
2. "when a single community is disrupted by civil war, and when one foreign power intervenes in support of this or that party, other powers can rightfully intervene in support of the other party"; and
3. "interventions can be justified whenever a government is engaged in the massacre or enslavement of its own citizens or subjects" (1980, 216–17).

Each of these conditions is, however, questionable or in need of revision. To take number 1 first: it is not clear why external agencies are always permitted to come to the assistance of a national minority when it is rebelling. Does it not depend on whether the national minority has good cause to rebel? Suppose that it is being treated fairly but rebels nonetheless; why is intervention to aid the rebels justified?

Number 2 is also suspect. Indeed, it suffers from a similar problem to number 1 in that it ignores the moral justifiability of those in conflict. It is peculiar to claim that one can always intervene to aid one side if the other side has already received help. Surely, whether one can intervene or not in support of one participant in a conflict should depend in part on their moral legitimacy. It matters whether one party to the conflict is the Khmer Rouge, say, or whether it is a persecuted minority trying to protect its fundamental rights (Doppelt 1978, 13; McMahan 1986, 47; Smith 1989, 15).

Finally, we might also criticize number 3. This is the most plausible condition of the three that Walzer affirms, but one might reasonably ask why Walzer justifies intervention only when people are being massacred or put into slavery—why not "political murder or torture" (Slater and Nardin 1986, 91)? why not when they do not have enough to eat?

When, then, is humanitarian intervention legitimate? Drawing on the case for humanitarian intervention outlined earlier, I would suggest the following account. Humanitarian intervention is legitimate when

1. its aim is to protect people's fundamental rights (where this includes rights to a decent standard of living as well as rights against torture, murder, imprisonment, or enslavement);

2. it is an effective way of meeting these objectives;
3. it does not have undesirable effects elsewhere that outweigh the benefits brought about by the intervention; and
4. intervention is undertaken by a legitimate body.

Conditions 1 and 2 are fairly self-explanatory, and similar conditions are given by others.[24] Condition 3 is also pretty uncontroversial: its claim is simply that "intervention should not do significant harm elsewhere" (Beitz 1988a, 189). Condition 4, by contrast, needs a little explanation. Many accounts of humanitarian intervention do not address the question of who should engage in humanitarian intervention (see, for example, Beitz 1988a). One might argue, however, that interventions can be legitimate only if they are implemented by a legitimate body. Much resistance to humanitarian intervention, I think, draws on this intuition, asking, in effect, "What gives you the right to intervene?" Furthermore, if we examine just war theory we find that many accounts insist that a just war can only be waged by certain authorities. The question that then arises is, *Which institution or institutions* possesses the *authority* to intervene? (Kymlicka 1995, 165 ff., 233, n. 15). This question merits an entire essay in itself, but a preliminary answer might be that an authority is legitimate to the extent that it is generally recognized throughout the world to be fair and evenhanded. It is, thus, better if an intervention is undertaken by genuinely representative international institutions and not by partisan bodies like individual states. However, because no current international institution enjoys such widespread support, two suggestions might be considered. First, in the long run we should seek to make the United Nations a more genuinely representative institution.[25] Second, in the meantime, we should normally encourage multilateral interventions in preference to unilateral interventions. Unilateral interventions are, quite reasonably, often perceived to be promoting a state's own ends (Donnelly 1993, 628–29). There is, therefore, a strong case for claiming that interventions should normally be undertaken by an agent incorporating as wide and ecumenical a coalition of support as possible. This may not always be possible, and it may not always be desirable (securing a multilateral alliance can take time, time in which atrocities are committed), but the more states involved, the more likely an intervention is to be accepted as legitimate.[26]

One final point should be made, namely, if we are considering whether external agencies have an *obligation* to intervene we should add the further condition:

5. intervention does not impose undue costs on the intervening authorities (Slater and Nardin 1986, 93–94).

Here the distinction between a right to intervene and an obligation to intervene is highly pertinent, for to establish the former one does not require this fifth condition. People can have a right to intervene even if doing so is costly or dangerous for them. Condition 5 is, however, extremely relevant if one wishes to argue that people have an obligation to intervene.

CONCLUSION

The discussion in the earlier sections has focused on the *moral* question of whether intervention is defensible and, if so, when. In this final section, I want to conclude and complete the analysis by noting briefly that even if we think (as I think we should) that there is sometimes a *moral* case for intervention, this does not establish that international law must grant a *legal* right to intervene. It is arguable that intervention is sometimes morally right but that international law should nonetheless disallow it (Slater and Nardin 1986, 95). One might argue, for example, that to entrench a right to humanitarian intervention in international law would have malign effects and would in practice allow not just humanitarian interventions but also nonhumanitarian interventions (Franck and Rodley 1973, 290). In other words, granting this legal right would produce worse moral outcomes than simply legally banning it. Clearly, as a consequentialist judgment, this requires a careful assessment of the possible effects of a legal right to humanitarian intervention.[27] And one might argue that it is possible to entrench a legal right to intervene that minimizes the problems (Mason and Wheeler 1996, 106). My point is simply that there is no straightforward relationship between the claim that external bodies have a moral right or obligation to intervene and the claim that such a right or obligation should be affirmed by international law.

This completes the analysis: what I hope to have provided is a clear definition of humanitarian intervention, an analysis of the moral justifiability of humanitarian intervention, and an evaluation of the situations in which humanitarian intervention may be attempted. We should, however, close with the thought that humanitarian intervention is essentially a "reactive" policy that is adopted after people's needs or rights have been harmed. Given the difficulties to which interventions are susceptible, there is a strong case for tackling the roots of these problems and seeking to prevent them from occurring rather than responding to them once they have arisen (Booth 1995, 121; Parekh 1997, 68; Pogge 1992, 100–01).

NOTES

I am grateful to an anonymous referee, Andrew Linklater, Hidemi Suganami, Andrew Valls, Nick Wheeler, and John Williams for their helpful comments. This work was completed during my tenure of a Leverhulme Research Fellowship. I am grateful to the Leverhulme Trust for its support.

    1. For further details, see R. Gordon 1994, 550–57; Griffiths, Levine, and Weller 1995, 51–52; Lewis and Mayall 1996, 107–24; Slim and Visman 1995; as well as Kieh's chapter in this volume.

2. For more on intervention in the former Yugoslavia, see Nagengast's chapter in this volume.

3. Most recently NATO intervened in Kosovo in 1999. This event occurred after this chapter had been completed and, therefore, could not be discussed here.

4. Others also define *intervention* in terms of "interference" and, thus, are vulnerable to this criticism too. Thus, Jack Donnelly defines *intervention* as "any coercive *interference* in the internal affairs of a state" (1993, 609, emphasis added). See also Vincent 1974, 13. This point also applies to Jeff McMahan's otherwise accurate definition of *intervention* as "coercive external *interference* in the affairs of a population organized in the form of a state" (1986, 27, emphasis added). Once the term *interference* is exchanged for *action*, McMahan's definition is, I think, a plausible one.

5. In this respect, my definition differs from that given by some. Michael Joseph Smith, for example, writes that "intervention can be defined as discrete acts which try to affect the domestic affairs of another state" (1989, 2). On this definition, noncoercive acts (like one leader trying to persuade another by force of argument) count as intervention.

6. He does, though, recognize the existence of nonmilitary ways of determining another state's conduct, preferring to call such action "quasi-intervention" (Donnelly 1993, 610).

7. Indeed, in line with his definition (see note 5), Smith argues against "trying to delimit intervention according to its means" and includes "propagandistic broadcasts" as a form of intervention (1989, 4). While I think Smith is right to challenge the claim that intervention requires force, my view is that, according to ordinary usage of the term, intervention is partly defined in terms of the means employed and that noncoercive acts should not be deemed to be interventionary.

8. For the moral assumptions underlying those critical of a principle of nonintervention, see the following: Beitz 1979a, 413–16; 1979b, 71–92; 1988a, 182–95; Doppelt 1980; Luban 1980a, 167–70, 173–76, 178–81; 1980b; Pogge 1992; and Teson 1988, 15–16, 111–23.

9. For lucid statements of cosmopolitanism, see Barry 1998, 144–45, 153; 1999, sec. 4, especially 35–36; Beitz 1979a, 417–20; 1988b, 191–93; 1994, 123–26; and Pogge 1994, 89–90.

10. See also Wicclair 1979, 147–48.

11. Some, like Gerard Elfstrom, deny that external agents have a duty to protect the rights of others; see Elfstrom 1983, 711–12, 715–16, 718.

12. Some describe such duties as "positive" duties (as opposed to "negative" duties). For a critique of this position, see Pogge 1992, especially 90. More generally, see also Henry Shue's excellent critique and analysis of the related distinction between "negative" and "positive" rights (1980, 35–64).

13. Some, it should be noted, seek only to argue for this weaker claim; see Teson 1988, 117.

14. I should stress that there are many other challenges to the case for humanitarian intervention besides those outlined in this section. Some, for example, challenge the idea of universal values like human rights (Brown 1997), and others challenge the mode of philosophical argument employed in the last section (Rengger 1993, 187–90).

15. There are a number of excellent discussions of defenses of nonintervention (Beitz 1988a; McMahan 1986). My position is most in keeping with that developed by Wicclair

(1979). The latter provides a useful classification of defenses of nonintervention, and, as we shall see in the text that follows, he makes persuasive critiques of each of them.

16. The claim that intervention is objectionable because it conflicts with the ideal of communal self-government has, it should be noted, been developed in other distinct ways; see Elfstrom 1983, 713, 715–18. Limited space precludes the examination of these arguments.

17. Jeff McMahan provides a more qualified and nuanced version of the "communal autonomy" argument that attempts to avoid some of the problems of Walzer's argument; see McMahan 1986, 34–35.

18. As Wheeler points out, Vincent's views evolved, and in later work he took a more human rights–sensitive view than Bull and than his own earlier work (Wheeler 1992, 478–80). See Vincent 1986, especially 111–28, and Vincent and Wilson 1993, especially 127–29.

19. For two good surveys of such arguments, see Mason and Wheeler 1996, 100–06, and Wicclair 1979, 149–53.

20. For more on the problems that plagued the intervention in Somalia, see Kieh's chapter in this volume.

21. See, for example, Murray's (1996) analysis of Morgenthau. I am grateful to Chris Brown for first drawing my attention to this point (and for referring me to Murray's work). The point is also noted by Smith (1989, 19; 1998, 71–72). For further analysis of the nature of the national interest and its relationship to morality, see Welch's chapter in this volume.

22. It is important to add here that resistance to intervention has moral significance in a number of ways independently of whether it prevents an intervention from achieving its humanitarian ends.

23. For other analyses of the moral justifiability of intervention, see Rengger 1993, 179–93, Smith 1998, and Vincent 1986, 111–28.

24. See, for example, Beitz 1988a, 188–89, and Slater and Nardin 1986, 93.

25. For an analysis of various proposals to reform the United Nations, see Archibugi 1995. See also Held 1995.

26. Smith (1998, 77–78) strikes the right note, arguing that in general collective intervention is best but on occasion unilateral intervention is justifiable.

27. For a good account of the possible advantages and disadvantages, see Chopra and Weiss 1992, 99–101.

9

Humanitarian Intervention in Civil Wars in Africa

George Klay Kieh

The postindependence era in Africa has failed to fulfill the high hopes of the African peoples for economic prosperity, political freedom, peace, and stability. Unfortunately, the region has been plagued with civil wars. Copson provides an excellent summary of the civil war epidemic: "During the 1980s, Africa was torn by nine wars, numerous other instances of large scale violent conflicts, and a kaleidoscope of coups and demonstrations. Those hostilities exacted a great toll on Africa in terms of the destruction of human life, cultural damage, economic disruption, and lost investment opportunities" (1996, 20). During the Cold War, the primacy of the Westphalian norm of the "sanctity of state sovereignty" hamstrung the international community in its ability to intervene in civil wars (Chopra and Weiss 1992; Hehir 1995; Smith 1998). As Hehir notes, "The wisdom of Westphalia, however, is a reminder that . . . a broadening of the reasons for intervention involves the risk that states will invoke humanitarian reasons while pursuing other objectives through military intervention" (1995, 9). However, since the end of the Cold War, the continual increase in the incidence of civil wars, their deleterious consequences for the global community as a whole, has brought about the rethinking of the norm of state sovereignty. Although the norm remains a major terra firma of international law, nevertheless, there is a growing chorus that its application now requires some flexibility in cases of humanitarian crisis. The reason is that such a new approach will provide the international community with the requisite "operating space" to engage in humanitarian intervention—the interposition of a military force and the provision of humanitarian assistance, among other things.

Against this background, this study will focus on what Minear, Weiss, and Campbell (1991) refer to as "military humanitarianism." Using four cases of the international community's intervention in civil wars in Africa—Somalia, Rwanda, Liberia, and Sierra Leone—this study will examine the following questions: First, were the military interventions by the international community in the civil wars humanitarian in nature? Second, what impact did these interventions have on these civil wars?

THE EMERGING EVALUATIVE CRITERIA FOR MILITARY HUMANITARIANISM

There is an ongoing debate both in the scholarly literature and within policymaking circles in international organizations and individual sovereign states regarding the formulation of criteria for determining when a military intervention can be considered humanitarian. Despite the debate, there is a growing consensus on some of the evolving elements of the criteria for military humanitarianism. At the base of the criteria is the requirement that a humanitarian crisis must exist. For example, there must be an immediacy of the violation of human rights (Lillich 1967; 1973). Similarly, there must be the widespread loss of lives (Moore 1969).

Second, the military intervention must be authorized by what J. Bryan Hehir terms the proper authority. In other words, multilateral authorization should be the norm (Hehir 1995, 9). This would entail that only the United Nations or a regional or subregional organization can legally authorize military intervention in a civil war. Operationally, the military intervention may be undertaken by either the international organization itself or a designated member state or group of member states. In the case of the former, a major requirement is the subordination of command and control of sovereign armed forces to a centralized instrument, authorized by the international community to act in the event of a crisis (Chopra and Weiss 1992).

Third, the means employed by the international community to undertake military intervention must be proportional to the imperatives of the civil war. In other words, under the principle of proportionality, the military force that is harnessed and deployed to help create the conditions for resolving the civil war must be tailored to the nature and the dynamics of such a war.

Fourth, the military intervention must positively impact the civil war. That is, it must help to alleviate human suffering and create the conditions for effective peacemaking. This criterion can be applied to a civil war both while it is ongoing and after it has ended.

The aforementioned criteria for military humanitarianism will be used to evaluate the intervention of the United Nations in the Somali Civil War, the United Nations and the Organization of African Unity (OAU) in the Rwandan Civil War, and the Economic Community of West African States (ECOWAS) in the Liberian and Sierra Leonean Civil Wars.

THE ROOTS AND DYNAMICS OF THE SOMALI CIVIL WAR

The civil war in Somalia is a by-product of the repressive and exploitative political economy that has its genesis in the colonial era. As elsewhere in Africa, colonialism formalized Somalia's incorporation into the emergent international capitalist system. Accordingly, the Somali political economy adopted certain features. At the vortex of the arrangement was the commercialization of kinship relationships. That is, a process of supplanting clan with class interest was set into motion. The incipient class structure pitted the colonial agents of British, French, and Italian colonialism and imperialism and their Somali collaborators, on the one hand, against the subaltern classes consisting of farmers and pastoralists. The consequent effects were tension and conflict between the two classes in one sphere and between the adherents to Somali traditionalism and its clan-based kinship relations and the advocates of the commoditization of relations transcending primordial ties.

The second contour of the colonial political economy was the reliance on state repression as the mechanism for consolidating and maintaining class relations and their relations of production. In other words, those Somalis who were resistant to the imposition of the colonial order were subjected to various punitive measures—harassment, beating, imprisonment, and so on. Amid the repression and exploitation, the majority of the Somali people took refuge in their clans. This was because these clans have historically served as the vehicles for political, economic, social, and cultural participation and as bulwarks of defense against external aggression.

Third, characteristically, the colonial economy was based on the production of bananas and livestock, as dictated by the needs of the colonial powers. Thus, the Somali people were deprived of the opportunity to use their ingenuity in the development of technologies that could have provided them with an industrial base. In essence, the collective energies of the Somali people were geared toward production for metropolitan consumption, while neglecting the development needs of the Somali masses.

At the dawn of independence in the 1960s, Somalia was plagued with the festering problems of neocolonialism—a subsistence-based, export-oriented dependent economy, a divided society, and so on. To make matters worse, as Lyons and Samatar observe, "[The] leaders of the independence movements construed the enterprise as a rare chance to win a personally profitable place in the new [state] structures, and only secondarily as an opportunity to construct new public institutions worthy of the great challenge ahead" (1995, 62). Accordingly, various problems arose. First, no effort was made to develop pan-clan and pan-regional democratic political institutions. For example, the various political parties politicized primordial ties. Hence, the eighteen and the sixty political parties that competed in the 1965 and 1969 national elections, respectively, were nothing more than "political cults" that revolved around their leaders.

The second problem was that the "elected governments" did not address the pressing issues of basic human needs—health, employment, education, and shelter, among others. In other words, although the Somali people participated in multiparty elections twice, those elections did not result in the formulation of public policies to address their needs. Instead, the elections gave various members of the bureaucratic wing of the new Somali ruling class the opportunity to engage in the private accumulation of capital.

Third, the government made little effort to remedy regional disparities and to decentralize political power. Consequently, it ignited mass disillusionment and regional tensions.

Importantly, the failure to construct a nationalist-based postcolonial order, and to address the malaise of underdevelopment, created the climate for the military coup of 1969 that brought General Mohammed Siad Barre to power. The new Barre regime proclaimed a socialist agenda, ostensibly designed to address the perennial problems of repression, exploitation, regional imbalances, class-based parochialism, mass poverty, and mass illiteracy. As Samatar notes, "Somalia seemed to have embarked on a quest for a progressive and socialist-oriented political economy" (1988, 3). This was evidenced by the mass-centered programs undertaken by the Barre regime in such areas as education and health. However, the pursuit of progressive policies was short-lived: Having consolidated power, Siad Barre began to demonstrate his authoritarian and despotic proclivities. For example, initially with the help of Soviet and then subsequently American aid, his regime committed human rights abuses, including the arrest and execution of political opponents both real and imagined. Significantly, the Barre regime manipulated clan cleavages by, among other things, encouraging interclan warfare and arming loyal clans. In essence, the Barre junta fostered internecine polarization among the various clans, akin to the colonial strategy of "divide and rule" (Kieh 1998, 69).

Unfortunately, the Barre regime's persecutions obliged the opposition to utilize their own clans as organizational bases for armed resistance (Adam 1996, 79). Accordingly, by 1978, various clan-based militias were beginning to form, with the common goal of deposing the Barre regime. The militias included the Somali Salvation Democratic Front (Mijerteen clan), Somali National Movement (Isaaq clan), Somali Patriotic Movement (southern based, Ogaden region), Somali Democratic Movement (Digil-Mirifle clan), and United Somali Congress (Hawiye clan). After a brutal civil war, the Barre regime was deposed in January 1991. Subsequently, the various militias decided to form an interim government of national unity. Unfortunately, the arrangement collapsed, and the militias engaged in a catastrophic war among themselves. The war had several adverse effects. Somalia was plagued with a devastating famine that occasioned hunger, starvation, and death. For example, in 1991–92, over 350,000 Somalis died. These deaths were a reflection of the war-induced burgeoning rates of mortality. According to the U.S. Centers for Disease Control (1992), the mortality rates in the Baidoa region were the highest in the history of famine worldwide. Also, over 500,000 Somalis became refugees in neighboring countries, and another 400,000 were internally displaced. The infrastructure—schools, hospitals, public and private buildings, and so on—was destroyed. Violence and crime became prevalent as armed militiamen used their control over the instruments of coercion to exact revenge and to rob and plunder.

THE MILITARY INTERVENTION IN SOMALIA

After various efforts by both regional leaders in the Horn of Africa and the United Nations to broker cease-fire agreements and to peacefully resolve the conflict failed, the United Nations decided to send in a peacekeeping force. Operating under the U.N. Operations in Somalia (UNOSOM I) authorized under Security Council Resolution 756, 500 armed troops and fifty unarmed peace observers were sent to Somalia in April 1992. The principal mandate of the peacekeepers was to safeguard humanitarian relief supplies—food, medicine, and so on. Unfortunately, the size of the peacekeeping force vis-à-vis the number of warring factions and the overall complexities of the civil war made the peacekeeping task difficult. Cognizant of the problem, UNOSOM I expanded to 4,200 security personnel. Again, the force could not stop the looting, crime, and carnage that were rained on defenseless Somali civilians by armed bandits and thugs from the various militias.

After about five months, the United Nations, acting under Security Council Resolution 794, decided to organize a large peacekeeping force under U.S. leadership. Accordingly, in December 1992, an additional force of 28,000 American troops was sent to Somalia. The mandate of the expanded peacekeeping force remained the securing of food routes through the prevention of looting, theft, and other acts of violence. By all accounts, the U.S.–led U.N. peacekeeping force succeeded in accomplishing its mission, as evidenced by the successful distribution of relief supplies to war-wearied Somali civilians.

Unfortunately, contrary to the U.N. mandate, the United States decided to impose a new post–civil war order on Somalia. Accordingly, the American peacekeepers, acting on the orders of Washington, expanded their mandate. For example, after the killing of some Pakistani peacekeepers by the Mohammed Aidid faction of the United Somali Congress, the United States decided to pursue and arrest General Aidid. Hence, the locus of the peacekeeping mission shifted from peace maintenance to a battle between the United States and Aidid forces. One of the consequences was strong opposition from the Somali people, who still had fresh memories of the contributions of the U.S. government to the civil war. For example, during the Barre regime, the United States gave Somalia over $800 million in economic and military aid. Clearly, the aid was designed to maintain the authoritarian Barre regime in power. Again, during the initial stages of the civil war, the United States supplied the repressive Barre regime with weapons. Ultimately, the American action elevated the warlord General Aidid to the status of a national hero, credited for resisting the reimposition of American neocolonialism and imperialism on Somalia.

The American quest to force a post–civil war order on Somalia led to a total disregard for the lives of Somali civilians. For example, in July 1993, U.S. helicopter gunships attacked Mogadishu and left fifty-four Somali civilians dead. There were other incidents of killing Somali civilians. When the issue was raised regarding the total number of Somali civilians who were killed by American troops, Colonel Fred Peck, the U.S. Marines spokesperson in Somalia, arrogantly stated that "the compilation of Somali casualties has no military utility" (*West Africa* 1993, 1238). Even some members of the U.S. Congress went on record to publicly protest the actions of the American military force in Somalia.

THE ROOTS AND DYNAMICS OF THE RWANDAN CIVIL WAR

The seeds of the Rwandan Civil War were planted by Belgian colonialism: The Belgian colonialists created the "Hutu–Tutsi ethnic divide" by categorizing people of essentially common ethnocultural background into two artificial but polarizing ethnic-cum-class strata. Subsequently, the Belgian colonialists developed a misleading racial ideology to justify their alliance with the Tutsi group: They argued that the Tutsi group was superior to the Hutu one. Thus, the members of the Tutsi group were given the "privilege" to gain education and to accumulate some wealth. As for the Hutus, they were marginalized and suppressed. The net effect was the development of antagonism and hatred between the two groups.

When Rwanda gained political independence in 1962, the Hutu–Tutsi conflict continued. Additionally, a new conflict emerged: The class conflict pitted the members of the "pan-ethnic" local ruling class against those of the subordinate classes. Interestingly, the Tutsis dominated the ruling class. However, the so-called Hutu–Tutsi ethnic conflict remained central and primary. Given the facts that the Hutus constituted 85 percent of the population and the Tutsis made up 14 percent, the latter made various efforts to use violence as the principal instrument for addressing the political, economic, and social disparities between the two groups. For example, in 1963, the Hutu–Tutsi "little war" left 20,000 people dead. Again, in 1972–73, a "second little war" occurred between the two groups that occasioned the deaths of more than 30,000, mainly innocent, people. Thereafter, a large number of Tutsis fled to Uganda in search of safety.

Amid the vicious cycle of tensions and war, in 1973 the military, under the leadership of Major-General Juvenile Habyarimana, the minister of defense, led a successful coup d'etat that toppled the civilian government of President Gregoire Kayibanda, the country's first president. The new military regime established a state of siege. For example, it banned all political activities and undertook a campaign of suppressing human and civil liberties. Interestingly, two years later, General Habyarimana attempted to "civilianize" military rule by making Rwanda both a de jure and de facto one-party state, under the reign of his political party, the Mouvement Revolutionnaire National Pour Le Development. Having consolidated power, the military regime continued its systematic campaign of raining terror on both Hutus and Tutsis, who were opposed to the regime. The repressive conditions of the Rwandan state were exacerbated by various economic crises that were characterized by increases in the cost of living and decreases in the standard of living. For example, during the 1989 economic crisis, hundreds of Rwandans died from starvation. In response, the military regime imposed a debilitating austerity program that made deep cuts in social programs.

While Rwanda was being plagued with political, social, and economic crises, the Tutsis who fled Uganda organized the Front Patriotique Rwandais or the Rwandan Patriotic Front (RPF). In order to give the organization a national complexion, some Hutu opponents of the regime in Kigali were admitted into membership. The primary goal of the organization was to depose the military regime. In October 1990, about 10,000 guerrillas from the RPF invaded Rwanda from Uganda. In response, the regime took two major measures. First, it received French, Belgian, and Zairean troops ostensibly to help repel the RPF attack. Second, the government instituted mass arrests. For example, during the first week of the hostilities, an estimated 8,000 people throughout Rwanda, of whom the vast majority were Tutsis, were arrested and imprisoned (Reyntjens 1997, 774). These steps did not help to solve the emerging civil war. Instead, the violence continued unabated. For example, in response to various incursions by the Tutsi-led RPF, the Rwandan government incited Hutus, especially in the rural areas, to attack their Tutsi neighbors. Consequently, thousands of people on both sides were killed and injured. The civil war was exacerbated by the death of Rwandan President Juvenile Habyarimana and his Burundian counterpart Cyprian Ntaryamira in a mysterious plane crash. The consensus is that the plane carrying the two leaders was shot down by dissident soldiers, who were unhappy with President Habyarimana's decision to make peace with the Tutsi-led RPF. Thereafter, the violence and bloodletting intensified and assumed an interesting form: There were divisions within the Hutu and the Tutsi groups between the pro–status quo and anti–status quo factions. The result was that Tutsis killed Tutsis, and Hutus killed Hutus, depending on which political alliance they belonged to. In short, the civil war revolved around three polarizing cleavages: "ethnicity," class, and political faction.

Cumulatively, the civil war led to the death of about one million people, mainly defenseless and innocent civilians; a refugee crisis that forced over two million Rwandans to flee their country and seek refuge in neighboring countries; and the collapse of the Rwandan state and its authoritative institutions. In other words, the civil war enveloped Rwanda in a state of mass killing, violence, and the destruction of the infrastructure.

THE MILITARY INTERVENTION IN RWANDA

Concerned about the carnage and destruction in Rwanda, especially its broad implications for both regional and subregional peace and stability, the United Nations sent a peacekeeping force to Rwanda. The force, consisting of 2,500 military personnel from twenty member countries, was given the mandate to help monitor and police a tenuous cease-fire between the warring factions. Characteristically, when the war got intense, the U.N. peacekeepers withdrew from Rwanda. Subsequently, in August 1992 the OAU deployed a peacekeeping force, NMOG. Unfortunately, it could not secure a lasting cease-fire (Sterns 1994). The problem was caused by the fact that France's involvement in support of its client Habyarimana regime made the rebel RPF apprehensive about conforming to a cease-fire.

Undaunted, the OAU again deployed a second peacekeeping force consisting of 120 soldiers from three member states. The peacekeepers' principal mission was to help create the conditions for successful peacemaking. The OAU peacekeeping mission had several successes. It contributed to the establishment of a cease-fire. Also, it enforced a demilitarized zone between the warring factions. Another contribution was that it provided the security environment that assisted parties in reaching the Arusha Peace Accord. The accord consisted of three major planks: (1) the establishment of a transitional government, (2) the formation of a new army, and (3) the development of electoral modalities. The performance of the OAU peacekeeping force won accolades from all factions in the civil war. For example, RPF Chairman Alexis Kenyarengwe said, "NMOG served the Rwandan people admirably, under difficult conditions" (Sterns 1994, 35). The OAU peacekeeping force succeeded for two major reasons. First, the peacekeepers had a good understanding of the conflict and, thus, related well to the warring parties. Second, the OAU demonstrated a rare political will, evidenced by its decision to make a second effort at peacekeeping after the failure of the first one.

After the expiration of its mandate, the OAU peacekeeping force was incorporated into a new U.N. peacekeeping force. The mandate of the new U.N. peacekeeping force was to help implement the Arusha Peace Accord. Unfortunately, the implementation of the peace accord was complicated by a variety of factors. The warring factions could not agree on the specifics of the interim governance structure. Some major factions were not committed to the peace accord. Also, there was serious mistrust among the various factions. Unfortunately, instead of helping to resolve these difficulties, the United Nations opted to withdraw its peacekeeping force. This action provided a vacuum. Accordingly, the cease-fire collapsed, and the fierce fighting resumed. The major consequence was one of the most horrendous campaigns of genocide in human history: Nearly one million Rwandans—Hutu and Tutsi, anti–status quo and pro–status quo, and rich and poor—were killed.

After more than a year of death and destruction, the RPF won a military victory and, thus, assumed control of Rwanda. The RPF organized a government of national unity and promulgated a five-year transitional program that would culminate in the holding of national elections. Importantly, as part of the postconflict peace-building process, the U.N. General Assembly passed Resolution 977 in February 1995, establishing an International Criminal Tribunal for Rwanda with headquarters in Arusha, Tanzania. The mandate of the tribunal is to put on trial those who committed war crimes during Rwanda's four-year genocidal civil war.

THE ROOTS AND DYNAMICS OF THE LIBERIAN CIVIL WAR

The seeds of the Liberian Civil War were planted in the early 1800s, with the repatriation of freed African American slaves. This development precipitated three types of conflict: African Americans versus the indigenes, the light-skinned African Americans versus the dark-skinned African Americans, and the ruling class versus the subaltern classes. When the African Americans arrived, they met sixteen indigenous ethnic groups in the area with their own political, economic, social, and cultural systems. Initially, these indigenous ethnic groups were receptive to the return of their brothers and sisters. However, having been subjected to the vagaries of the southern plantation system, the African Americans wished to re-create the American slave system in Liberia. Under such an arrangement, they would become the masters, and the members of the indigenous ethnic groups would become their servants. The African Americans or Americo-Liberians, as they became known, promulgated a philosophy that was based on their superiority, because they had lived in the United States, and the inferiority and barbarity of the indigenes. This philosophy provided the basis for the caste system that was developed. Under that arrangement, the members of the indigenous groups were placed in the lowest stratum. This led to a series of wars between various indigenous ethnic groups, on the one hand, and the Americo-Liberians, on the other hand. With American military and financial support, the Americo-Liberians were able to defeat the indigenous ethnic groups.

Another major conflict involved differences between the light-skinned African Americans and the dark-skinned ones. The former argued that because they were better educated—most of them were lawyers, preachers, and entrepreneurs—they should therefore control the political and economic system, while the other group would concentrate on the agricultural sector. These differences were reflected in the relationship each group had to the colonial bureaucracy: The agents of the American Colonization Society, who governed Liberia from 1818 to 1839, aligned with the light-skinned African American cluster against the dark-skinned one.

Another dimension of the conflict was based on class status. Under this arrangement, very often the obvious but static caste distinctions, based on skin color and ancestral origin, coincided with class differences defined by the relationship of each group to the means of production and the state (Burrowes 1983, 27). Specifically, in terms of the class structure, 1820–39, the agents of the American Colonization Society occupied the upper tier; the light-skinned African Americans were at the middle level; the dark-skinned African Americans were one lower; and the indigenes and Congoes remained in the lowest tier.

By 1926, a major development occurred in the Liberian political economy: The country was formally incorporated into the global economy, beginning with the penetration of foreign investment (Kieh 1998, 3). One of the major outcomes was the emergence of a class-based political economy. Under this rubric, pan-ethnic ruling and subaltern classes emerged; however, the ruling class was dominated by the "Americo-Liberian ethnic stock." That is, although some members of the various indigenous Liberian ethnic groups became members of the local bourgeoisie, nevertheless, the settler stock controlled both the state and the local sector of the commercial wing of the ruling class. The emergent relations of production benefited the ruling class while exploiting and suppressing the members of the subordinate classes. Subsequently, every Liberian regime—from King to Tolbert—sought to perpetuate this exploitative and repressive political economy.

Although Liberia experienced a military coup d'etat in 1980, which was led by noncommissioned officers from the subaltern classes, nevertheless, the institutions and the relations of production remained intact. The few superficial changes occasioned by the coup were the expansion of the size of the local sector of the ruling class and a change in the personnel of the leadership. However, substantively, the postcoup era witnessed a precipitous decline in the standard of living, spiraling unemployment, the deterioration of social services, and the expansion of the repression multiplex, particularly with the formation of a state-sponsored death squad.

Consequently, there was growing mass discontent. This atmosphere provided Charles Taylor and his National Patriotic Front of Liberia (NPFL) with the pretext to launch a rebellion against the Doe regime, beginning on 24 December 1989. This set into motion a genocidal civil war that witnessed the wanton killings of civilians, the creation of a refugee crisis, and the eventual collapse of the government.

THE MILITARY INTERVENTION IN LIBERIA

The ramifications of the Liberian Civil War for subregional and regional security prompted the Economic Community of West African States (ECOWAS) to make the determination to militarily intervene. As then-President of Gambia and former Chair of ECOWAS Dauda Jawara affirms, "Immediate action was required to prevent Liberia, a member state, from sinking further into anarchy and destruction" (Aderiye 1992, 131). But the decision by ECOWAS to militarily intervene in the Liberian Civil War sparked a bitter conflict within the leadership of the organization: On the one hand, a group of francophone member states led by Côte d'Ivoire contended that the organization had not properly authorized the creation of ECOMOG, the peacekeeping force. On the other hand, another group led by Nigeria argued that ECOWAS had provided the authorization for both the formation of the peacekeeping force and its subsequent intervention in Liberia. The fact that both the United Nations and the OAU endorsed the military intervention addressed the "proper authority" issue.

Operationally, the ECOMOG military posture was based on both traditional peacekeeping and peace enforcement. In the case of the former, the peacekeeping force with an initial size of 6,000 (the number rose to about 12,000 later) had the mandate (1) to end the hostilities among the three warring factions—the Doe faction, the Taylor-led NPFL, and the Prince Roosevelt Johnson–headed Independent National Patriotic Front of Liberia (later, the Liberian Peace Council, ULIMO-J, ULIMO-K, and the Lofa Defense Force emerged as four additional warring factions); (2) to establish a security zone; (3) to impose a cease-fire; (4) to interdict weapons; (5) to supervise the disarming and the encampment of combatants; and (6) to assume responsibility for security for the entire country until a new government was elected. ECOMOG conducted its peacekeeping function in several cycles. The post-cease-fire imposition cycle (late 1990) involved the establishment and monitoring of a cease-fire. Another cease-fire cycle (late 1992) involved ensuring that the NPFL did not engage in any military operation. The post–April 1996 bloodbath cycle (May 1996) revolved around ensuring that the Johnson-led ULIMO-J, on the one hand, and the Taylor-led NPFL and the Kromah-run ULIMO-K, on the other, did not engage in further armed battles.

The peace enforcement posture was designed to pressure the warring factions to abide by the terms of the various peace accords. Specifically, the operations included taking control of Monrovia, the capital city, from the warring factions, the pacification of the country, the prevention of arms and ammunition from going to the various warring factions, and the engagement in "limited offensives." The purpose was to take the necessary military action to effect the delivery of social services and to create order (Kieh 1998, 24).

Cumulatively, the peacekeeping and peace enforcement operations of the peacekeeping force produced several positive results. The warring factions observed a general cease-fire from November 1990 to 15 October 1992. Also, a security zone was created in Monrovia and its environs. Another benefit was that a safe corridor was created for the delivery of essential social services to civilians. Politically and administratively, efforts were made to reinstate the state's authority over territorial Liberia.

On the other hand, the peacekeeping and peace enforcement operations had two major shortcomings. The fact that the peacekeeping force on occasion collaborated with some warring factions against others raised serious issues about the force's neutrality. For example, during a counteroffensive against the NPFL in 1992, ECOMOG worked with the remnants of the Doe faction. Second, and relatedly, some of the warring factions, especially ULIMO-J and ULIMO-K, used their collaboration with ECOMOG to seize and hold territory.

Overall, the role of the peacekeeping force was pivotal to creating the conditions for peacemaking. For example, it was the threat to launch full-scale peace enforcement by the leaders of ECOWAS, among others, that forced the various warring factions to engage in meaningful disarmament and demobilization of combatants. In turn, this led to the holding of national elections in July 1997 and the subsequent formation of a new government led by former warlord Charles Taylor.

THE ROOTS AND DYNAMICS OF SIERRA LEONEAN CIVIL WAR

The civil war in Sierra Leone was caused by the combination of contingent and proximate factors. In the case of the former, the evolution of the state requires examination. The Sierra Leonean state is the product of British colonialism. Like other colonial powers, Britain constructed and organized a repressive state that predominantly relied on violence as its motor force. Economically, labor and natural resources were exploited for the benefit of the British ruling class. Customarily, in order to maintain its stranglehold, the British fostered conflict between the settler Creole ethnic group (black repatriates) and the various indigenous Sierra Leonean ethnic groups—Mende, Temne, and so on. Under the "Creole–country man" division, the Creoles had better access to education and jobs (Kandeh 1996, 390).

The postcolonial state retained the repressive and exploitative complexion of the colonial one. A new pan-ethnic ruling class consisting of members from the various ethnic groups replaced the colonial one. Characteristically, the barons of the local ruling class used ethnicity as an instrument for mobilizing support for the purpose of enhancing their bargaining positions during intra–ruling class negotiations. Besides the regime of Sir Milton Margai, the first prime minister (1961–64), every regime in Sierra Leone fostered a repressive political economy and its values of class inequities, exploitation, the suffocation of civil society, and unbridled corruption, among others. For example, during the administration of Albert Margai (1964–67), the one-party system was institutionalized, and ethnicity became a tool of political manipulation. One of the consequences of these developments was the emergence of a regional divide between the North and the South. The Temnes and Limbas in the North maintained that the Mende ethnic group in the South was dominating the political landscape and consequently marginalizing them. This schism gave rise to the formation of the All People's Congress (APC) as the North's response to what was perceived as the Mende-dominated ruling Sierra Leonean People's Party (SLPP).

After a bitter election in 1967 in which the ruling SLPP attempted to fraudulently hold onto power, the military intervened in the political arena. Initially,

Brigadier David Lasana staged a coup designed ostensibly to restore the SLPP to power. However, this coup was countered with another, led by Lt. Col. Juxon-Smith. Consequently, the first military government was established under the banner of the ruling council, the National Reformation Council (NRC) (1967–68). However, the NRC government was deposed in 1968 by the "Sergeants Coup." In turn, the coup makers handed power to Siaka Stevens, the leader of the APC and the winner of the election for prime minister. Prime Minister, and later President, Stevens ruled Sierra Leone like his personal fiefdom from 1968 to 1985. During his reign, corruption became a "national sport," as evidenced by the wholesale and pervasive looting of the national treasury by various government functionaries led by President Stevens himself. Also, the Stevens regime undertook a systematic destruction of democratic institutions within both the government and civil society. The clear purpose was to weaken opposition to his despotic and kleptocratic rule. Another major contour of "Papa Siake's" style of governance was the repression of groups in civil society, individuals, and ordinary citizens. The broad-based repression multiplex was designed to instill fear in the populace in order to foster the unbridled plundering and pillaging of the national coffers.

Amid intense mass dissatisfaction precipitated by horrendous economic conditions, President Stevens was forced to "retire." Rather than redeeming himself by setting into motion the process of democratization, he instead handpicked his illiterate chief of military staff, General Joseph Momoh, as his successor. President Momoh continued "Stevenism without Stevens"—corruption, the mismanagement of resources, repression, and the continual pursuit of malaise-inducing policies.

The proximate causes of the civil war were the debilitating effects of the national economic crisis on the military and the spill-over effects of the Liberian Civil War. In the case of the former, the Sierra Leonean military was disgruntled because of poor conditions of service—low salaries and the lack of equipment, among others. In the latter case, the Charles Taylor–led NPFL played a pivotal role in assisting the Revolutionary United Front of Sierra Leone (RUF), led by former Army Corporal Foday Sankoh, in its quest to depose the Sierra Leonean government. While the RUF was waging war against the Momoh regime, a group of junior military officers staged a coup in 1992. However, the new military regime under the leadership of Captain Valentine Strasser was ineffective in both formulating and pursuing policies that would have arrested the socioeconomic malaise and promoted political pluralism. Instead, the military leaders became the new barons of the ruling class and continued the perpetration of human rights abuses and the plundering and pillaging of national resources amid mass poverty, unemployment, high inflation, and overall social and economic stagnation. To make matters worse, the NRC focused its attention on the exploitation of the rich diamond mines in an effort to foster the private accumulation of capital by the leaders of the military junta. This predatory orientation helped fuel the rise of the "sobel phenomenon": Following the example of their leaders, some members of the Sierra Leonean military were soldiers only in the day and became rebels at night. In the latter capacity, they joined the fighters of the RUF in plundering the diamond mines and robbing defenseless civilians of their possessions. Interestingly, in order to protect the regime's economic interest in the diamond mines, the Strasser government contracted the services of Executive Outcomes, a mercenary group based in South Africa. The group's main mandate was to prevent both the RUF and the sobels from exploiting the diamond fields. All factions in the conflict engaged in wanton human rights violations—the killing of civilians, rape, and so on.

THE MILITARY INTERVENTION IN SIERRA LEONE

Sensing the possibility of a subregional conflict epidemic—with the civil war raging in Liberia—and its attendant cataclysmic consequences, ECOWAS decided to militarily intervene in the Sierra Leonean Civil War through ECOMOG, their peacekeeping force, in 1991. The troops for the force (about 2,000 initially and 5,000 later) came primarily from Nigeria and Guinea. Clearly, ECOWAS made the determination for the peacekeeping force to collaborate with Sierra Leonean government troops against the RUF. This was evidenced by various military offenses by the peacekeeping force against RUF positions. Such a posture violated the neutrality proviso of peacekeeping. Despite its alliance with the government forces, ECOMOG failed to help create the conditions for the resolution of the civil war.

By 1995, an internal power struggle occurred within the ranks of the ruling NRC: the council's vice chair, Brigadier Bio, staged a coup that ousted Head of State Strasser from power. The Bio regime continued the policies of exploitation, thuggery, and repression. Hence, it could not mobilize the national population to address the escalating civil war.

Amid the collective efforts of ECOMOG and the mercenary force Executive Outcomes to defeat the RUF militarily, ECOWAS and the rest of the international community hastily pushed for the holding of national elections in Sierra Leone, as the panacea to the civil war. As expected, the elections were opposed by both the Bio military government, which wanted the civil war to continue so that it could pursue its policy of looting and pillaging, and the RUF, which wanted to seize power through the barrel of the gun.

Despite the intense NRC–RUF opposition, national elections were held in 1996, and Tejan Kabbah of the SLPP was elected president. To the dismay and disappointment of the Sierra Leonean masses, the Kabbah regime failed to develop a new national blueprint for promoting democratization and economic revitalization. Furthermore, the civil war continued unabated, with its consequent toll of death and destruction. Exploiting the incompetence and ineffectiveness of the

Kabbah regime, a group of junior military officers toppled the government in a coup on 25 May 1997. Major Johnny Paul Koroma was installed as the head of state and chair of the Armed Forces Ruling Council (AFRC), in a coalition government consisting of the military and the insurgent group RUF as partners. Consequently, ECOMOG increased its military involvement and further shifted its focus from peacekeeping to the restoration of the Kabbah government. After months of intense fighting between ECOMOG and the combined forces of the AFRC and the RUF, the former defeated the latter and reinstated the Kabbah regime. However, this has not ended the civil war. Instead, the combined RUF and AFRC forces are still attacking towns and villages and raining death and destruction on defenseless civilians.

CONCLUSION

This chapter has attempted to examine whether the interventions by the United Nations in the Somali Civil War, the United Nations and the OAU in the Rwandan Civil War, and ECOWAS in the Liberian and Sierra Leonean Civil Wars fulfilled the requirements of military humanitarianism. The military intervention by the United Nations in the Somali Civil War did meet all of the criteria for humanitarian military intervention, except the one pertaining to impact. Specifically, the military intervention was in response to a humanitarian crisis; a proper authority authorized it; and the means were proportional to the nature of the crisis. In terms of its impact, the intervention did succeed in securing the routes for delivery of much needed food to the starving civilians. However, the decision by the United States, the leader of the operation, to engage in peace building was contrary to the requirements for humanitarian intervention. Moreover, the killing of Somalian civilians by American troops undermined the very essence of the humanitarian military intervention. Ultimately, the intervention did help the delivery of much needed relief supplies, but it did not help to create the conditions for ending the civil war.

In the case of Rwanda, both the OAU and the United Nations did fulfill all the requirements for humanitarian military intervention, at least at first. In terms of impact on the conflict, the OAU intervention was pivotal to creating the conditions for peacemaking. That is, it helped to create the conditions for peacefully resolving the civil war. Unfortunately, the OAU turned over a successful peacekeeping operation to the United Nations. Characteristically, the United Nations did not demonstrate the political will and resolve that the OAU had. Accordingly, when the Arusha peace process faltered, the United Nations withdrew its peacekeeping force. Clearly, the departure of the U.N. peacekeeping force helped to create the vacuum that made the commission of genocide possible. Overall, the U.N. peacekeeping operation did not help to create new conditions that were better than those existing prior to the military intervention. In essence, the U.N. intervention did not help to create the conditions for ending the civil war.

The military intervention of ECOWAS in the Liberian Civil War did fulfill all of the requirements for humanitarian militarism. Clearly, the humanitarian crisis—the massive killing of civilians, the refugee crisis, and the collapse of the state—justified the intervention. Also, a "proper authority" did authorize the intervention, despite the initial conflict over the matter. Similarly, the means employed were proportional to the crises. However, given the scope of the civil war—seven warring factions—the means were often outstripped by the enormity of the crises. Despite this, the intervention helped to create the conditions for peacemaking and the eventual end of the civil war.

In the Sierra Leonean Civil War, ECOWAS did fulfill the provisions requiring a humanitarian crisis, proper authorization, and the proportionality of means to ends in its first military intervention. However, the ECOMOG alliance with the government against the RUF violated the neutrality expected of peacekeepers. In terms of impact, the intervention did not help to stop the killing and destruction. The second intervention in 1997 did not meet the requirements of military humanitarianism. This is because it was designed primarily to effect domestic politics in Sierra Leone by restoring a regime that had been deposed in a coup. In other words, the merits of restoring the "process of democratization" notwithstanding, the second ECOMOG intervention did not meet the minimum standards for a humanitarian military intervention. In fact, the intervention contributed to the escalation of the civil war, especially the deaths of innocent civilians and the further destruction of the infrastructure.

Finally, much work remains in the formulation of fully developed and refined preconditions for military humanitarianism. Such a framework would serve as a generalized and objective compass for navigating the often rough seas of intervention. Particularly, it will separate military intervention motivated by raw national interests from humanitarian military intervention triggered by the international community's commitment and resolve to address crises that have broad ramifications for maintaining peace and security in the international system.

10

German and U.S. Intervention against Yugoslav Sovereignty

Emil Nagengast

Germany's decision to extend diplomatic recognition to the secessionist Yugoslav republics of Croatia and Slovenia in December 1991 marked the beginning of international intervention in Yugoslavia. Considering Germany's disastrous history of blatant disregard for the territorial integrity of East European states, it is understandable that Germany's apparent eagerness to dismember Yugoslavia aroused widespread condemnation (e.g., Glenny 1993; C. O'Brien 1993; Woodward 1995). According to one scholar, Germany's violation of Yugoslavia's sovereignty was morally irresponsible and "unquestionably one of the most precipitous acts in post–Cold War Europe. With it the Bonn government in effect renounced the legitimacy of the existing Yugoslav state and pressured other European governments to do the same. Within weeks the Yugoslav federation came apart at every seam" (Hodge 1998, 1).

According to Raju Thomas, "Yugoslavia was dismembered through a selective and prejudicial international recognition policy of its internal 'republics' " (1997, 17). Thomas singles out former German Foreign Minister Hans-Dietrich Genscher and former U.S. Ambassador to Yugoslavia Warren Zimmermann as the two individuals responsible for the dismemberment and devastation of Yugoslavia: "There could have been peace without war and human tragedy if Yugoslavia's territorial integrity had been preserved" (1997, 17). Likewise, Donald Horowitz condemns Germany's determination to violate Yugoslavia's sovereignty: "Led by Germany, European and American recognition of the former Yugoslav republics was accomplished in disregard of international law doctrine forbidding recognition of secessionist units whose establishment is being resisted forcibly by a central government" (1995, 1).

This chapter examines Germany's political intervention in 1991 and the U.S. path to military intervention in Yugoslavia in 1995. Until Germany "internationalized" the Yugoslav crisis through diplomatic recognition of the breakaway republics, the international community treated the conflict largely as a civil war. Throughout 1991 the United States, France, the United Kingdom, the European Community (EC), and the United Nations were determined to salvage a unified, sovereign, multiethnic Yugoslav state that would serve as a model for the rest of Eastern Europe and the Soviet Union. The Germans, however, asserted the priority of defending humanitarian principles in 1991. This case study captures the tension between the principle of nonintervention derived from respect for state sovereignty, on the one hand, and the transnational responsibilities required of the pursuit of humanitarian principles, on the other hand.

The German, and to a lesser extent, the U.S., decision to intervene in Yugoslavia must be understood as a manifestation of what Stanley Hoffmann describes as the contemporary "normative revolution that erodes the content of sovereignty and restricts the rights, derived from sovereignty, that states were free to exercise at home" (1995–96, 31). Michael Walzer's (1992) standard of justified intervention provides an ethical foundation for Germany's widely misinterpreted, but successful, effort to force the international community to accept the necessity of intervention against the remnants of the Yugoslav central government.

One of the tragic ironies of the Yugoslav conflict is that German leaders learned that their idealist attempt to defend certain norms was out of step with the realist principles that played a central role in guiding the behavior of their allies. The international response to the war in Yugoslavia and, in particular, the cynical diplomatic and scholarly assessment of German foreign policy are a troubling indication of the discrepancy between rhetoric and behavior concerning ethics and intervention which characterizes the priorities of the "international community" in the post–Cold War era.

OVERVIEW OF THE YUGOSLAV CRISIS

Slobodan Milosevic's decision in 1987 to exploit ethnic tension in the autonomous Yugoslav province of Kosovo as a means to seize power of the Serbian Communist Party marked the beginning of the end of Yugoslavia. Milosevic's imposition of martial law in Kosovo and his nationalist strategy to increase the strength of Serbia within the Yugoslav Federal Council confirmed the views of many leaders in Croatia and Slovenia that the Yugoslav Federation needed to be drastically decentralized or completely abandoned. After 1987 the legitimacy of a unified Yugoslav state was called into question with increased intensity in the non-Serb regions of Yugoslavia. According to Michael J. Smith, "State sovereignty, in short, is a contingent value: its observance depends upon the actions of the state that invokes it" (1998, 78). Milosevic's violation of Kosovo's autonomy, his intimidation of the Yugoslav Federal Council, his primitive nationalist rhetoric, his unconstitutional efforts to block the ascension of a Croat to the presidency of the Federal Council in 1991, and his refusal to accept a decentralization of the Yugoslav federal system together removed any significant resistance in Croatia and Slovenia to the argument that Yugoslavia's sovereignty and territorial integrity had become little more than instruments of self-interested Serb rhetoric.

In spring 1991, Croat and Slovene officials appealed to the international community to accept the illegitimacy of the Federal Republic of Yugoslavia and to support their secessionist movements. Despite the widespread international condemnation of Milosevic's policies, there was no serious support outside Yugoslavia for the dissolution of this multiethnic state. Against intense international pressure, in June 1991 Croatia and Slovenia declared their independence. In response, the Yugoslav People's Army (JNA), which quickly became a Serb army, waged military campaigns against the breakaway republics. The fighting ended after only ten days in Slovenia, largely because of the fact that Slovenia was an ethnically homogeneous republic. Within the borders of the Croatian republic, however, there lived over 600,000 Serbs. As long as Yugoslavia remained one country, these Serbs could rely on the protection of the federal government against any nationalist, discriminatory Croatian policies. But if Croatia became an independent state, the fate of these Serbs would be in the hands of Croatian leaders. To make matters worse, Franjo Tudjman's Croatian government revived primitive nationalist symbols and rhetoric from Croatia's fascist past. During World War II a Croatian fascist government, allied with Hitler, massacred over 500,000 Serbs. In 1991 the Serbs interpreted the breakup of Yugoslavia in terms of their wartime suffering at the hands of an independent Croatian state. For the Serbs it was, thus, no coincidence that the Germans played the key role in supporting Croatian efforts to destroy the multiethnic state.

The fiercest fighting began in July 1991 in the regions of Croatia with large Serb populations. In December 1991, Germany announced that it would recognize the sovereignty of Croatia and Slovenia, thereby forcing the rest of the international community to begin diplomatic and, later, military intervention in Yugoslavia. Following the establishment of a cease-fire between Croat and Yugoslav federal (i.e., Serb) forces in January 1992, the fighting began in March 1992 in Bosnia when the Muslim-led government in Sarajevo also declared its independence from Yugoslavia. It was not until fall 1995 that a cease-fire was reached in Bosnia with the signing of the Dayton Accords and the intervention of U.S.–led NATO troops.

GERMANY AND THE INTERNATIONAL RESPONSE TO THE YUGOSLAVIA CRISIS

At the beginning of 1991, German leaders shared the view of their West European partners that a unified Yugoslavia was in Europe's best interest. German Chancel-

lor Helmut Kohl made it clear that his government was prepared to support Yugoslavia's wish to join the process of European integration but that this support
was endangered by Serb policies in Kosovo (*Frankfurter Allgemeine Zeitung*, 6
December 1989). A delegation of German parliamentarians in Belgrade warned
the Serb leadership that Yugoslavia's "European option" depended upon respect
for established European standards of human rights (*Frankfurter Allgemeine Zeitung*, 12 November 1990). In February 1991, the consensus among all mainstream German parties was that Yugoslavia should remain unified in some form
but that this unity could not be based on the threat or use of military aggression
or on the basis of Serb political hegemony (*Stenographischer Bericht des Bundestags*, 21 February 1991, 404–16).

By June 1991, however, German interests changed dramatically. As the Croats
and Slovenes prepared their declarations of independence, German officials grew
frustrated with the tepid international response to the crisis. On the one hand,
Kohl was determined to toe the EC line, which maintained that the Yugoslav crisis was an internal matter. Helmut Schäfer, a member of Kohl's government, explained Kohl's position: "Together with our partners we stand for the peaceful
preservation of pan-Yugoslav structures. . . . The form of these structures must
be decided by the nations of Yugoslavia themselves" (*Stenographischer Bericht
des Bundestags*, 19 June 1991, 2560). On the other hand, members of the German
parliament (the Bundestag) grew frustrated with the EC priority of respecting
Yugoslav sovereignty. Parliamentarian Friedrich Vogel captured the mood in
Bonn: "Through the incantation of Yugoslavia's integrity . . . the [EC] has supported the Serb communists, who find themselves increasingly in the minority,
yet who fight fiercely to gain power in a unified Yugoslav state" (*Stenographischer Bericht des Bundestags*, 19 June 1991, 2564). On June 23, the German
government joined the unanimous EC vote not to recognize Slovenia and Croatia
if they chose to secede unilaterally from Yugoslavia.

After the Croats and Slovenes ignored this last-ditch EC effort and declared
independence on 25 June 1991, German foreign policy makers feared that the
Serb leadership would view the passivity of the international community as justification for crushing the secessionist movements. German Foreign Minister Hans-
Dietrich Genscher warned his Yugoslav counterpart Budomir Loncar that the renunciation of aggression was a fundamental element of post-1945 European
peace. Furthermore, as a member of the Conference on Security and Cooperation
in Europe (CSCE) and a signatory of the Charter of Paris, Yugoslavia had agreed
that the use of military force to resolve political disputes was no longer acceptable in Europe (Genscher 1995, 936).

Once military force entered the equation in Yugoslavia in June and July, all
levels of the German foreign policy community saw the crisis as a serious challenge to established principles of acceptable state behavior. In Bonn the conflict
was viewed as a test of the capacity of European institutions (primarily the EC
and the CSCE) and of the European powers to take an unequivocal stand to assert

the priority of the renunciation of military force as the foundation of post–Cold War European peace. Genscher was asked about the contradiction of violating the sovereignty of a CSCE member in order to defend CSCE principles. He defended Germany's demand for intervention with the argument that human rights were anchored in the Charter of Paris as rights that supersede the principle of sovereignty (*Kieler Nachrichten*, 18 November 1991).

More troublesome was the principle of free national self-determination, which the Germans had just used to reunify their own nation. The principle of national self-determination was also a central issue for German officials concerning the ethnic clashes in Yugoslavia, but, according to Reinhard Schäfers (interview by the author, June 1994), one of Kohl's advisers on East European affairs, the German government was aware of the difficult implications of this concept for the national separatist movements in Spain, France, and the United Kingdom. For this reason, and because the immediate danger to the post–Cold War "European peace order" was perceived to be the weak international response to the use of force, the Germans focused primarily on stopping Serb militarism.

Confronted with a united block in the Bundestag which included traditionally bitter parliamentary opponents, Kohl and Genscher realized that they were rapidly becoming domestically isolated in arguing that a unified EC foreign policy was more important than standing up for moral principles. Even many members of the German Green Party turned away from their pacifist platform to demand international intervention in Yugoslavia as a powerful statement against militarism in Europe (Edith Müller, Green Party representative at the European Parliament, interview by the author, October 1995). According to Uwe Stehr, an East European expert in the German Social Democratic Party (SPD), frustration with the passivity of the EC, the United Nations, and the United States led many Germans to believe that Bonn needed to play a leading role in forcing the international community out of its "halfheartedness" concerning the situation within Yugoslavia (interview by the author, June 1994). Cyrill Nunn, an analyst from the Department of Yugoslav Affairs in the German Foreign Ministry, explained that for most Germans it was incomprehensible in the summer of 1991 that the Western powers tolerated the blatant violation of established norms in Europe. According to Nunn, many people in the German Foreign Ministry believed that the preference for diplomatic patience over intervention was at least partly because the United States, France, and Britain, as active military powers, had become desensitized to military conflicts around the world which fit the description of "civil wars" (interview by the author, June 1994).

In July 1991, the EC (under the Dutch presidency of Hans Van de Broek) was determined to play the role of mediator. The EC was careful to maintain close negotiating ties with what remained of the Yugoslav federal government, as opposed to simply accepting the end of Yugoslav unity and dealing instead with the independent Serb and Croat governments. The EC also tried hard to remain neutral and resist pressures to lay blame on one side or the other in the conflict. The

EC went as far as to make a bizarre appeal to the JNA and Croat forces to unify their efforts and conduct joint patrols to keep the peace in Croatia (*Belgrade Tanjug*, 26 July 1991, reprinted in *US Foreign Broadcast Information Service–West Europe*, 29 July 1991).

On 7 July 1991, the leaders of Croatia, Slovenia, and the Serb-dominated Yugoslav government signed the EC–brokered "Brioni Accord." This agreement called for an end to the fighting and the initiation of negotiations to establish some form of unified but loosely confederated Yugoslavia. Croatia and Slovenia agreed to a moratorium on their declarations of independence for three months while the EC tried to arrange a political solution to the conflict. The federal government agreed to recall all JNA troops to their barracks. Kohl was unsuccessful in trying to persuade his EC partners that the EC should at least announce that diplomatic recognition of Croatia and Slovenia was a possibility when the three months had expired—if the JNA continued its military operations (*Frankfurter Allgemeine Zeitung*, 19 July 1991).

The Brioni Accord succeeded in halting JNA actions in Slovenia, but the Serbs quickly turned the JNA against Croatia. In a radio interview, Genscher and Luxembourg Foreign Minister Jacques de Poos both blamed the Serbs for violating the cease-fire agreement. According to Genscher and de Poos, the Serbs lacked the political will to maintain the cease-fire and aimed at the expansion of Serb-controlled territory as a fait accompli for any future negotiations. Genscher's message was that the JNA actions justified the international community's abandonment of respect for the unity and sovereignty of the Yugoslav federation (*Fernseh- und Hörfunkspiegel*, 5 August 1991).

At a special session of the Bundestag on 4 September 1991, Kohl read a statement from the August 27 EC meeting of foreign ministers: "The [EC] will never accept a politics of *fait accompli*. [The EC] will not recognize border changes achieved through violence" (*Stenographischer Bericht des Bundestags*, 4 September 1991, 3022). Speaking after Kohl at this special session, SPD Chairman Bjorn Engholm supported Kohl's view of the Charter of Paris as the source of German foreign policy priorities, but he attacked Kohl and the EC for allowing their misplaced devotion to Yugoslavia's integrity to trample the basic principles of the charter. Genscher concluded the session with a direct threat to Yugoslav federal authorities:

> I wish to inform those responsible at the head of the JNA; with every shot from your tanks, the hour of recognition gets closer for us. We will not simply sit by and watch. . . . Our approach to the conflict is grounded in freedom, democracy, human rights and self-determination. These values led us to German unification, and these values will also form the foundation of a pan-European home. [*Stenographischer Bericht des Bundestags*, 4 September 1991, 3045]

After repeated violations of cease-fires negotiated by the EC, Genscher tried to head off further unrest within Germany by insisting that the forthcoming sec-

ond round of the Conference on Yugoslavia in The Hague (under the chairman-
ship of Lord Carrington) would either stop the fighting or force the EC to accept
diplomatic recognition as the only remaining option. Genscher reassured his EC
colleagues that Germany would not take unilateral action, but he requested that
the EC consider an internationalization of the crisis as the most effective means
to stop Serb military aggression in Croatia. The importance of diplomatic recognition as a political strategy, Genscher argued, was not merely to send a strong
political signal regarding principles; just as important, recognition would interna-
tionalize the Yugoslav conflict and bring in the United Nations. Unlike the CSCE,
he noted, the United Nations had well-established crisis mechanisms and the authority to pass binding resolutions against its members (*Heute Journal*, 6 September 1991). Genscher raised the issue of sending peacekeeping troops in the context of the EC or CSCE. He also supported the suggestion of French Foreign
Minister Dumas to inform the U.N. Security Council of EC negotiations. This
proposal, however, was resisted by a number of EC states, foremost by the United
Kingdom (Genscher 1995, 945).

Marten H. A. van Heuven writes that in September 1991 "there was a curious
contrast between the European public impression that little useful was being
done, and the self-satisfied view of EC diplomats who were seeking to manage
the Yugoslav issue through a succession of verbal exhortations that proved futile"
(1993, 59). By November, fourteen EC–brokered cease-fire agreements had been
broken. The international perception of the Serbs as the military aggressors was
strengthened by the Serb siege and shelling of Vukovar and Dubrovnik (which
was a U.N. Educational, Scientific, and Cultural Organization world cultural
landmark). After the fall of Vukovar in November, the Serb forces executed several hundred wounded men and women in the city hospital.

In Germany, public outrage and pressure for international action produced a
Bundestag resolution that was unequivocal in stating that there was no longer any
chance for a continued existence of a Yugoslav state in its latest structure. The
resolution blamed the Serb leadership for the destruction of a state in which all
ethnic groups could coexist on the basis of equality. The Bundestag supported
the efforts of Kohl's government to create the preconditions for international recognition of those republics that sought independence and would guarantee the
rights of their ethnic minorities (Libal 1997, 75–76). On 25 November 1991,
Genscher responded to a question about Germany's willingness to recognize
Croatia and Slovenia if Serb military aggression was not halted by the December
10 deadline (as agreed on by the EC members at the outset of Carrington's Conference on Yugoslavia):

> We would quite certainly not be alone, in that I cannot imagine that our partners,
> who did not contradict the position that after December 10, if the political process
> has not found a solution, recognition would be on the agenda, I cannot imagine that
> someone would deviate from this. If someone does deviate, then he would act more

unilaterally than Germany, who would certainly not remain alone. [*Fernseh- und Hörfunkspiegel*, 25 November 1991]

At the end of November 1991, Kohl sent Christian Tomuschat, a German expert on international law and a member of the U.N. Human Rights Commission, to Zagreb and Ljublana to ensure that Croatia and Slovenia had moved beyond far-reaching pronouncements concerning minority rights and had established specific legal frameworks that met the standards of the Council of Europe and the CSCE. Shortly after the Croatian parliament passed the necessary legislation on minority rights in early December, Kohl told Tudjman that Germany would not take action until after the December 16 special meeting of EC foreign ministers, but Kohl assured Tudjman that with the new minority rights legislation, Croatia could count on German recognition before Christmas.

In the days leading up to the December 16 meeting, Genscher and U.N. General Secretary Javier Pérez de Cuéllar engaged in a heated exchange of public letters over the appropriateness of intervening with recognition of Croatian and Slovenian sovereignty. Pérez de Cuéllar was concerned with the wider ramifications of this step for other parts of Yugoslavia—particularly for Bosnia-Herzegovina and Macedonia. Genscher was atypically aggressive in his rebuttal to Pérez de Cuéllar's warning against an "uncoordinated approach" to diplomatic intervention. For a significant time already, Genscher responded, the German government had worked carefully to move its EC partners toward a concrete multilateral statement in defense of certain international norms: "The denial of recognition of the republics which seek independence would certainly lead to further escalation of the use of force by the federal army, because the JNA would see this as a validation of their policy of conquest" (*Frankfurter Allgemeine Zeitung*, 16 December 1991).

Shortly before the foreign ministers' meeting, the German and French governments issued a "Catalog of Principles" that delineated the proposed criteria for any new East European state seeking international recognition. Among the criteria listed in the catalog were reliable protection of minority rights, respect for the CSCE principles, and respect for the inviolability of existing borders and of the territorial sovereignty of other states. With small changes this German–French catalog was eventually officially adopted by the EC as "The Guidelines on the Recognition of New States" (*European Political Cooperation Press Release* 1992).

After a round of negotiations at the 16 December meeting, the twelve foreign ministers announced that the EC and its member states would recognize those Yugoslav republics that had met the specific criteria regarding minority rights. The "implementation" of the decision on recognition, the statement explained, would take place on 15 January 1992. In the interim the Badinter Commission, comprising five European judges, was to assess whether or not the independent republics met the criteria. The German government waited neither for the results of the Badinter Commission nor for January 15. On December 24 the German government announced its recognition of Croatia and Slovenia. Although Germany did not wait for the results of the Badinter Commission, Genscher and Kohl, according to Tomuschat (interview by the author, June 1994), had already received an extensive "legal evaluation" from him on Croatia's minority rights legislation. At the 16 December foreign ministers' meeting Genscher made it clear to his EC colleagues that the German government was certain the Badinter Commission would merely confirm Tomuschat's assessment (Genscher 1995, 960–63). On 11 January 1992, the Badinter Commission announced that Croatia and Slovenia had fulfilled the criteria of minority rights legislation as described in the EC guidelines for recognition. On 15 January 1992, the other EC member states recognized the new states and, along with Germany, opened diplomatic relations with Croatia and Slovenia (but not with Macedonia because of Greek opposition within the EC). The Yugoslav central government condemned this intervention as a violation of "the sovereign rights of Yugoslavia, which are based on fundamental, modern international legal documents" (*Washington Post*, 16 January 1992).

After the Yugoslav crisis was transformed from a civil war to an internationally recognized war of aggression against Croatia, the Germans were forced to play a passive role as the international community moved toward military intervention because the German constitution did not allow German troops to be deployed outside NATO territory. The Germans were the most determined to violate Yugoslav sovereignty in defense of universal norms of acceptable state behavior, but the Germans were also incapable of taking the necessary military steps to legitimize their political intervention. Conversely, the United States was the country most capable of stopping Serb military aggression, but U.S. foreign policy makers were also among the strongest opponents, first, of dividing Yugoslavia through recognition of the breakaway republics and, second, of military intervention.

THE U.S. PATH TO MILITARY INTERVENTION

In 1991 the U.S. government held to the position that the Yugoslav crisis was an internal matter that should be resolved by the Yugoslavs themselves. President Bush believed that the conflict did not involve U.S. national interests and that the United States had no compelling reason to intervene (Woodward 1993). According to former U.S. Ambassador to Yugoslavia William Zimmermann (interview by the author, October 1994), Secretary of State James Baker became so disgusted with his inability to make any progress with Milosevic, Tudjman, and other Yugoslav leaders that he left it to the EC to negotiate an arrangement that would salvage Yugoslav unity. A senior State Department official summed up the U.S. view: "If they want to find someone who will help them to stop shooting and start negotiating, they should look to West Europe, or most particularly to the EC" (*Washington Post*, 22 September 1991).

Senator Orrin Hatch condemned "Western policy makers" for their "policy of moral equivalence," that is, of treating the secessionist republics and the hard-line Serb government as equally responsible for the bloodshed. Hatch called on the U.S. government to defend universal principles such as democracy and self-determination: "If we fail to do so, the offensive by the federal army could set a perilous precedent: military forces will have been used to dismember or destroy a democratic republic [i.e., Croatia] in the heart of Europe" (1991).

The U.S. government was also concerned about setting a perilous precedent, namely, allowing minority ethnic groups to provoke a horrendous civil war as a means to gain international sympathy for their secessionist movements. Near the top of U.S. security concerns in 1991 was the fear of a proliferation of ethnic civil wars across East Europe and the Soviet Union (Glenny 1993, 236). A clear example of this concern was the U.S. government's halfhearted support for the independence movements of the three Soviet Baltic republics—despite the fact that the United States had never officially recognized the incorporation of these republics into the Soviet Union. U.S. policy concerning Yugoslavia's territorial integrity changed after the Soviet Union was legally dissolved on 25 December 1991 and after January 1992 when the United States followed the Europeans in extending diplomatic recognition to the breakaway Yugoslav republics.

Following the international recognition of Croatia and Slovenia and the cessation of fighting in Croatia in January 1992, international attention shifted quickly to the Yugoslav republic of Bosnia-Herzegovina. With Croatia and Slovenia no longer serving as counterbalances to Serbia in the federal Yugoslav government, the Bosnian Muslims and Bosnian Croats refused to live in a Serb-dominated Yugoslavia. But, just as in Croatia, the Serbs in Bosnia refused to live under a non-Serb or non-Yugoslav government. The Serbs (in Bosnia and in Serbia) warned the Muslim-led Bosnian government in Sarajevo that a Bosnian declaration of independence would lead to a civil war even more horrific than what had occurred in Croatia. Based on the results of a popular referendum in Bosnia (which the Bosnian Serbs boycotted), the Bosnian government declared independence from Yugoslavia in March 1992. The Bosnian war began almost immediately as the Muslims, Croats, and Serbs each fought to control as much of Bosnian territory as possible.

In January 1992 Genscher argued that because military force had not yet replaced the search for political solutions to the Bosnia crisis, recognition of Bosnia as a sovereign state should be withheld (interview by the author, June 1998). In stark contrast to U.S. passivity in 1991, in early 1992 the United States took the lead in gaining international recognition of Bosnian independence. According to Zimmermann, "Our view was that we might be able to head off a Serbian power grab by internationalizing the problem" (*New York Times*, 29 August 1993). James Baker attributes the shift in the U.S. view of the Yugoslav crisis to the fact that in spring 1992 over 14,000 U.N. peacekeeping troops were deployed in the territory of the former Yugoslavia—the largest U.N. deployment since the 1960s in Congo (*Washington Post*, 11 March 1992).

Although the United States intervened diplomatically in the Bosnian crisis first, by encouraging the government in Sarajevo to declare independence and then by quickly recognizing the new sovereign state of Bosnia-Herzegovina in April 1992, it was not until 1995 that the U.S. government intervened militarily to defend Bosnian sovereignty. Baker's remark that "we got no dog in this fight" captures the spirit of the "disciplined standoffishness" of the Bush administration concerning the fighting first in Croatia in 1991 and then in Bosnia in 1992 (Danner 1997, 61). President Clinton became increasingly disturbed by the massacres in Bosnia, but he followed the example of his predecessor in rejecting U.S. military intervention. Three factors caused Clinton to order a massive attack against the Bosnian Serbs in August and September 1995. First, the U.S. government feared that growing international Muslim frustration over the lack of support for the Bosnian Muslims would lead to direct military intervention by a Middle Eastern state or by Turkey. The potential strategic consequences of external Muslim involvement made it impossible for U.S. policy makers to view the Bosnian conflict as merely regional (Glenny 1993, 237). Second, the daily coverage of concentration camps, massacres, rapes, and mass graves generated a powerful moral outrage within the United States which demanded that something be done. Most significant in this regard was the Serb destruction in July 1995 of Srebrenica, which had been designated as a U.N. safe haven. The atrocities committed against the Muslims by the Serbs in Srebrenica had a significant impact on Clinton's attitude regarding the necessity of military intervention (Woodward 1996). Third, Clinton was convinced that the U.S. policy of nonintervention ran counter to U.S. national interest: "Our position is unsustainable, it's killing the U.S. position of strength in the world" (quoted in Woodward 1996, 260).

On 28 August 1995, the Bosnian Serbs defied a NATO–imposed cease-fire by launching a shell into a crowded Sarajevo market. Clinton immediately ordered NATO air strikes against the Serbs with the conviction that the failure to act would undermine the legitimacy of NATO, further weaken the United Nations and other international institutions, and make a mockery of attempts to promote international norms as the foundation of the post–Cold War international system (Danner 1997).

The fruit of the NATO air strikes was the Dayton Accord, which was signed by Milosevic, Tudjman, and Izetbegovic (the leader of the Bosnian Muslims) in November 1995. The NATO attacks ended three years of Bosnian Serb military successes against the outgunned Muslims. For the first time the Serbs were on the defensive, especially because the Muslims and Croats exploited the moment to launch ground attacks against the Serbs. This new military situation forced the Serbs to accept a negotiated settlement in Dayton which made Bosnia a unified, independent state and brought in NATO ground troops (including 20,000 U.S. troops) to enforce the agreement.

Whereas the NATO air strikes represented U.S. military intervention against one side in the Bosnian war, the placement of U.S. troops in Bosnia was agreed on by all three warring factions in Bosnia. In his address to the American public, Clinton was careful to make it very clear that U.S. troops were not intervening against any particular forces in Bosnia but were instead assisting the Serbs, Croats, and Muslims to defend their own peace agreement:

> When I took office, some were urging immediate intervention in the conflict. I decided that American ground troops should not fight a war in Bosnia because the U.S. could not force peace on Bosnia's warring ethnic groups. . . . But as the months of war turned into years, it became clear that Europe alone could not end the conflict. . . . Finally, just three weeks ago, the Muslims, Croats and Serbs came to Dayton, Ohio, in America's heartland, to negotiate a settlement. There, exhausted by war, they made a commitment to peace. They agreed to put down their guns; to preserve Bosnia as a single state; to investigate and prosecute war criminals; to protect the human rights of all citizens; to try to build a peaceful, democratic future. And they asked for America's help as they implement this peace agreement. [Presidential Speech to the Nation, 27 November 1995]

THE VIOLATION AND DEFENSE OF NORMS

In his virulent attack on German and U.S. foreign policy makers for their violation of Yugoslav sovereignty, Raju Thomas (1997) reiterates an argument commonly made by the Serbs but seldom discussed in the United States, namely, that Serb military aggression against the secessionist republics was no different than Abraham Lincoln's "war between the states." As it forcefully resisted secessionist movements within the USSR, the Soviet leadership was also frustrated by what was perceived to be the U.S. refusal even to consider the inconsistencies between our condemnation of Soviet military aggression to preserve the federal USSR, on the one hand, and our veneration for our own devastating campaign to crush southern secessionism, on the other hand. George Will's article "Lithuania and South Carolina" (1990) is an interesting, but still controversial, attempt to justify the rather hypocritical U.S. approach to contemporary secessionist struggles.

The Yugoslav crisis is a troubling example of the suffering that the international community will tolerate under the guise of a "civil war." Looking back on U.S. policy, Zimmermann writes, "The failure of the Bush administration to commit American power early in the Bosnia war was our greatest mistake of the entire Yugoslav crisis" (1996, 15). The behavior of the Serb leadership in Belgrade and Bosnia between 1991 and 1995 supports the argument that the Serbs perceived the international emphasis on the principles of territorial integrity and nonintervention as "carte blanche" for their centralist, militarist policies (Weller 1992). German foreign policy makers were the first to recognize the manner and degree to which the Serbs were abusing the norms of sovereignty and nonintervention. As the Serbs grew increasingly defiant in their use of force against the various secessionist movements, the Germans could not understand why their European allies had made nonintervention an end in itself—regardless of the day-to-day situation within Yugoslavia. Once they recognized that Yugoslav unity was impossible and that the norm of nonintervention was responsible for increased suffering, German officials saw full internationalization of the ethnic war as the essential first step toward defending other universal norms, in particular, the abrogation of military force.

Hans Maull (1995) suggests that during the Cold War West German foreign policy makers made a "leap of faith" into a new paradigm of international relations which he describes as "principled multilateralism" and "interwoven interests." Alexander Mühlen (1992) draws on this argument to assert that German assertiveness concerning international intervention in Yugoslavia was a direct product of the "policy of responsibility" *(Verantwortungspolitik)* that Germany had adopted during the Cold War as a negation of the pre-1945 German pattern of open disregard for international norms. Michael Libal, who headed the German Foreign Ministry department dealing with the Yugoslav crisis, summarizes Germany's core interests in 1991:

> If there was anything that German diplomacy dreaded, it was what has been termed a "renationalization" of foreign policy in Europe. The course of German unification had amply reconfirmed the primacy of multilateralism in the conduct of German foreign policy. But multilateralism depends on the credibility of international norms and institutions, and German policy makers had no doubt whatsoever that the policies pursued by Serbia constituted an open and very serious challenge to the principles that were supposed to govern the behavior of states in post–Cold War Europe. [1997, 104]

Germany's unilateral push for international intervention in Yugoslavia has been described by some as evidence of a "normalization" of German foreign policy, that is, that post–Cold War unified Germany would shift away from its previous priority of multilateralism and toward the unilateral pursuit of national self-interest (e.g., P. Gordon 1994). But this case study suggests that Germany's Yugoslavia policies clashed with the "normal" interests of the Americans and the EC states precisely because the Germans retained an excessive devotion to the *principles* of multilateralism in 1991.

Amir Pasic and Thomas G. Weiss describe the Yugoslav crisis as one of the clearest examples of the tension between the transnational "humanitarian impulse" of modern foreign policy and the traditional norm of respect for sovereignty. The humanitarian impulse, they write, "has seeped into foreign ministries and security agendas as heads of states proclaim the virtues of 'doing the right thing,' despite the usual warnings that moral sentiments should not guide the ship of state" (Pasic and Weiss 1997, 106). The authors warn against excessive eagerness to relegate the norm of sovereignty to a second tier below humanitarian values, but they also argue for a dispassionate view of this norm: "We should not delude ourselves into thinking that [sovereignty] is a natural fact" (Pasic and Weiss 1997, 123–24).

Walzer writes that "the recognition of sovereignty is the only way we have of establishing an arena within which freedom can be fought for" (1992, 89). But Walzer also describes circumstances that demand a violation of national sovereignty: "Humanitarian intervention is justified when it is a response . . . to acts that shock the moral conscience of mankind. [I]n such cases, we praise or do not condemn these violations of the formal rules of sovereignty" (1992, 107–08). Stanley Hoffmann believes that a moral sense of duty should have precipitated earlier and more forceful action to end the suffering in Yugoslavia. The contemporary, eroded norm of sovereignty, he writes, "allows for collective intervention when a state's condition or behavior results in grave threats to other states' and peoples' peace and security, and in grave and massive violations of human rights" (1996, 23). Walzer's and Hoffmann's standards for justified intervention support the argument of German officials that the Serbs themselves, through their militarism and violation of human rights, had forfeited the protection of sovereignty from outside intervention.

CONCLUSION

German and U.S. foreign policy makers derived contrasting lessons from their intervention in the Yugoslav secessionist conflicts of 1991–95. While the Germans were thrown into turmoil over the correctness of their decision making, the Americans felt a sense of vindication. The lessons derived by the United States from the Yugoslav crisis from 1991 to 1995 can be summarized as the following: First, the Europeans are incapable of coping with a serious military conflict—even in Europe. Second, decisive military engagement is an essential element of effective intervention against a military aggressor. Third, intervention with ground troops is permissible only when all the combatants want peace.

In stark contrast, officials in the German Foreign Ministry commonly describe their experience with the Yugoslav crisis as "having burned our fingers on the stove." Germany's lessons can be summarized as the following: First, their international partners did not trust Germany to take the lead on such an important issue. Second, their international partners neither shared nor understood Germany's determination to place humanitarian values above the norm of nonintervention in 1991. Third, a devotion to international norms cannot yet serve as a guide to foreign policy making because the norms of nonintervention and human rights are inherently contradictory and because the international community has turned the norm of nonintervention into a convenient excuse for its unwillingness to get involved in complicated "civil wars." Fourth, until Germany is in the position to back up political intervention with military intervention, it must follow, and not attempt to lead, the United States, France, and the United Kingdom in future interventions.

Libal sums up the frustrating experience of German foreign policy makers with this crisis: "Even the most profound analytical perspicacity and the most justified and well-intentioned moral rhetoric are in themselves not sufficient to provide strength and persuasiveness to a foreign policy, especially when it lacks conviction in other parts of the international community" (1997, 164). Hopefully, the international community has recognized the extent to which the misplaced faith in Yugoslavia's territorial integrity in 1991 only served to multiply the suffering on all sides of the conflict. The fact that in 1991 the international community sat back and, although filled with moral outrage over the events in Yugoslavia, felt that it was an "internal Yugoslav matter" adds much weight to Hoffmann's plea: "Every opportunity for a morally justified intervention—whether it is created by the media or by atrocities that shake the public out of its complacency . . . needs to be seized and pushed as far as it can be so that the gap between what we *ought* to do and what is politically feasible will narrow" (1995–96, 49).

PART V

GLOBAL JUSTICE

11

Global Distributive Justice

Peter Jones

The application of ideas of distributive justice to a society's internal arrangements has a pedigree stretching back at least as far as the ancient world. The application of ideas of distributive justice to the international world has a much more recent and less secure history. One reason for the relatively late emergence of ideas of global distributive justice is that it is only recently that we have been in a position to trouble ourselves about the global distribution of resources. Before the development of modern technologies, including modern systems for gathering information, proposals that we should assess the distribution of resources across humanity and refashion that distribution according to a conception of justice would not have been practicable. Even now, our political structures are not well suited to treating humanity as a single all-encompassing unit of distribution. Another reason is that questions about how justly resources are distributed across humanity have been prompted by radical economic inequalities between societies, and those radical inequalities have developed only during the last two centuries. Before the Industrial Revolution, some societies would have been wealthier than others, but economic inequalities between societies would not have been of the magnitude to which we are now accustomed and would have been less conspicuous than inequalities within societies (Brown 1992, 155–58).

In addition to these historical factors, however, the very idea of global distributive justice is still far from widely accepted. Many people resist attempts to extend ideas of distributive justice to the international domain. The human race has always been divided into separate political units of one sort or another. For the most part, those units are now semiautonomous states, and many people take the view that, as long as humanity remains so divided, just distribution is something that should go on within states rather than between them. Of course, not everyone accepts even that; some libertarians argue that it is a mistake, even within the bounds of a state, to subject the spread of resources across a population to a test of distributive justice (e.g., Hayek 1976). But many of those who do not share that libertarian view are still unwilling to extend the idea of distributive justice beyond the bounds of the state.

THEORIES OF GLOBAL DISTRIBUTIVE JUSTICE

Why, then, should we not be content with that common state-centric view? Perhaps the most powerful thought that leads people to propose global principles of distributive justice is also the most simple. If we believe that resources should be distributed justly within societies, how can we not also believe that they should be distributed justly among societies? It seems odd that our concern for distributive justice should come to an abrupt halt when we reach the borders of a state. In particular, how can those who strive for greater equality within societies remain indifferent to inequalities among societies? What satisfaction can they derive from a world in which people are reasonably equal in relation to their fellow citizens but radically unequal in relation to the citizens of other societies? In fact, there are justifications that might be offered for allowing the borders of states to set the boundaries of distributive justice, and we shall consider those later, but those defenses run counter to the powerful thought that people are human beings first and foremost and that it is across humanity as a whole that we should secure distributive justice.

Natural resources are particularly susceptible to the claims of global justice (Barry 1991, 196–200; Beitz 1979b, 136–43; Pogge 1989, 250–52, 264–65; Richards 1982, 287–93). Natural resources are resources that are made available by nature; no one creates them and no one deserves them. Who then has a claim to them? Prima facie, it would seem that we all do; no one can reasonably claim to come into the world with a greater entitlement to the bounties of nature than anyone else. Nature has spread its resources unevenly across the globe, but, morally, that uneven distribution is a matter of mere chance and should be of no significance. The geographical distribution of natural resources is, to use Rawls's phrase, "arbitrary from a moral point of view" (1971, 72). It would seem indefensible, therefore, that access to those resources, or to the benefits that flow from them, should be limited to those who happen to be standing on them or near them. That principle of distribution would mean that, merely by the accident of their birth, some people would find themselves hugely favored and others hugely disadvantaged. Yet that is effectively how we distribute natural resources across mankind at the moment. In allowing each state an exclusive right to the natural resources that fall within its territory, we allow some people to benefit far more than others from the gifts of nature. A just approach to the allocation of natural resources would try to find some way in which their value could be spread more evenly across mankind.

Differences in their endowments of natural resources go some way, but only a limited way, toward explaining why some societies are wealthier than others. They explain why Kuwait is richer than Mali but not why Japan is richer than Nigeria. Much, and frequently more, depends on the humanly created circumstances that societies inherit. Some of those theorists who argue that we should treat natural resources as goods to which all human beings are, prima facie, equally entitled argue that we should view the legacies of the human past in the same way (Barry 1991, 199–200; Richards 1982, 290–93). Whether people find themselves heirs to goods such as "productive capital, good systems of communication, orderly administration, well-developed systems of education" (Barry 1991, 199), and the like is as much an accident of birth as whether they find themselves members of societies that are rich or poor in natural resources. The same is true of the knowledge, skills, and technologies that we inherit from the past. That being so, we might treat the current distribution of these more or less fortunate legacies across mankind as no less fortuitous than the geographical distribution of natural resources. That, in turn, implies that we should try to find some way in which the benefits of those legacies might be spread fairly across all humanity. People's economic well-being should not be determined by their ancestry.

Theorists who challenge the existing global distribution of resources in these ways often turn to the conceptual apparatus developed by John Rawls (1971) to make their case (Amdur 1977; Beitz 1979b; Brewin 1978; Pogge 1989; Richards 1982). Suppose that we accept that all human beings have equal moral standing and that all stand in a contingent relation to the resources that are made available by nature and the human past. How can we work out what would be a fair distribution of those resources across mankind? We might do so by turning to a global version of Rawls's "original position." That entails a thought experiment in which we imagine that all of the world's populations have to agree on the principles that are to govern the distribution of resources among themselves. However, they have to reach that agreement behind a "veil of ignorance" that prevents their knowing whether they have been born into resource-rich or resource-poor societies. After they have reached their agreement and the veil of ignorance has been lifted, individuals might discover that they are citizens of the United States, Switzerland, or Dubai, but they might also discover that they are citizens of the Philippines, Botswana, or Bangladesh.

What would people agree to under these conditions of uncertainty? There has been much controversy over whether the principles that would emerge from Rawls's domestic version of his original position would really be those that Rawls himself derives from it. However, those who have proposed an international version of Rawls's original position have generally agreed that it would issue in a global version of his "difference principle": resources should be distributed equally across mankind unless an unequal distribution would work to the general advantage, particularly the advantage of the least well-off group. So there would be a general presumption that each human being has an equal claim to the world's resources, and departures from that presumption would be tolerated only insofar as inequalities would have the effect of improving the economic condition of mankind generally, particularly its worst-off section.

This focus on resources that current human beings confront as "givens" derives from the thought that social arrangements are unjust if they prejudice people's lot in life because of features of their situation for which they themselves are not responsible. But what about goods that are produced by the current generation of human beings? Should they be subject to a global difference principle? Rawls himself regards political societies as cooperative schemes in which individuals join together for their mutual advantage, including their mutual economic advantage. The fruits of a society's cooperation are to be distributed justly among its cooperators, and that, for Rawls, means that the society's economic arrangements should be governed by the difference principle. Charles Beitz has argued that we should extend this way of thinking to the world as a whole (1979b, 143–53). International economic interdependence is now so great that it warrants our treating all of humanity as a single cooperative community across which the fruits of international cooperation should be distributed justly, that is, according to a global difference principle. However, this argument has not found favor among many who are otherwise sympathetic to the idea of international distributive justice (e.g., Barry 1991, 170–77, 193–95; Nielsen 1984; Richards 1982, 288–90). The extent of economic interdependence is uneven, trade is not the same as cooperation, and mutual advantage is arguably not a prerequisite of just relations. Beitz himself has come to accept that the case for global distributive justice should not depend on claims about international economic cooperation (1983, 595). Nevertheless, the more the world moves in the direction of a single globalized community, the less persuasive is a sharp distinction between principles that apply within states and principles that apply beyond them.

JUSTICE AMONG WHOM?

Who are the proper subjects of global distributive justice? Among whom should we be just? Generally, theorists who subscribe to the ideas of global justice that I have been describing answer, "individual persons." Indeed, there is a natural association of ideas here. If we believe that, in the international no less than in the intranational domain, individual human persons are the ultimate units of moral standing and that states have no moral standing that is not finally reducible to the standing of their individual members, we shall be more inclined to take a global view of justice. State boundaries will have no moral significance, or only contingent moral significance, and that removes a possible obstacle to our adopting a global approach to justice. This sort of cosmopolitan view need not ignore the existence of states; given the political make-up of our world, cosmopolitans often feel obliged to look to states to play an instrumental role in bringing about global justice. But, even if they give states that role, cosmopolitans still regard the just distribution for which we should strive as a distribution among individuals.

Formally, however, there is no reason why we should not regard states as the proper subjects of global distributive justice. Indeed, some who adopt a Rawlsian approach to international justice take that view and so regard states as the parties that should be represented in the original position and be governed by the difference principle (e.g., Brewin 1978). Rawls (1971, 377–79; 1993a) himself treats states, or "peoples" understood as corporate entities, as the ultimate units of standing in the international domain, although he refrains from subjecting the international society of states to any principle of distributive justice (see Jones 1996). There is also good reason, as Gerald Elfstrom argues (in this volume), to treat other sorts of corporate entity, such as multinational corporations, as bearers of rights and obligations in the international domain, although, in what follows, I shall focus only on states.

If we treat states rather than individuals as the subjects of global justice, it makes a considerable difference. We shall then be concerned with how resources are distributed among states rather than within them, and the justice of an international distribution will be quite independent of the way in which states deploy their resources. Resources might, for example, be redistributed from rich states to poor states only to end up in the hands of the most privileged sections of poor states. It is this absence of concern with the internal arrangements of states that leads many theorists to reject a state-centric approach to distributive justice and some governments to favor it (Hoffman 1981, 144–47).

Another reason why many theorists refuse to recognize states as the subjects of distributive justice is a simple reluctance to accept that states, like persons, can be moral subjects in their own right. If we share that view, must we deny that a political community can make collective claims of any sort? Not necessarily. Instead of conceiving the claims of a political community as the claims of a corporate entity, we might think of them as claims that the members of a community hold jointly rather than severally. In that way, we can acknowledge the possibility of collective claims while still holding that the bearers of those claims are the individuals who make up the political community rather than their state conceived as a corporate entity that has some sort of moral existence independent of them. That is particularly important if we want to bring public goods within the compass of justice—goods that, because of their public nature, cannot be disaggregated into the separate entitlements of separate individuals. For example, during the last thirty years there has been much talk of a "right to development." If there is such a right, it can hardly be an individual right because development is meant to enhance the infrastructure and general economic condition of an entire society. The right to development really makes sense only as a group right. But we can still think of that group right as a collective right held jointly by the citizens of a developing society rather than as a corporate right held by a state (Jones 2000).

THE MORAL RELEVANCE OF POLITICAL BOUNDARIES

Theories of global distributive justice frequently confront us with a simple conflict between the world as it ought to be and the world as it is. On the one hand, we have theories that demand a radical redistribution of resources across humanity and that frequently ask us to give no moral weight at all to state boundaries; on the other hand, we have the actual world of states whose conduct is driven by an amoral realism and a selfishness that makes them impervious to the claims of justice. However, not everyone sees the world in that way. Some philosophers, as well as some politicians, argue that, far from being morally irrelevant, the division of humanity into separate political communities is of primary moral significance, so much so that we should reject attempts to extend the idea of distributive justice beyond state boundaries.

We have already encountered one reason why Rawls himself refuses to extend his difference principle to the international domain. Because he conceives a political society as "a cooperative venture for mutual advantage" (1971, 4), he holds that only the participants in that venture have a just claim to the fruits of their cooperation. A principle that distributes those fruits to the members of other societies would be unjust because it would take resources from those who were entitled to them and give them to those who were not. Rawls does not mean to deny the existence of an international economy. He makes clear that his conception of political societies as "closed" is a simplifying assumption that eases the development of his theory rather than a true description of our world (1993b, 12). But presumably he still thinks it sufficiently true to play some part in explaining why we should apply the difference principle within states but not across them. Even so, his appeal to the morality of social cooperation relates only to the fruits of cooperation. It does nothing to counter claims that the current distribution of natural and inherited resources among societies is morally arbitrary and in need of radical adjustment if it is to be just. Rawls's reluctance to acknowledge that claim seems to derive from a conventionalism at the heart of his thinking which makes him unwilling to challenge well-entrenched and widely accepted orthodoxies.

That conventionalism relates to another justification Rawls gives for not extending his difference principle beyond state boundaries: the fact of international cultural diversity (1993a). The so-called later or new Rawls derives his liberal principles of justice from ideas implicit in the public culture of liberal democratic societies (1993b, 13–15). He intends those principles to apply only to societies that are already committed to the liberal democratic public culture from which they derive. It would be quite wrong, Rawls believes, for liberal societies to impose their cultures, and the principles of justice grounded in them, on nonliberal societies. Well-ordered nonliberal societies have their own principles of justice grounded in their own cultures, and their nonliberal principles of justice are no less "just" and worthy of respect than liberal principles. The difference principle is, he suggests, a liberal principle (1993a, 75–76); its global application would, therefore, mean that liberal societies were imposing their culture on nonliberal societies. That would be an act of international injustice directly analogous to the injustice that occurs within a liberal society when some citizens use political power to impose their controversial beliefs on other citizens. Thus, if we were to extend the difference principle to the international domain, we would treat unjustly both people cooperating together in liberal societies and people belonging to nonliberal societies who would experience the difference principle as an alien imposition.

Michael Walzer (1983; 1994) and Terry Nardin (1983, especially 23–24, 109–12, 260–71) also regard cultural diversity and the different and conflicting conceptions of justice associated with it as conclusive reasons for not adopting a global conception of distributive justice, although Nardin is less concerned to defer to cultures as such than to safeguard "international society" from the disintegrative effect of attempts to commit it to the pursuit of controversial ends. Appeals to cultural diversity often claim to be motivated by concern and respect for the cultures of non-Western societies. But when those appeals provide obstacles to transfers from First World to Third World societies, we may reasonably wonder whether they are not calculated more to protect the First World from the Third than the Third World from the First.

A related but distinct argument appeals to the idea of national self-determination. The doctrine that each people has a right, and an equal right, to be self-determining is now very widely accepted. But if a people claims that right, it must bear the consequences that go with it. We would not think it reasonable for an individual to insist that he must enjoy freedom unrestrained by others while also demanding that others must come to his aid whenever he finds he has made an unwise use of that freedom. He cannot reasonably demand untrammeled freedom but also a right that others shall pick up the bill for his use of that freedom. Similarly, if a people insists on its right to autonomy, it must live with the consequences of its use of that right. If two self-determining peoples opt to pursue different economic policies, one successful, the other unsuccessful, the unsuccessful people cannot insist that, as a matter of justice, the costs of their unwise decision must be borne by the successful people. Justice requires us not merely to compare peoples' conditions but also to consider how their conditions have come about.

This argument has some force but considerably less in practice than in principle. First, in reality, societies are not sealed units whose fates are entirely in their own hands. Second, the analogy between self-determining peoples and self-determining individuals cannot be drawn too simply. For one thing, those who decide on the course of economic policy are usually governments rather than peoples, and governments can be unrepresentative of, or endorsed by only a section of, their populations. For another, we should consider whether we should punish children for the sins of their parents. If generation X decides unwisely, should generation Y have to endure the consequences? A world of genuinely self-determining peoples would be one in which peoples would have only limited responsibility for one another's condition; but our world is one in which populations have created their own economic circumstances only in very limited measure. If we appeal too simple-mindedly to the idea of self-determination, we risk treating victims as culprits.

Perhaps the most frequently given reason for containing distributive justice within political boundaries is that the members of a political community stand in a special moral relation with one another. As members of the same community they have rights and obligations with respect to one another that they do not have with respect to humanity at large. In its weakest form, this claim might appeal only to the fact of statehood as an adventitious feature of our world. The human race could be organized for political purposes differently from the way it is at present; it has been in the past, and it probably will be again in the future. But as long as humanity remains divided into more or less independent states, it is idle and unreasonable to hold that this should make no difference to people's rights and responsibilities.

In its stronger forms, the claim protests against abstract universalist moralities and insists that human beings are necessarily embedded in particular communities and that, morally, they must function as members of particular communities (Sandel 1982; Walzer 1983; 1994). The containment of distributive justice within "bounded communities" reflects not the mean-spiritedness of the human race but its proper moral condition. One version of this communitarian view holds that humanity is divided into nations that have more than merely political identities and constitute ethical communities whose members are tied to one another morally as well as sociologically and culturally. Indeed, Miller suggests that a substantial conception of social justice will take hold only among populations that think of themselves as a nation and as, therefore, having special obligations to one another; that is one of a number of reasons he gives for trying to match the boundaries of states with those of nations (1995, 83–85, 91–98).

This issue is much larger than the issue of distributive justice, and I cannot examine it properly here (for a range of views, see Cohen 1996). Nor is it an issue that is easily settled by argument. However, we need not accept that we are faced with a simple and exclusive choice between either our co-nationals or humanity at large as the proper objects of our moral concern. Even if we have special obligations to our fellow citizens, we can still have some obligations to human beings in general. Moreover, the question of where we should locate the dividing line between those two sets of obligations gives rise to a spectrum of possible answers: we can fix it so that special obligations are many and general obligations few, but we can also set it differently so that the balance between special and general obligations shifts in favor of the latter. Thus, even if we accept that political communities give rise to special obligations that should, in turn, affect the way we think about distributive justice, we can still insist that people have some obligations to one another merely as fellow human beings and that the spread of resources across humanity is not entirely beyond the reach of distributive justice.

HUMAN RIGHTS AND BASIC NEEDS

Their readiness to recognize special moral ties and to give significance to the separateness of political communities leads some people to present more modest ideas of global distributive justice than those we have considered so far. At its fullest, the idea of global distributive justice implies that we should make the totality of the world's income and wealth our concern, subject it in its entirety to a test of distributive justice, and reapportion it as justice dictates. However, critics of the existing spread of resources across humanity frequently have less comprehensive ambitions. Often they are concerned less to reshape the entire global pattern of resource holdings than to secure for everyone a certain minimum of economic well-being. In other words, they are concerned not to prescribe how the entire global cake should be sliced but to insist only that everyone should have an adequate slice. This more limited ambition of securing a basic minimum of well-being for all is implicit in approaches that focus on "basic needs" and the elimination of world poverty.

Whereas ambitious theories of global justice can seem a million miles from what, for the foreseeable future, is likely to happen in our world, the more modest goal of meeting people's basic needs may seem less utopian. Indeed, it is a goal to which the world would seem already committed. The U.N. Universal Declaration of Human Rights (1948) proclaims that each human being has rights to a variety of socioeconomic goods including rights to food, clothing, housing and medical care; to education and social security; and to whatever other economic, social, and cultural goods are "indispensable for his dignity and the free development of his personality" (Articles 22–27, in Brownlie 1992, 25–26). The U.N. International Covenant on Economic, Social, and Cultural Rights (1966) goes on to elaborate these rights in greater detail. However, these bold assertions of right are less global in intention than they might seem. They are typically made against a background assumption that individuals' socioeconomic rights are rights that they hold against the political communities of which they are citizens rather than against the world at large. Given that assumption, we may wonder whether they are properly described as "human" rights at all, as opposed to local rights that individuals hold only as members of the particular societies to which they belong (Cranston 1973).

Can there be genuinely universal rights that yield only local obligations? Cosmopolitans sometimes suggest that the division of humanity into states has a certain utility in that it facilitates a division of moral labor. Universal rights may yield universal duties, but, in practice, those universal duties can be more effectively discharged if humanity divides itself into separate societies and assigns each society responsibility for providing for the universal rights of its own members (Goodin 1988). For practical purposes, therefore, we can translate the universal duties of mankind into the particular duties of citizens. That proposal is not without merit, but, in the case of socioeconomic rights, it encounters an obvious objection. If some societies are wealthier than others, some will be better placed than others to provide for the socioeconomic needs of their citizens. The current division of the world into states cannot pretend to be merely a division of moral labor; it is also a division of humanity into unequal resource holders, so that the socioeconomic rights that a society collectively can deliver to its members severally will be radically different if the society is Norway or Canada rather than India or Malawi. Under these circumstances, it is simply fraudulent to pass off the different welfare rights enjoyed by people in different societies as merely different local instantiations of the same set of human rights.

The idea that all human beings possess the same rights to certain social and economic goods is consistent with some variation in local provision. Different climates make for different housing needs, differences in the geographical spread of disease require differences in medical provision, and cultural differences legitimate differences in the education that societies provide for their children. But these differences do little or nothing to justify the inequalities of provision that characterize our world. Sometimes the value of a good is relative to the society in which it is held (Goodin 1990; Weale 1983, 35–38, 76–91). If, for example, social security provision is to enable individuals in America and individuals in Pakistan each to function at equivalent levels as members of their own societies, an American will need to receive a more generously resourced form of social security than a Pakistani. In the same way, Americans might be alleged to need more and better education than Pakistanis if education is to have the same value for Americans and Pakistanis as members of their respective societies. But to argue that is, of course, to accept a background of inequality and to adjust people's entitlements to that inequality rather than to challenge the difference in economic condition of the two societies. Moreover, not every good can be relativized in that way. It would be quite implausible to hold, for example, that differences in the quantity and quality of medical care that First World and Third World societies can provide for their citizens are of no consequence because the badness of bad health is diminished several times over for people who live in poor societies.

The interpretation of individuals' rights to socioeconomic goods as rights that should be met only from the pool of resources held by their own society is really a triumph of statism over cosmopolitanism. The United Nations is an organization of states, and it is unsurprising that it is unwilling to go very far in compromising the traditional rights of states, particularly the rights of states over their "own" resources. The first Article of the International Covenant on Economic, Social, and Cultural Rights asserts that "all peoples may, for their own ends, freely dispose of their natural wealth and resources without prejudice to any obligations arising out of international economic cooperation" (1966). Article 11 does commit the state parties, "recognizing the fundamental right of everyone to be free from hunger," to taking measures "to ensure an equitable distribution of world food supplies in relation to need" (Brownlie 1992, 114, 118). But Article 25 provides that "nothing in the present Covenant shall be interpreted as impairing the inherent right of all peoples to enjoy and utilize fully and freely their natural wealth and resources" (Brownlie 1992, 122). It would seem then that, for the United Nations, the property rights of states or "peoples" trump the needs of individuals. Pressure for formal recognition of the sovereign rights of states over resources within their own territories came from Third World states who were reacting to their experiences of colonialism; ironically, it is people in those states who stand to lose most from a system that locks resources into states.

If we take seriously the idea of human rights and if we link it to the idea of basic human needs, needs-based human rights will be the same for everyone, and the obligations they impose will be uninhibited by state boundaries (Jones 1994, 157–69). It makes no sense to suppose that the human rights of people suddenly diminish in content if those people happen to live in, say, India or Pakistan rather than America or Canada. So, if we take humanity as our canvas and if we give priority to meeting basic needs, we should do so in a truly cosmopolitan spirit that treats people's needs-based rights as genuinely global entitlements. If those entitlements can be met adequately for all human beings through the state system, there need be no objection to providing for them in that way. But if some societies lack the resources necessary to respond to the human rights of their members, the populations of other societies should not be able to dismiss that shortfall as no concern of theirs.

If we work with the idea of every human being having a right to a basic minimum, how do we establish what that minimum should be? One strategy, proposed by Henry Shue (1980), is that we should identify a set of rights that are "basic" in that their possession is essential for the enjoyment of all other rights. Shue argues that basic rights, so understood, must include a right to subsistence, as well as rights to security and certain kinds of liberty, and that the global duties imposed by everyone's right to subsistence include a duty not to deprive others of their means of subsistence and, for the affluent, a duty to aid those who are without subsistence.

More commonly, people turn to the concept of "need" to establish a global minimum (e.g., Doyal and Gough 1991; Vincent 1986). Taken on its own, that concept is insufficiently discriminating to do the job. In its ordinary use, need is an instrumental notion that implies some purpose beyond itself. When someone asserts that they need something, we can always ask, "What for?" and our response to their claim of need will depend on the answer they give. Thus, someone might say, "I need water—to survive," but also, "I need water—to fill my swimming pool"; or, "I need clothing—to avoid death from exposure," but also, "I need a new suit—to look my fashionable best." That is why we have to discriminate among needs if we are to use them to establish universal human entitlements. Hence we have the idea of "basic human needs."

But what makes some needs "human" and "basic"? One answer is that they encompass what human beings must have if they are to survive. So, for example, we can identify food, water, and breathable air as basic human needs. But people are often reluctant to restrict the idea of basic need to mere survival. After all, people can survive even if they live in grinding poverty. A less parsimonious conception of basic need would relate it to a condition such as human flourishing or human well-being. There is certainly scope for identifying needs that are common to human beings if they are to flourish and enjoy well-being. But flourishing and well-being are, of course, much more open-ended in what they might require than mere survival and, therefore, yield much less determinate notions of need. They also make the idea of basic need potentially more controversial. We may agree, for example, that by a test of human flourishing housing and education must qualify as basic needs, but just what quantity and quality of living space and education should count as basic?

In truth, our idea of a basic minimum to which all human beings are entitled is more likely to be driven by a conception of the minimum quality of life that everyone should be able to enjoy, given the resources that are available and the strategies that are possible in our world, than by a fixed set of absolute and unchanging human needs. And it is not merely that we may want to set that minimum somewhere above what is strictly necessary if human beings are to survive. Survival itself may sometimes require more than people can reasonably demand as of right, as is evident from the vast expenditure that might be devoted to medical technology.

JUSTICE OR HUMANITY?

I have previously indicated that the idea of securing a minimum level of well-being for all of the world's population is rather different from that of applying an idea of distributive justice to the world's resources as a whole. That is why some of those who reject the general idea of global distributive justice nevertheless allow that there can be international obligations to relieve people from poverty and starvation (e.g., Rawls 1993a). Indeed, even though the language of justice is often associated with that of rights, the morality that underpins this commitment to a minimum level of well-being for all might be better characterized as a morality of humanity than as one of distributive justice. It derives not from an idea of fair shares but from a conviction that human beings owe one another a basic concern and respect that, in turn, obliges them to assist one another if their material circumstances slip below a certain level.

People are often reluctant to exchange the language of justice for the language of humanity because they believe that duties grounded in humanity must be weaker than those grounded in justice. For example, people often suppose that we ought to provide humanitarian aid, but that "ought" falls somewhere short of strict obligation. But there is no reason why duties of humanity should be any less imperative than duties of justice (Campbell 1974). Certainly, if we subject the question of meeting people's basic needs to the test of a Rawlsian original position, it is highly plausible that the parties in that position would agree on strict rights and duties of mutual aid, particularly in cases in which the benefit for the aided was substantial and cost to the aider relatively slight (Richards 1982, 282–87).

Nor need a duty of humanity have a less demanding content than a duty of justice. In a celebrated essay, Peter Singer argues that people in affluent societies are duty bound to relieve suffering and to prevent death in famine-stricken societies (1972). He does so by invoking an analogy with the duty of a passer-by to rescue a drowning child from a shallow pond, even though, in wading in and saving the child, the passer-by would incur the minor cost of muddied clothes. The principle that links the two cases for Singer is the following: "if it is in our power to prevent something bad from happening, without thereby sacrificing anything of comparable moral importance, we ought, morally, to do it" (1972, 231). The cost to affluent societies of relieving famine in poor societies is relatively slight compared with the benefit to be gained by those suffering from famine; people in affluent societies should therefore regard themselves as duty bound to provide that relief. Singer goes on, however, to subscribe to a much stronger principle: "that we ought to give until we reach the level of marginal utility—that is, the level at which, by giving more, I would cause as much suffering to myself or my dependents as I would relieve by my gift" (1972, 241). That stronger principle requires affluent societies not merely to attend to the basic needs of people in poor societies but to go on transferring resources to them until the relative conditions of donor and recipient come close to equality.

Singer subscribes to this strong principle because he is an uncompromising utilitarian who holds that resources should be distributed, or redistributed, in whatever way will maximize the aggregate well-being of humanity. Any prescription based in utilitarianism must be highly contingent on an empirical assessment of which course of action will, in fact, maximize human utility. Others of a consequentialist cast of mind have made empirical assessments different from Singer's and so have proposed strategies fundamentally opposed to his. Neo-Malthusians, in particular, have suggested that Third World poverty results from overpopulation and that international relief of poverty will only exacerbate that problem, so making matters worse for humanity in the long run (e.g., Hardin 1995). Hence, working from the same sort of moral premises as Singer, they oppose international redistribution in the very circumstances in which he believes it to be most urgent.

The idea of basic needs does not have the significance for maximizing utilitarians that it has for rights theorists who need some way of giving content to the rights they ascribe to human beings and also some way of limiting the demands they can make on one another (Fishkin 1986). But some who appeal to the idea of basic needs and make these the objects of strong international obligations do so while dispensing with rights and utilitarianism as well. According to Onora O'Neill (1986; 1988), one problem with a rights approach to world poverty is that any particular person cannot be said to hold his or her needs-based right against any particular other (see also McKinsey 1981). But if a person's right does not clearly ground another's duty, its status as a right becomes very doubtful. Hence, O'Neill herself suggests that we should make obligation rather than rights the primary moral concept when we approach issues such as world hunger. We can be obligated to contribute to the relief of hunger and poverty even though the obligation of any particular person is not owed to any particular other. Moral philosophers describe this sort of obligation to unassigned others as "imperfect obligation," but the adjective *imperfect* indicates only that it is an obligation that is not owed to a specific other; it does not imply that it is somehow defective or any less imperative than a perfect obligation. Hence, O'Neill, in dispensing with claims of right and replacing them with obligations of beneficence, does not in any way relax the moral demands that world hunger makes on the affluent. The imperfect obligation to meet people's basic needs remains a strict and morally enforceable obligation.

Finally, we must note the possibility that the morality of international transfers can be located within the realm of supererogation. Supererogatory acts are acts that are good to do but not wrong not to do; they are acts that exceed the demands of duty. On this understanding of the morality of international transfers, rich societies, if they assist poor societies, do so as matters of charity rather than justice or strict obligation. Poor societies have no right to receive resources from rich societies, and rich societies have no duty, strictly speaking, to transfer resources to poor societies, even though there may be moral merit in their doing so. Many people, including both politicians and ordinary citizens, are inclined to think of international transfers in this way. Even if they applaud "overseas aid," they associate it with the morality of giving; they think of that aid as a gift—perhaps a gift that their society "ought" to make but a gift nonetheless—rather than as something that answers to the demands of right, duty, or justice.

If we do place international transfers within the realm of supererogation, it becomes open to question whether states should be involved with these at all. If transfers to other societies do not form part of the duties of a body of citizens but, rather, are merely matters of discretionary virtue, those citizens can reasonably object to their governments using taxation to compel them to make those transfers. Arguably, supererogatory international transfers should derive only from the voluntary contributions of private individuals and private associations and not from compulsory contributions exacted by governments.

CONCLUSION

There is, then, a wide range of positions that we might occupy in relation to global distributive justice. Its strongest advocates urge us to give no significance to state boundaries or other ways in which humanity might be divided and to apply the idea of distributive justice equally to all of the world's population and to all of the resources available to that population. Its strongest opponents urge us to give primacy to people's membership in particular communities and to resist proposals that we should extend conceptions of distributive justice beyond those communities. Among those sympathetic to the idea of global distributive justice, some treat individual persons as its ultimate subjects, and others regard states or peoples as those subjects. Some aim to fashion the entirety of the world's income and wealth according to a principle of distributive justice, whereas others aim only to secure a minimum of well-being for all so that their basic needs are met and their basic human rights are honored. Even if we dispense with the idea of global distributive justice, the value of humanity may still provide us with reason to be concerned about the material condition of the world's population. The value of humanity may itself be interpreted differently: either as a source of obligations, perfect or imperfect, that are every bit as strict as obligations of justice or as a source of "oughts" that have a less imperative character.

I began this chapter by observing that the idea of international distributive justice is a relatively recent one historically and that it has still to gain widespread acceptance. As the demise of the 1970s vision of a New International Economic Order illustrates (see Cason, this volume), it is an idea whose progress remains uncertain. One of many practical obstacles that theorists of global distributive justice confront in making a reality of their theories is that the world is not currently structured in a way that matches their view that, morally, humanity constitutes a single unit of distributive justice. There are some supranational organizations such as the United Nations, the European Union, and the Organization of African Unity, but those organizations remain very much creatures of their member states, and states remain the dominant political units of our world. In principle, states and their governments might function as instruments of global redistribution, but in practice they are likely to have greater effect as obstacles to that redistribution. Ideas of global distributive justice may play some part in gradually eroding the state system, but, as long as that system remains institutionally unmodified, it is hard to believe that theories of global distributive justice will be realized in any but very limited and imperfect ways.

NOTE

I wrote this chapter during my tenure of a Nuffield Social Science Research Fellowship. I am grateful to the foundation for its support.

12

The Ethical Responsibilities of Multinational Corporations: The Case of the North American Aluminum Companies in Jamaica

Gerard Elfstrom

Since gaining independence from Great Britain in 1962, Jamaica has been among the western hemisphere's poorest and least developed nations. Bauxite is among its few economically significant natural resources and has been mined since the early 1950s. By 1962, all four of the major North American aluminum companies were active in Jamaica. Though these enterprises profited handsomely from their activities, Jamaicans received relatively little economic benefit. In the early 1970s, the Jamaican government headed by Michael Manley made determined efforts to wrest increased control of Jamaica's bauxite and greater profit from its exploitation. Though they initially seemed disposed to cooperate with Manley's efforts, the companies soon reduced bauxite production in Jamaica, closed some of their Jamaican operations, and shifted their investment and production elsewhere (Edie 1991, 93–96; Manley 1987, 15–40).

THE ISSUE

This case touches a number of contentious issues, but I wish to focus on just one, that of whether the aluminum corporations had a moral obligation to adopt policies designed to assist the economic development of an impoverished nation. However, stated in this way, the question is entirely too sweeping. It requires greater refinement before it can usefully be examined. First, we need to consider the question of just how great a sacrifice the companies should be expected to

185

shoulder. For example, are they obligated to help only insofar as this can be done without sacrificing profits? Should they assist to the degree that corporate viability is weakened? Are they obligated to sacrifice some profits, though not to the extent that the corporation is imperiled? Second, we need specification of the ways in which they should seek to be of assistance. Are corporations obligated to devise workable programs of economic development for nations lacking either the resources or motivation to do so? Are they expected to combat local governments that impede a nation's economic advance by being corrupt or inept, or should they help local corporations improve their efficacy and enable them to compete more effectively? Should they make investment funds and economic expertise readily available to the local community in order to assist its development efforts? Or should corporations pursue the significantly more modest goals of vowing to pay their workers decent wages, offering them opportunity to improve their skills, and bringing further investment and technology into the country when it is feasible for them to do so?

To help focus discussion and begin to address the above questions, I will rely on several assumptions. First, nations, through the agency of their governments, must bear the largest burden of responsibility for improving the material welfare of their citizens. I believe this principle supports the inference that corporations, however wealthy and powerful, do not hold primary responsibility for any nation's economic progress, even when that nation is woefully underdeveloped. Second, I will assume that capitalism is morally defensible. This is a controversial presumption, but, without it, the case at hand is moot, for the corporations would have no moral claim to exist as capitalist enterprises. This assumption has important and nontrivial implications, for capitalism is a system in which business enterprises are devoted to the acquisition of profits as a fundamental goal. Further, under the capitalist system, business enterprises compete with one another for market dominance; the arena of commerce is, and is intended to be, a cockpit of corporate life-and-death struggle. From this set of assertions, I draw the further inference that, unless exceptional circumstances exist, corporations are not obligated to sacrifice profits to the extent that their viability is threatened, though the question of whether they need sacrifice any profits at all, and, if so, how large a portion, remains open to question.

In addition, I will presume that capitalism has brought considerable prosperity to a substantial portion of humanity; there is no convincing evidence that it is inferior to socialist systems in its ability to improve human beings' material welfare; and there is no convincing evidence that capitalist ventures violate human beings' rights more frequently or cause them greater harm than do alternative economic schemes. I believe that this set of assumptions supports the inferences that there is no compelling moral argument favoring socialist economies over capitalist and that the leaders of national governments have no general moral obligation to endorse socialist programs or seek to destroy capitalist ventures. The above does not support the inference that socialist systems are unjustified or less admirable than capitalist ones. These matters remain open to discussion.

Finally, I will presume that no agency, whether an individual human being, a government, or a corporation, can be obliged to endeavor to satisfy the entire array of human needs or address all the ills that beset human beings. No single human agency or institution has the power, the resources, or the expertise for these tasks. More crucially though, the attempt to right all wrongs and satisfy all needs would inevitably result in infringing the autonomy of some agent, whether an individual human being or a national government.

With the above presumptions in hand, I believe the core issue of this case study can be formulated as follows: Corporations cannot be expected to sacrifice profits, expertise, business acumen, and so on to the extent that their viability and continued profitability are threatened. However, it is an open question whether they are obligated to sacrifice any profits at all. Second, corporations do not bear the major responsibility for seeking the material advance of any nation or people, but, if they have some responsibility of this sort, they are obligated to work with the representatives of that nation to assist in its plans for economic improvement. Hence, the issue at hand is that of whether the aluminum corporations should be expected to sacrifice some resources to aid Jamaica and whether they should be willing to work with the Jamaican government to pursue its programs of material improvement.

BACKGROUND

Jamaica is blessed and cursed with a balmy tropical setting and ample deposits of bauxite, the ore from which aluminum is produced. For better or worse, agriculture, tourism, and bauxite extraction are the three pillars of its economy, though the latter pair generates the vast bulk of its foreign exchange income (Manley 1987, 30). This foreign exchange income is exceedingly important for Jamaica, for, as a small island nation, it must import the vast bulk of goods and materials its citizens need to sustain their lives (Hewan 1994, 67–69; Kirton 1992, 12–14). Nearly everything from basic foodstuffs, to construction materials, to machinery must come from abroad, and foreign exchange is required to pay for them. Tourism and bauxite extraction, however, depend on outsiders, whether they be travel agencies, airlines, and cruise ship operators and their dollars or the handful of gigantic aluminum companies that mine bauxite, process it into aluminum, and then bring it to market. Though tourism has contributed greater foreign earnings since 1983, bauxite was the more important source of foreign exchange income for Jamaica in the 1970s (U.S. Department of State 1996, 2). In that decade bauxite contributed 35 percent of Jamaica's foreign exchange earnings, attracted the lion's share of foreign direct investment, supplied the bulk of the island's supply of skilled and relatively remunerative jobs, and was a major avenue for the import of sophisticated technology and business expertise (O'Flaherty 1978, 144). As it happens, the world's aluminum industry is dominated by a few enormous multinational corporations. These enterprises, based in economically advanced and prosperous nations, are vertically integrated and control the global market for aluminum, a commercially valuable and militarily important product. Hence, a most promising domain of Jamaica's economy was dominated by powerful outside corporations (Hewan 1994, 26–31).

Jamaica is also blessed and cursed by its close proximity to the United States. ("So near the United States, so far from God," as a vivid phrase puts it.) U.S. markets and wealth are vital for Jamaica's prospects, but the U.S. government also believes that Jamaica's location puts it squarely within the domain of U.S. influence and zone of national security (Hewan 1994, 3–4, 71–74). Also, the United States considers aluminum to be essential for its economy and its military security. Furthermore, in the 1970s some 50 percent of the U.S. supply of bauxite came from Jamaica (Payne 1984, 29). As a result, it displayed an all-too-keen interest in Jamaica's economy, its politics, and Prime Minister Michael Manley's efforts to gain increased control over its bauxite resources (O'Flaherty 1978, 150–58).

Finally, Jamaica was blessed and cursed by Prime Minister Manley and his leadership (Keith and Keith 1992, xxi). Manley was a most engaging and mercurial leader. Enormously articulate and energetic, he aspired to improve the material status of his people by squeezing additional benefit from Jamaica's bauxite resources, and he also wished to ease Jamaica free from the dominating influence of the great aluminum corporations and the United States. In pursuit of these ends, Manley played an active role in creating the group of nonaligned nations, a loose structure designed to serve the twin goals of plotting a third way between the United States and the Soviet bloc and creating means for the world's poorer and less powerful nations to pool resources and energy so as to allow them to cope more effectively and strongly with powerful governments and vast multinational corporations (Edie 1991, 90–91; Keith and Keith 1992, 11–12; Manley 1987, 46–48; O'Flaherty 1978, 146–47). More directly, inspired by the success of the Organization of Petroleum Exporting Countries (OPEC), though dismayed by the consequences that its success in boosting the price of petroleum had on Jamaica's balance of foreign exchange, Manley worked to establish a consortium of bauxite-producing nations, the International Bauxite Association or IBA (Hewan 1994, 69–70). He hoped that the nations' pooled resources and cooperation would allow them to gain control over the bauxite market analogous to the dominance over the petroleum market that OPEC achieved in 1973 (Bradshaw 1978, 10; Payne 1984, 24).

Manley added further complexity to the equation when, in 1974, his political party (the Peoples' National Party) gave its formal endorsement to the principles of socialism, albeit a loosely formulated socialism (Hewan 1994, 62–64; Payne 1984, 30–31). He also stoked U.S. anxiety, and that of the aluminum corporations, by striking up a close and admiring relationship with Fidel Castro (Edie 1991, 91; Hewan 1994, 71; Marable 1993, 24; O'Flaherty 1978, 155–56; Payne 1984, 29–30). Hence, though Manley repeatedly stated that he bore no hostile intent against the aluminum corporations and that he firmly believed that private enterprise should coexist peacefully and profitably with his government, the U.S. government and the aluminum corporations had grounds for suspecting that his reassurances were disingenuous at best (Gardels 1992; Manley 1993, 153; Marable 1993, 24–26; Rohter 1997).

This anxiety was nurtured by several additional factors. First, as a leader of the nonaligned nations, Manley repeatedly stated that capitalist enterprise stood solidly in the way of poor nations' efforts to gain control of their fates (Manley 1987, 222–23, 235–36, 266–67; Mufuka 1978, 71, 88; Payne 1984, 39). Indeed, in that era he frequently expressed hostility toward capitalist endeavors, once asserting that capitalism must be dismantled "brick by brick" (Rohter 1997). Second, Manley nationalized several Jamaican firms and asserted that the "commanding heights" of the Jamaican economy should be under public control (Edie 1991, 101). He did not press for total control of the aluminum corporations at least partly because he believed the effort would not succeed (Hewan 1994, 47, 68). Indeed, these policies and others aroused the suspicions and hostility of Jamaica's business community, which soon came to oppose him (Edie 1991, 105–07).

In sum, Manley's efforts to deal with the aluminum corporations had several facets. First, he established a consortium of bauxite-producing nations to attempt to wrest control over the world market price of bauxite and gain a larger share of the proceeds for themselves. Also, he hoped that if the bauxite-producing nations grouped their resources into a common pool, they would be better situated to cope with the great wealth, resources, and political clout of the aluminum companies. Second, he labored to secure greater information about the aluminum companies' operations and the technology required for bauxite extraction and smelting. Last, he dealt directly with the aluminum companies. What he sought from them, and what he finally received, was relatively modest. He gained a boost in taxes paid on the bauxite and aluminum the corporations shipped out of the country. He also sought, and gained, 51 percent ownership of the companies' operations within Jamaica (Edie 1991, 93–96; Manley 1987, 50–54; Mufuka 1978, 72; Payne 1984, 27–28). With no particular enthusiasm, the companies agreed to Manley's conditions. However, they soon trimmed bauxite production in Jamaica, shifted production and investment elsewhere, and closed some of their operations.

In the sections following, I will examine a range of views about the moral responsibility of multinational corporations to assist the economic development of impoverished nations and explore the ways they can be applied to the case of the aluminum corporations in Jamaica.

LIMITED MORAL RESPONSIBILITY

Milton Friedman is a well-known proponent of the view that business enterprises have no moral responsibilities beyond the obligations to follow the wishes of their owners, which are generally to seek maximum profits, and to obey the law (1990, 153). He asserts that corporate executives are morally obliged to serve as the agents of owners and abuse their office if they seek different ends (1990, 154). Hence, were he to address the case at hand, Friedman would likely argue that the aluminum companies had absolutely no obligation to assist Jamaica's programs of economic development. In fact, he would likely insist that any efforts to aid Jamaica which imperiled profits would be a violation of the companies' fiduciary responsibilities to their owners.

However, Friedman does assert that corporations are obligated to obey laws (1990, 153). Possibly, then, he would endorse one facet of Manley's program: the effort to gain more information about the aluminum companies' local operations. Manley's hope was that, with this information in hand, his government would be able to examine and verify the companies' assertions about production, losses, investments, and so on and ensure that Jamaica could then garner its agreed share of corporate profits. Hence, even Friedman might agree that the companies should have been more forthcoming about the workings of their plants and given greater cooperation to Jamaica's efforts to control them.

However, Friedman would also likely insist on two things: first, that corporations are duty bound to seek maximal profits, because he believes this is the only goal stockholders will unanimously endorse, and, second, that capitalism only works for the welfare of all when corporate endeavors seek profits to the exclusion of all else. Hence, he likely would assert not merely that the aluminum companies had no obligation to assist Jamaica's development program but that they would have abrogated their fiduciary duties to their owners if they had sought to do so. I will examine these points in turn.

It seems incontrovertible that people who invest in corporate stocks expect that corporations will endeavor to provide a return on their investments. However, it is not obvious that shareholders or corporate executives believe that the corporations are, therefore, obliged to seek maximal profits for their shareholders. Friedman appears to believe, however, that this is the only goal all shareholders are likely to endorse (1990, 154–55). As a matter of fact, corporations generally do not follow this policy. That is, they rarely return all profits to their stockholders. Portions of their profits are commonly devoted to expansion, repaying debt, amassing cash reserves, and even buying back shares of stock to remove them from the market. If Friedman is to be taken at his word, these choices would be unjust if there is reason to believe that any stockholder would oppose them. However, policies that are not aimed at maximal profitability would likely all be defended by executives as sound business practice, justified by the need to ensure the long-term viability of the corporation.

Corporate leaders often assert that their obligation is to manage the enterprises in their charge in competent and professional fashions, and, in service of these ends, they occasionally oppose the wishes of stockholders. Moreover, corporations commonly dedicate considerable sums of cash to build corporate goodwill, gain political support, and even support charitable activities. Worse, they often spend more money on their employees than is strictly required for efficient corporate operation. Friedman might be willing to accept some of these practices on grounds that they may help secure maximal profitability over the long term. However, it is also the case that the virtuous life for human beings is commonly touted as the surest path to flourishing over the course of a lifetime, so the fact that moral practices may result in long-term viability need not imply that they are no longer genuinely grounded in moral aspiration.

Furthermore, Friedman's argument founders on its own fundamental premise, that corporate managers are morally obliged to follow policies that all stockholders, without exception, endorse. He claims that any other course of action will result in overriding the wishes of some shareholders. First, he is certainly well aware that stockholders rarely achieve complete agreement about corporate policies. Hence, the desires of at least some stockholders will be overridden nearly every time corporate policies are put to a vote. Second, there is little reason to suppose that stockholders value profits above all else and would be unwilling to sacrifice profits for the sake of other goals. So, on Friedman's own terms, there is little support for the view that corporate leaders are bound to seek profits and only profits.

However, if in fact corporations are not inevitably bound to seek maximal profits in each and every circumstance, another possibility emerges. It is possible that corporations may dedicate themselves to assisting the impoverished *simply* because they believe it is the morally decent thing to do. That is, they may wish to perform these good deeds simply because they benefit human beings rather than from the expectation of future benefit for the corporation.

Moreover, even if the above comments are inept, corporations have means to reformulate the terms of their fiduciary responsibilities. At shareholders' meetings, in financial reports, and in data made available to potential investors, corporate leaders are able to invite comment on policies dedicated to aiding the development of impoverished nations where they conduct operations.

Friedman's second assertion is that capitalism and capitalist endeavors flourish only when they devote themselves single-mindedly to maximal profits. However, it is not certain that corporations that devote themselves single-mindedly to profits are more likely to flourish and dominate their markets than those that are less single minded. This observation does not support the inference that profits should be unimportant to corporations. Rather, it gives credibility to the view that there are other factors to consider as well, and, on occasion, these factors may outweigh the devotion to profits. Hence, it appears that Friedman's arguments do

not preclude the aluminum corporations from adopting policies expressly designed to assist Jamaica's program of economic development.

FUNDAMENTAL RIGHTS

Thomas Donaldson is among the most influential and respected commentators on
the moral obligations of multinational corporations. He asserts that corporations
are morally bound to respect a fixed array of basic human rights, a moral bedrock,
but they have no moral obligations to their employees or their host nations beyond this commitment. He begins with a useful distinction between the moral
minimum and the moral maximum (1989, 62–64). The moral minimum is the
fundamental set of moral obligations, which no corporation is justified in ignoring. From Donaldson's perspective, the moral minimum for corporations consists
of upholding a set of ten basic human rights that all individual human beings
enjoy and which all moral agents, including governments and corporations, are
obligated to respect (1989, 81). Donaldson's moral maximum consists of a spectrum of heroic or saintly actions that are clearly worthy of admiration but cannot
be classed as moral obligations. A corporation that devotes a portion of its profits
to feeding and housing impoverished people may be lauded, but its acts are properly classed as part of the moral maximum, and, therefore, they cannot be considered obligatory. Depriving people of life, the means of life, or bodily security,
however, clearly falls well below the moral minimum for corporations and, therefore, cannot be justified. More crucially, Donaldson believes that a corporation
whose conduct drops below the minimum standard has lost its entitlement to
exist. So it may be stripped of its resources and dismantled if its actions result in
bodily harm to human beings (Donaldson 1989, 98).

As is implicit in the above paragraph, Donaldson argues that corporations have
a moral status that is significantly different from that of individual human beings
(1989, 84–85; 1994, 368–69). Corporations are properly classed as moral agents
and are, therefore, morally accountable for their actions and can be expected to
uphold an array of moral standards. However, they do not enjoy the inalienable
rights to life or well-being of individual human beings. Rather, they are artificial
creations, erected to serve human purposes and advance human welfare. Should
they fail to achieve the goals set by their human creators, or should their actions
fall below the moral minimum, they can be destroyed (Donaldson 1989, 98).
Though corporations' moral status does not match that of individual persons,
Donaldson believes that the set of duties constituting their moral minimum is also
narrower. For example, they lack the duties of loving care and concern for others
that are central features of the moral life of individuals. Once again, this narrow-
ness results from the fact that they are artificial creations devised to advance
human well-being.

Donaldson concludes that assisting impoverished nations is not part of the moral minimum corporations are obligated to uphold. Should they pledge themselves to do so, they have attained the moral maximum and may be applauded, but it would be mistaken to assert that they have a moral obligation to commit themselves to corporate moral saintliness.

Donaldson performs a genuine service by distinguishing between the moral minimum and the moral maximum. The insight that not all actions properly deemed morally laudable are also morally required is important. However, he apparently overlooks the possibility of an array of morally significant actions that range between the minimum and maximum. That is, there may be actions that corporations are morally obligated to perform which are not sufficiently obligatory that nonperformance will drop the corporations below the moral minimum. Certainly acts of this sort, those ranging between the moral minimum and the moral maximum, are an important domain of the moral lives of ordinary human beings. One is certainly morally obligated, for example, to repay the $5 one has borrowed from a colleague for lunch. Paying our debts is not morally optional. However, should we fail to do so, we have not committed a grievous moral wrong. Our moral lives do not continually veer from the saintly to the demonic and back. Rather, they mostly inhabit the domain in between the two, the domain of keeping promises, showing kindness, and hewing to moral scruple.

Though Donaldson may be correct in asserting that the moral standing of corporations differs from that of individual human beings, there is little reason to believe that their moral domain is composed entirely of the minimum and maximum. For example, a corporation may carefully seed a number of hints that it will expand its operations in a certain state, resulting in significant additional jobs, if it receives a healthy tax reduction. Intrigued political leaders may then reduce its tax burden, but the company then might find an excuse for expanding elsewhere instead. It would seem that the corporation has indeed been dishonest and manipulative, immoral in other words, but it is unlikely that its transgressions are so wicked that it has forfeited its right to exist. Moreover, as is the lot of ordinary persons, failings of this sort constitute the broadest domain of corporate life.

If the above is correct, corporations may be morally obligated to assist impoverished nations, though failure to do so is not a mortal transgression. Donaldson believes corporations have no such obligation. Furthermore, he apparently views most impoverished nations' pleas for assistance from corporations as requests for gratuitous gifts (1989, 62–64). The difficulty is that Jamaica's jousting with the aluminum companies clearly is not merely a request for corporate charity. Jamaica and the aluminum companies had a complex and long-standing relationship. Furthermore, the corporations had greatly benefited from their presence in Jamaica and were vigorously exploiting Jamaica's prize resource, for bauxite exploitation was the centerpiece of its program of economic development. Because of this, the Jamaicans' efforts to gain additional benefit from the companies' presence was not equivalent to seeking gratuitous charity. Rather, they were seeking to acquire greater benefit from one of the island's own resources, a resource that was extremely important to their lives and well-being. Hence, it is not obvious that the aluminum corporations had no obligation to cooperate with Jamaica, though neither would failure to cooperate be a venial sin.

THE APPEAL TO JUSTICE

Richard DeGeorge is firmly convinced that multinational corporations have an obligation to assist the economic development of underdeveloped nations. In fact, he asserts that this principle should be one of the fundamental tenants that guide the conduct of multinational corporations (1993, 49). DeGeorge bases his contention on a multifaceted analysis of justice, for he believes that considerations of justice impose this moral obligation on multinational corporations.

He begins with a distinction between national justice and international justice (1993, 26–33). DeGeorge believes that corporations, like individuals, have a richer and more compelling array of obligations and relationships to inhabitants of their home nations than to outsiders. However, DeGeorge asserts that this general circumstance is counterbalanced by a different set of concerns when multinational corporations set up shop in underdeveloped nations. Hence, he believes an American corporation does indeed have fewer obligations to citizens of Great Britain than to citizens of the United States, but its operations in an underdeveloped nation like Jamaica may well be subject to weightier obligations.

Human beings in a wealthy and advanced nation, the United States for example, can rely on an imposing set of institutions and machinery established to insure that corporations obey laws, that business transactions are conducted fairly, and that means are available to assist people who are unable to work, lose their employment, or have special needs. The international arena, however, has no such protections. Further, many underdeveloped nations also lack them. One consequence of this disparity is that an unemployed person in the United States commonly enjoys a variety of benefits designed to protect him or her from destitution.

Laborers in underdeveloped nations, though, too frequently lack such protection. If they are thrown out of work, neither they nor their families are likely to have access to governmental resources provided to soften the blow (DeGeorge 1993, 31–32). Further, poor nations commonly lack the legal structures and oversight bodies equipped to enforce statutes to regulate business conduct, ensure that business dealings are fair and honest, and ensure that business activity is undertaken in a manner that benefits the larger society. Also, such nations commonly lack the body of expertise and experience needed to equip them to negotiate effectively with multinational corporations seeking access to them. Therefore, a multinational corporation that single-mindedly follows its own corporate interests in a developing nation is far more likely to cause harm to that nation and its citizens than when it functions in a developed nation. Because these corporations cannot rely on other institutions to forestall harm that might result from their activities, DeGeorge believes they are morally obliged to do so on their own initiative.

In addition, DeGeorge asserts that the vast differences in wealth, power, and expertise that divide multinational corporations from underdeveloped nations imply that these nations are not well situated to negotiate with multinational corporations as equals (1993, 43–45). Hence, agreements reached via negotiation are apt to be skewed in favor of the stronger party, the corporations.

DeGeorge offers a number of useful insights. Nonetheless, when applied to the case of Jamaica, his analysis suffers from two limitations. First, though it is easy to agree that powerful multinational corporations are obliged to aid the economic development of impoverished nations, DeGeorge offers little guidance on the important questions of how much aid corporations are obliged to provide, whether they should actively seek out opportunities to benefit impoverished nations, and whether they are obliged to transfer advanced technology and sophisticated manufacturing processes to such nations in order to help advance their programs of economic development. When discussing the extracting industries in general, DeGeorge says only that they should avoid exploitation and that they should offer adequate compensation to the host nation (1993, 74–79). Though he acknowledges that *exploitation* and *adequate compensation* are vague terms, he offers little concrete explanation to help give them greater precision.

Second, however, DeGeorge appears to believe that the moral foundation of his principles of justice is a type of egalitarianism; that is, he appears to believe that, given the disparity of wealth and power that separates multinational corporations from impoverished nations, poor nations' citizens will not receive their due as the equals of all other humans unless the corporations shoulder a substantial additional burden or moral obligation when dealing with them (1993, 34–35, 37). Unfortunately, this response seems to cement the unequal relation between the parties into a status quo. Genuine equality is not achieved because the corporations are presumed to have the upper hand and to retain a greater moral burden.

More fundamentally, however, the real foundation of DeGeorge's concern appears to be his analysis of the negative consequences for nations and peoples when multinational corporations do not shoulder a greater burden of obligations. That is, his fundamental concern is that nations and peoples will be harmed by unfettered corporate activity, but, more pertinently, he also believes they will be denied the opportunity for economic advancement if corporations do not undertake the burden of assisting their development. Thus, DeGeorge's primary concern appears to be that of utilitarian consequences rather than egalitarian justice. It is not inevitable, for example, that two equal parties to a bargain must receive equal benefit, and it is not obvious that injustice has occurred if they do not. DeGeorge's assertion that corporations should commit themselves to aiding the economic development of impoverished nations, in other words, appears to be motivated by utilitarian concerns rather than those of the justice of reciprocity.

A UTILITARIAN PERSPECTIVE

Manuel Velasquez has devoted considerable attention to the Jamaica case (1995). He is quite emphatically convinced that the North American aluminum corporations were morally obliged to commit themselves to providing far greater assistance to Jamaica's efforts at economic development than he believes they were prepared to provide. His approach is notably eclectic, for he believes that appeals to human rights, justice, and utility must all be employed to achieve the proper resolution of the Jamaican case (1995, 865). However, his analysis is disturbingly post hoc. He appears to have decided a priori what must be done in Jamaica and then searched around for moral principles to provide support for his beliefs. Hence, he asserts that human rights theory, justice, and utilitarianism each supplies a different, but partial, piece of the picture of moral obligation. Apparently he accepts Donaldson's theory of rights and DeGeorge's theories of justice without serious question. He simply believes their theories are not capable of supplying the full panoply of obligations required of the multinational corporations (Velasquez 1995, 879–88). He also considers utilitarianism, specifically a version developed by me, to fill in the missing piece (Velasquez 1995, 873–75). However, he does not supply the background discussion required to adequately determine what utilitarian obligations are required of the multinational corporations in this context. That is, utilitarian theory must rely on an estimate of the consequences of an array of options and then select one of them based on a projection of the benefits and harms likely to result from each. Hence, a utilitarian analysis, particularly in a concrete case like that at hand, demands an analysis of the circumstances at hand.

ANALYSIS

Given the considerable need of the Jamaican people, and given the aluminum corporations' considerable ability to improve their lot at very little cost to their profits or corporate viability, the corporations were indeed morally obligated to cooperate with Manley's efforts to gain increased benefit from their operations. Thus, the aluminum corporations were obliged to negotiate in good faith with Manley on the matter of diverting a greater portion of their profits back to Jamaica, in terms of both tax revenue and investment. Further, they were obliged to assist Manley's efforts to secure greater knowledge of the details of their operations and to assist his efforts to ensure that Jamaica received a fair return from their activities. The foundation of these obligations is the prospect of the significant benefit to the people of Jamaica likely to result from these changes. That said, a careful look at the circumstances of Manley's dealings with the aluminum corporations reveals a more nuanced picture.

It does not appear that the aluminum corporations were morally obliged to yield to Manley's insistence that his government receive controlling ownership of their Jamaican operations. It is not clear what concrete benefits Manley hoped to gain from this shift. Apparently he believed that controlling ownership would give Jamaica increased control over local exploitation of bauxite and vastly expanded information about the companies' inner workings. However, because the companies' decisions about investment and operating strategy were made elsewhere and they retained control of technology and marketing, it is difficult to determine how much concrete benefit Manley could hope to gain from his narrow margin of local ownership. He did hope to persuade the companies to establish more processing facilities on the island, for smelting plants require a far greater monetary investment, provide more jobs at higher wages than extraction, and employ vastly more sophisticated technology. There are grounds for believing that Manley's socialist convictions were also significant factors in his decision because he seems to have been wedded to the belief that means of production should be under social control. However, the experience of the past two decades gives support for the view that capitalist systems are better suited to advance peoples' material prosperity than socialist ones and are, at the very least, no more apt to cause harm or violate human rights. Hence, Manley had no clear moral obligation to adopt socialist principles, and the aluminum corporations had no clear moral obligation to yield to his efforts to advance his principles.

The facts of the matter remain unclear, but if it can be shown that the aluminum corporations scaled down their operations in Jamaica and shifted production elsewhere in retribution for Manley's negotiations, the corporations behaved badly and deserve moral censure. Nonetheless, in this case, as in life in general, there is plenty of blame to pass around. A utilitarian conception of guilt can be constructed on evidence that parties have acted in ways that prevented the greater good from being achieved or made the greater good more difficult to attain. In the case at hand, it appears that the U.S. government was concerned almost entirely with its own national security, its prosperity, and the welfare of its major corporations, but it displayed scant concern for Jamaica's needs or its efforts to improve its lot. So, to the extent that the U.S. government worked to undermine Jamaica's stability, helped create a climate of mutual distrust and uncertainty among the principals to the Jamaica case, and encouraged corporations to retaliate, it also deserves moral censure (Hewan 1994, 77–84). Michael Manley does not escape a portion of blame, either, though his error seems to be more one of miscalculation, uncritical acceptance of socialist dogma, and, quite likely, imprudently seeking the limelight that attended his friendship with Castro and his efforts to become a world leader of the movement of nonaligned nations. Manley was a gifted and charismatic figure, and, like many of that type, he tended to match his rhetoric to his audience. He was capable of asserting, on the one hand, "I was promoting democratic processes, private-sector development" (Marable 1993, 25), and, "We thought an interventionist state and a strong market could exist in tandem, each complementing the other" (Manley 1993, 153). But, on the other hand, in other settings he was also prone to claim, "Capitalism should be demolished 'brick by brick' " (Rohter 1997, 52). His anticapitalist rhetoric was, at best, imprudent, and his avowed espousal of socialist principles and national-ization of Jamaican businesses certainly helped create a climate in which the cor-porations were legitimately uncertain of his goodwill and future intentions (Edie 1991, 92; Payne 1984, 39–40).

However, all the parties involved are at least partially exculpated by the gen-eral turmoil of the 1970s. The OPEC oil embargo threw the entire world into an economic tailspin (Mufuka 1978, 88). During the period of negotiations between Manley and the aluminum corporations, inflation reached astonishing levels in the most prosperous nations, including the United States, unemployment was ap-proaching levels that threatened social stability, and the world first began to come to terms with grave problems of environmental pollution and degradation and explosive population increases, all of which threatened social stability and eco-nomic welfare. It is the era in which the Club of Rome issued a report that as-serted that the world would exhaust its supply of petroleum by the year 2000 and many of its remaining resources soon thereafter (Meadows and Meadows 1974). Hence, even relatively prosperous nations were anxious and uncertain.

Moreover, it was a period when many had legitimate doubts that the capitalist system was capable of continuing to advance the well-being of the people of the world. Certainly, many doubted that the benefits that capitalist enterprise had brought for prosperous nations would ever reach those who were poor. In addi-tion, this period was also the era of the North-South debates, the array of often heated exchanges in which prosperous and impoverished nations engaged in sharp discussions of control of natural resources and the obligations of the wealthy to the impoverished (see Cason's chapter in this volume). Multinational corporations were accustomed to conducting their overseas operations in colonies of European states or in former colonies that nonetheless continued to follow the old practices of the imperial powers. These enterprises were, thus, unprepared to function in circumstances in which impoverished nations were disposed to battle vigorously for a larger portion of the world's wealth. Hence, the corporations often reacted defensively, clumsily, and with scant sensitivity to the concerns and needs of impoverished nations.

For their part, the Third World nations converged on the view that they must fight more aggressively for greater power and prosperity, but they were suspi-cious of the colonial powers and viewed multinational corporations as their agents. Further, many governmental leaders came to espouse socialist ideology to provide an intellectual framework and justification for their efforts at national liberation. As a result, they tended to view corporations as enemies, or at best as threatening and untrustworthy, rather than as institutions that could be trusted and counted on to bargain in good faith. To make matters worse, the impover-ished nations generally lacked the resources of law, technology, or information which would enable them to deal with huge multinational corporations confidently and on equal terms.

In sum, all parties were entering a new world of relations with one another, and all were uncertain of how to conduct themselves. The atmosphere was made tense and difficult by difficult economic conditions the world round and the hostile atmosphere left over from battles against imperialist powers.

In the two decades following his negotiations with the aluminum corporations, many of the problems that concerned Manley have received attention, though, obviously, much remains to be done. Leaders of the underdeveloped world, including Manley himself, came to have a different and somewhat more benign view of multinational corporations and a more positive conception of the benefits they may provide. They are inspired by the enormous success of nations, such as South Korea and Taiwan, impoverished two decades ago but now prospering and the home bases of several formidable multinational corporations that are eagerly establishing themselves in less developed nations. The most commonly accepted prototype of national economic advance at present is founded on the notion that nations must attract investment, expertise, and business enterprise from elsewhere, and less developed nations view multinational corporations as the necessary vehicle through which these benefits must flow. Moreover, the nations of the world are in the process of creating the structures of a genuine global economy that will function in a more orderly and equitable fashion than earlier. Because of these new circumstances, it seems unlikely that the clumsiness, misunderstanding, mutual recrimination, and ill-will that characterized the Jamaica bauxite case would be repeated today. Multinational corporations have learned from their recent experiences, and so have national leaders, including, most notably, Michael Manley, a recent convert to the wisdom of capitalist enterprise.

CONCLUSION

Focusing tightly on Jamaica and the aluminum corporations has the great advantage of adding precision to the present discussion. The bare question of whether corporations have an obligation to aid impoverished nations is entirely too broad. However, this precision has a price, for it leaves open the question of whether Jamaica's experience offers any guidance for other corporations dealing with other underdeveloped nations. I believe that it does, provided that we recall the working assumptions listed earlier. If we presume that the capitalist system is morally justified, and agree that this implies that corporations are entitled to seek profits and that they make a contribution to human well-being by doing so, then we can conclude that corporations need not assist impoverished nations through acts of gratuitous corporate charity. That is, they are not obliged to donate vast sums of money to impoverished nations or establish unprofitable operations for the sake of economic development. Nor are they obliged to allow themselves or their subsidiaries to be hamstrung by intrusive and predatory government regulations that impair their ability to operate in businesslike fashion. Furthermore, they are not morally obliged to cooperate in schemes designed to create militantly socialist economic systems that aim at their destruction.

Nonetheless, corporations are commonly eager to enter underdeveloped nations for the good economic reason that they hope to profit from their endeavors. Impoverished nations need not depend on corporate charity. At the present time, corporations rush into poor nations to gain access to natural resources, cheap labor, or new markets. They are keenly aware of the opportunities and benefits that poor nations have to offer. However, as in Jamaica, when they march into these nations, they are obligated to cooperate wholeheartedly with local governments to attempt to ensure that their activities bring genuine benefit for the nation. Further, they should cooperate with nations in their efforts to establish equitable taxation, legal oversight, and environmental and worker safety mechanisms.

Of course, Jamaica is unusual in one important respect: Michael Manley, whatever his failings, did seem to be genuinely concerned to improve the lot and prospects of his citizens. Many nations have entirely corrupt governments. Many are run by tight oligarchies that control the nations for their own enrichment and gladly exploit their citizens to benefit themselves. Hence, corporations that establish operations in such nations do not assist their broad economic development. Rather, they help ensure the continued rule and prosperity of a privileged few. Thus, corporations dealing with nations of this sort cannot presume that cooperating with the local government will result in discernible benefit for the general citizenry.

Multinational corporations have both the expertise and the means to determine which nations and which governments are corrupt or inept. Because they are able to make these discriminations, and because they control expansion into new nations and control investment and corporate strategy in those where they have operations, corporations are obliged to assist governments genuinely working to improve the lots of their citizens and to avoid establishing operations in nations that are corrupt and repressive.

13

Whatever Happened to the New International Economic Order?

Jeffrey Cason

From the perspective of the late 1990s, the demands for a New International Economic Order (NIEO) made by poorer countries in the mid-1970s seem quaint. These demands—which were, in effect, demands for a global redistribution of wealth—are certainly not taken very seriously by policy makers in industrialized countries, and most poor countries have also abandoned hope that an NIEO could be adopted. But at the time the proposals were made, they were taken seriously. International conferences were dedicated to the topic. The United Nations was filled with discussions on the kinds of policies that should be implemented to make the NIEO a reality. Some in rich countries also supported these demands and argued in favor of the global redistribution that was implied by the proposals.

But by the mid-1980s, the demands for an NIEO had faded, and the initiative had failed. There were no new conferences addressing the need for this sort of global distribution, and an ethic of self-help reigned in the international community when it came to evaluating what it would take for poor countries to pull themselves out of poverty. Indeed, as the international economy has become ever more integrated, many of the demands for and concessions of real benefits for those less advantaged in the world system have disappeared from international discourse and political reality.

What happened to the NIEO? Why did it rather suddenly disappear from the realm of realistic policy scenarios? This chapter addresses this question and provides the following three-part answer: First, the NIEO disappeared in part because the conditions that allowed for its creation—a feeling of empowerment on the part of poorer nations, particularly in the wake of the first oil crisis in 1973—disappeared. That is to say, the leverage that poor countries thought they had, including, in particular, control over valuable mineral resources that industrialized countries wanted, vanished. Second, the debt crisis that hit developing countries with particular ferocity in the early 1980s put them on the defensive, and the drying up of international finance removed another element of power that the poorer countries had at their disposal: access to money without many strings attached. After the debt crisis began, strings were attached to everything, and those leaders who attempted to assert that the goals of the NIEO still mattered—such as Peru's ill-fated president, Alan García—were punished for their reckless behavior. Third, the triumph of Reaganism/Thatcherism in the ideological realm, with its emphasis of market-based solutions for economic problems, pushed the NIEO off the agenda. If—as Reagan and Thatcher asserted—even domestic-oriented policy should eschew government-mandated redistribution, why should new international institutions be created to carry out global redistribution?

This argument will be demonstrated in three steps: First, the main demands of the NIEO will be laid out, so that the substance of the NIEO is clear. Second, I discuss the two material changes that led to the rise and decline of the NIEO: the potential power of raw material producers and the effects of the debt crisis. The third section of the chapter addresses the ideological dimension of the NIEO, considering in particular the impact of the Reagan/Thatcher triumph, and discusses how the end of the Cold War has only accelerated this trend, making the reemergence of an NIEO nearly impossible. After the elaboration of this argument, the chapter turns to an evaluation of NIEO viability, considering in particular the ways in which domestic political and economic structures would make the fulfillment of its goals difficult. Finally, the concluding section focuses on the future of NIEO–like demands, particularly given the continuing enormous inequality in the international system.

DEMANDS FOR A NEW INTERNATIONAL ECONOMIC ORDER

The demands for an NIEO can be seen simply as a demand for global distributive justice that was advanced by the poorer countries in the world system. The roots of these demands emerged shortly after World War II, when those developing countries that were independent (primarily in Latin America) sought to organize the international trading system in a way that would be advantageous to the poorer nations (Hart 1983, 36; Spero and Hart 1997, 161–62). Primarily, these pre–NIEO demands were for commodity stabilization arrangements that would make it easier for developing nations to count on stable prices for their main exports of primary products. These initial efforts were not at all successful, and the International Trade Organization (ITO) (that would have implemented these policies) was never created. Instead of ITO, the General Agreement on Tariffs and Trade (GATT) was established as a long-lasting temporary coordinator of trade, one that focuses on reducing tariff barriers of trade, which was a particular interest to the wealthier nations in the world economy.

Dissatisfied with their lack of influence in the international political economy, developing countries—bolstered by an increase in numbers after decolonization—began to push their own agenda in the 1960s. This developing country agenda included a wide variety of issues and focused on, according to Hart,

> (1) sovereignty over their economies and natural resources, (2) increasing their control over the level and nature of foreign investment, (3) maintaining or (preferably) increasing the purchasing power of raw material and commodity exports, (4) increasing access to commercial markets of developed countries, (5) reducing the cost of technology transfers, (6) increasing the flow of official development assistance, (7) alleviating the debt burdens of certain developing countries, and (8) increasing the decision-making power of the developing world in the United Nations and the IMF [International Monetary Fund]/World Bank system. [1983, 33]

What developing countries were asking for was a more powerful role for international organizations that could transfer resources from North to South, that is, from rich countries to poor ones. This was indeed an ambitious agenda, and what was surprising was that poor countries—which are themselves quite diverse in their circumstances and interests—could unite, at least temporarily, around this program.

The demands themselves were made most explicitly at the sixth special session of the U.N. General Assembly in 1974. At this special session, developing countries united around a Declaration and Action Programme on the Establishment of a New International Economic Order (Gilpin 1987, 298). The declaration asked for new institutional arrangements and resource transfers "to eliminate the widening gap between developed and developing countries" (Brunner 1996). In effect, developing countries were attempting to advance what Jones (in this volume) considers a rather maximalist position in favor of international redistributive justice.

These demands can be justified theoretically, as Beitz (1979b) makes clear. In particular, Beitz points out that as interdependence increases in the international political economy, obligations for resource transfers on the North can be justified (1979b, 127–28). This does not mean that such demands will be met but merely that there is a case to be made—even within liberal political theory—that there is some obligation on the part of the richer nations in the world economy to assist those that are poorer. That said, as Brunner points out, the demands for an NIEO hardly had a liberal bent and at times adopted socialist rhetoric.[1]

Nevertheless, even though at times their demands for an NIEO sounded radical, these nations were hardly trying to overthrow the global capitalist order. Jacobsen and associates report that even at the height of the negotiations over an NIEO in the mid-1970s, many of those who were doing the bargaining on behalf of developing countries adopted rather moderate positions on some of the most important issues (for example, they viewed multinational corporations [MNCs] in a partly positive light) (1983, 356–62). The NIEO was not trying to overthrow the established international political and economic system; rather, it was an attempt to force richer countries to provide more assistance to developing countries.

And the case was made in multiple forums, including, in particular, the United Nations and its organizations, such as the U.N. Conference on Trade and Development (see 1996). What it involved, as Krasner (1985) points out, was an attempt to move away from market allocation of resources. Rather than by market allocation, resources would be allocated by decisions made by new or existing institutions that would give substantial advantages to developing nations.

By and large, those who advocated an NIEO failed, with a few minor exceptions. Krasner has argued that the success or failure of developing nations has been determined by three factors: the existing institutions of the international political economy, the strength of the United States, and the ideological coherence of the developing country's demands (1985, 59). Gilpin (1987, 300) asserts that developing countries could not maintain unity in the face of their own distinct national interests. To these explanations, I add two others, discussed here: global change on an ideological level and international economic conditions that affected the power of the South. These factors will be discussed in the next two sections.

THE CHANGING GLOBAL ECONOMIC CLIMATE

One of the most important stimulants to the demands of developing countries for an NIEO was the ability of oil-exporting countries to increase the price of oil during 1973. This gave hope to many developing countries that they had power that they had heretofore not imagined. It demonstrated, quite dramatically, that the South could impose economic adjustment on the North. Developing countries saw evidence that through united action, they could in fact increase their power, in effect subverting the power and corporations of the North. This was clearly an event of substantial import.

The oil shock of 1973 had an unintended side effect that also increased the willingness and desire of developing countries to push for more resources: it created petrodollars. Because the oil-exporting countries were now suddenly flush with resources after the increase in the price of oil, and because they could not (or did not want to) immediately spend all of these new resources, they deposited the new earnings in international banks, which were then suddenly brimming with cash that could be loaned in Eurocurrency markets (Stallings 1982). This increase in the availability of capital in developed countries' banks led the banks themselves to search for new customers for loans. And, of course, the oil-importing developing countries were particularly anxious to borrow money to finance their balance-of-payments deficits that had emerged along with the oil shock. Developing countries that exported oil were also prime customers for banks looking for a way to make money on the money that they had on their hands. As a consequence, the total level of developing country debt increased immensely after the oil shock, as table 13.1 indicates. The table demonstrates the general increase in developing country debt, as well as its greater relative weight in developing country economies: in most countries, debt increased substantially both as a percentage of gross national product (GNP) and as a percentage of export earnings.

Table 13.1 also demonstrates some heterogeneity in the developing world. Latin American countries, in particular, demonstrated a rather spectacular growth in their foreign debt levels, with the exception of Chile, which nonetheless had a high level of debt service compared with many other countries. In addition, not all countries wound up with an unsustainable level of debt service. Moreover, some countries (notably South Korea and, to a lesser extent, Indonesia) were able to increase exports sufficiently to make debt service more tolerable. What the table does indicate, beyond any reasonable doubt, is that many developing countries saw an impressive increase in their debt levels after the oil shock.

This debt was not simply used to pay for oil, even in the oil-importing countries. As Stallings (1987) and Frieden (1981) have observed, this increased debt also financed industrial or other development objectives of those countries that were able to borrow on international financial markets. Obviously, not all developing countries had access to these funds, though many in Latin America did, as

Table 13.1   Selected Developing Country Foreign Debt Indicators, 1970 and 1982

	Foreign Debt		Debt as a Percentage of Gross National Product		Debt Service as a Percentage of Export Earnings	
Country	1970	1982	1970	1982	1970	1982
Brazil	3.23	47.59	7.1	16.9	12.5	42.1
Chile	2.07	5.24	25.8	23.7	18.9	18.8
Indonesia	2.44	18.42	27.1	21.1	6.9	8.3
Mexico	3.21	50.41	9.1	31.1	23.6	29.5
Morocco	0.71	9.03	18.0	60.8	7.7	36.8
Nigeria	0.48	6.09	4.8	8.7	4.2	9.5
Peru	0.86	6.90	12.6	33.5	11.6	36.7
Philippines	0.57	8.84	8.1	22.5	7.2	12.8
South Korea	1.80	20.06	20.4	28.3	19.4	13.1
Zambia	0.62	2.38	37.0	66.3	5.9	17.4

Source: World Bank 1984, 248–49.
Note: Total debt in billions of U.S. dollars.

did some in Africa (notably Nigeria and Algeria) and East Asia (particularly South Korea). This ability to borrow suddenly increased the capital available for development and in some cases allowed developing countries to drive harder bargains with multinational corporations that wanted to invest in their markets.[2]

In other words, the oil crisis increased the power (or perceived power) of developing countries in two ways: first, it increased the bargaining power of developing countries in at least one key commodity and led to hopes that this sort of increased bargaining power could be achieved in others as well. In addition, it added to the potential resources that developing countries had to finance their own development programs and led to the hope that such resources could increase their structural power.

Krasner also points out that the early to mid-1970s presented a unique opportunity for developing countries. This was a period during which the international ideological environment still favored assistance to developing countries, and this, combined with an increase in the number of countries that had achieved independence, led to an increase in the weight of developing countries in international forums where an NIEO could be debated. At this point, Krasner points out, countries in the North had not yet defected from supporting these international institutions, and some in the North were indeed favorably disposed toward the demands of developing countries (1985, 91). In 1980 one could have expected the debate over the NIEO to continue well into the next decade.

But this brief window of opportunity did not last long because of events in the global political economy. These events, in fact, dictated a "new" understanding of the NIEO. In particular, change was initiated by the onset of global recession in 1981 and the ensuing debt crisis of developing countries that was triggered by Mexico's declaration that it could not pay its foreign debt in August 1982. All of a sudden, banks were no longer willing to loan to developing countries, viewing them all as substantial credit risks. This unwillingness of banks to loan to developing countries meant that quite suddenly a power resource available to developing countries was taken away, as many countries were cut off from access to foreign financial resources. This access would not be restored on a widespread scale until the beginning of the following decade, by which time substantial changes had occurred in the world economy.

In addition, the worldwide recession of the early 1980s depressed commodity prices, including the price of oil. Suddenly, the hope that developing countries could put pressure on the nations of the North to revise their economic policies and transfer more resources to the South, based on some sort of economic threat, evaporated. The international recession meant that developing countries had the rug pulled out from under them, and, thus, they were no longer in a position to make many demands.

To put it simply, conditions in the international political economy suddenly put developing countries on the defensive. The NIEO was a strategy that only made sense if developing countries had the potential to act collectively to cause economic harm to wealthier countries. The major threat they had at their disposal after the advent of the debt crisis was that of not repaying their foreign debts. The response of developed countries and international banks to this threat was one of divide and conquer: whenever a country made a move to act more aggressively against foreign lenders—Peru in 1985 or Brazil in 1988, for example—these countries were forced to pay a steep price by international financial institutions for falling out of line. The banks would refuse to offer short-term lines of credit, for example, which are crucial for conducting the normal business of international trade. This elimination of what is normally routine put enormous stress on the economies of these "disobedient" nations. As a consequence, any unity on the part of debtors was discouraged, which meant that developing countries no longer had much of a hand to play in negotiations over any new international economic structure.

IDEOLOGICAL CHANGE AND THE NIEO

This scenario may sound overly deterministic, in economic terms. Nevertheless, while material forces are important, and in many cases crucial, they cannot, on their own, explain why particular economic policies are followed at a particular point in time or why international negotiations take a particular turn. Ideology and ideas matter as well, and this was certainly the case with the NIEO.

How did ideas about the NIEO change? Biersteker, in his analysis of a broader and related phenomenon—the "triumph" of liberal economic ideas in the developing world—suggests four possibilities: (1) economic elites in developing countries had been "educated" and had "seen the light" when it came to the virtue of liberal economics, (2) international financial institutions (particularly the IMF and the World Bank) had imposed such change, (3) countries had been forced to rethink their economic policies because of changes in the global economy and in particular in light of the success of export-oriented development strategies in East Asia, and (4) the old models of development (such as import-substitution industrialization) had been exhausted (1995, 180–81).

All of these explanations are related to changes in international economic conditions, with the possible exception of the first. In the end, Biersteker concludes that the independent role of ideas must be considered in any thoroughgoing understanding of what happened in developing countries over the course of the 1980s. Clearly, the election of Margaret Thatcher in Britain and Ronald Reagan in the United States affected the development policy debate, putting emphasis on market allocation of resources. These market-oriented ideas were quite opposed to the goals of the NIEO, which wanted to replace market allocation with more authoritative allocation coming from international institutions. As Krasner points out, demands for change coming from the developing world were based on arguments that "major aspects of the international economic system are flawed be-

cause the underlying mechanisms of exchange are unequal. Market-oriented regimes are inherently problematic because they provide unfair advantage for
larger and more knowledgeable economic actors" (1985, 86–87).

The ideas of Thatcher and Reagan could not have been more opposed to this
position. Their much more conservative position asserted that countries were
poor because they had intervened *too much* in the market, not too little. If this
were the case, then why should developed countries help, *enable,* developing
countries to continue to avoid the salutary effects of the market? It was, after all,
the market that allowed for the most efficient allocation of resources, and to the
extent that developing countries were trying to avoid this sort of allocation, they
were doomed to a future in poverty. This is, at any rate, the logic of the argument.

And the argument did not work just in rhetoric. As Biersteker points out, the
Reagan administration in particular was quite involved in stocking international
organizations with appointees that would advance its agenda: "The atmosphere
was highly politicized, and there was little reluctance on the part of the new administration about using U.S. power and influence in international organizations
to assert the ideological hegemony of its ideas" (1995, 183). There was, in other
words, an assault on both the domestic and international levels to delegitimize
ideas that argued in favor of redistribution of economic resources, on either a
national or an international scale. The NIEO was hardly welcome in such an environment.

It also became clear during the 1980s and the triumph of Reaganism and
Thatcherism that developing countries could not expect much in the form of
"handouts" from those who were wealthier, and this is reflected in the overall
level of aid provided by the wealthier countries. Table 13.2 shows the general
provision of aid since the beginning of the 1970s. What is remarkable about these
figures is that aid, while generally increasing over time (in current, not constant,
dollars), has declined precipitously in the late 1980s and 1990s, especially when
viewed as a percentage of GNP, and *all* G-7 countries (the countries listed, minus
Sweden) provided a lower level of aid in 1996 than they did in 1985–86. None
of the G-7 countries is even close to providing aid at a level of even 1 percent of
its GNP (an initial NIEO goal), and even Sweden, a country that prides itself on
its overseas assistance, is short of that goal. In other words, there was little effect
on aid flows from the NIEO debate, and although aid continues to go to developing countries, there clearly has not been a commitment to large resource transfers
from developed to developing countries. In the end, the desire for "handouts" on
the part of developing countries has come to naught and is hardly legitimate in
the current global economic and political climate.

In addition, it is even less likely in the current international ideological context
that other goals of the NIEO, such as greater regulation of multinational corporations, might be accomplished. Currently, there is little movement for such regulation, even if there might be the occasionally expressed complaint—Malaysian
Prime Minister Mahathir Mohamad comes to mind—about the excesses of the

Table 13.2   Official Overseas Development Assistance, Selected Countries

	1970		1975		1980		1985–1986		1991		1996	
	$ᵃ	%ᵇ	$	%	$	%	$	%	$	%	$	%
Canada	.34	—	.88	—	1.08	—	1.67	.48	2.60	.45	1.79	.32
France	.74	—	1.49	—	2.89	—	3.59	.58	7.39	.62	7.45	.48
Germany	.60	—	1.69	—	3.57	—	3.39	.45	6.89	.40	7.60	.33
Italy	.15	—	.18	—	.68	—	1.75	.35	3.35	.29	2.42	.20
Japan	.46	—	1.15	—	3.35	—	4.72	.29	10.95	.32	9.44	.20
Sweden	.12	—	.57	—	.96	—	.97	.86	2.12	.90	2.00	.84
United Kingdom	.48	—	.90	—	1.85	—	1.64	.32	3.20	.32	3.20	.27
United States	3.15	—	4.16	—	7.14	—	9.48	.23	11.26	.20	9.38	.12
Org. for Econ. Coop. and Dev.	3.71	—	13.25	—	26.20	—	32.3	.34	56.88	.33	55.49	.25

Source: Calculated from figures from the Organization of Economic Cooperation and Development (1998a; 1998b).
Note: 1985–1986 figure is an average of those two years.
ᵃ Figures in billions of U.S. dollars, at current prices.
ᵇ Figures as a percentage of gross national product.

international capitalist system and its unjust effects. Despite these occasional protests, developing countries are doing whatever needs to be done to attract additional multinational corporation investment. There is nothing left of whatever "solidarity" once existed to rein in the practices of MNCs; they are now welcomed with open arms wherever they might want to set up shop, and developing countries openly and aggressively compete with one another for this investment.

In sum, the ideological climate has turned against nonmarket-based allocation of resources in the world economy and against the notion that new institutions should be created to foster greater development in the poorer countries in the world economy. Now the overwhelming sentiment is in favor of market allocation of world resources, and developing countries must present themselves to be as "market friendly" as possible. Long gone are the days when there was some hope of developing country unity that would force the more developed nations of the world economy to transfer resources to those less well-off.

THE VIABILITY OF AN NIEO

An NIEO—or some other version of a program for global distributive justice—depends on two assumptions that have not yet been examined here. The first is that the changes demanded by the poorer countries would have the real effect of increasing the welfare of the majority in poorer countries. The second—and per-

haps more important—is that elites in developing countries would have the best
interests of their populations in mind when they implemented policies that would
come out of global redistribution.

On the first issue, authors such as Kreinin and Finger (1976) have argued that
most of the reforms proposed by developing countries to redistribute global resources, such as commodity cartels or preferential trading arrangements, would
not do much to improve their overall lot. At best, they argue, the improvements
would be only marginal. This is indeed a question for economists who could develop models that would predict what would happen to the economies of developing nations if the NIEO demands were met. If this analysis led to conclusions
that the changes would not greatly affect welfare in developing countries, then
certainly more appropriate policies could be designed that could take advantage
of resource transfers from North to South. Nonetheless, as Onwuka points out,
"little consensus has emerged on the development issues, the priorities tagged to
them and on the policies required to promote development in the underdeveloped
areas of the world" (1986, 2).

In the end, Kreinin and Finger do not think that developing countries would
benefit from most of what they propose; they believe that "economic development is essentially a process of *internal* transformation of society" (1976, 511).
While this last point may be arguable, it does bear keeping in mind that bringing
poor nations out of their poverty does not require simply a transformation of the
international system (though such a change is probably essential); it requires substantial change of policies and governments in the countries that are poor, and
debate rages in the economic development literature about what policies would
be most appropriate to promote growth and improve equity in developing countries.

In addition, to the extent that the NIEO might move countries in a more socialist direction, these countries might very well have a harder time making it out of
poverty. Elfstrom suggests that "capitalism has brought considerable prosperity
to a substantial portion of humanity" and that "there is no convincing evidence
that [capitalism] is inferior to socialist systems in its ability to improve human
beings' material welfare" (this volume, 186). If an NIEO were to encourage a
more socialist (or statist) economic development path, there is hardly any guarantee that this will alleviate the most pressing problems of poor countries.

This is not to argue against social democracy, which may in fact be a more
effective political and economic strategy for poor countries. Rather, it is to suggest that a statist solution to developing country woes is fraught with danger.
A nonmarket-based transfer of resources to developing nations could have great
potential for improving the lot of the majority of the population in developing
countries. It is necessary to consider, however, how these resources will be used.

This line of argument leads to the second assumption that underpins the NIEO,
which must also be considered. Although elites in developing countries have
often made eloquent statements about the need for global redistributive justice,

these statements have carried with them the notion that the leaders have the interests of their populations at heart. This is not necessarily the case, especially with authoritarian regimes. It is not that political leaders do not think that they are doing the right thing for their citizens; indeed, they might. More likely, however, these elites have the interests of particular sectors or classes in mind, and these sectors or classes are not necessarily the poorest, the sectors and classes that need assistance most dramatically. Indeed, to the extent that demands for an NIEO would lead to greater industrialization, such demands might contribute to the "urban bias" of so many development policies, in effect squeezing the countryside, where most of the poorest live (Lipton 1977).

Consider, for example, Langley's description of the NIEO: "The proposed NIEO sought to uproot all of this [dependence on the advanced countries]: to centralize financial and economic matters, to subject them to popular political control and to suggest general models and definitions for modernization other than the North's" (1990, 60). It is hardly likely that an NIEO would have subjected financial and economic matters "to popular political control." After all, many of the states asking for this global redistribution were far from models of democratic political participation. Even if the elites could assert a desire to help those who are least fortunate, their political systems would have made it very difficult for them to act so as to put effective policies into practice. They always had a domestic political calculus to consider, and this calculus did not necessarily lead to the most enlightened policies, even in those cases in which leaders were genuinely interested in improving citizens' standards of living.

In other words, there are not necessarily "good" and "bad" sides in the NIEO debate; as in much of life, matters are more complex than public rhetoric would have us believe. Many would agree that rich countries have some obligation to transfer at least some resources to poorer countries. However, getting from such a general sentiment to the desired practical effects of improving living standards in poor countries is not at all simple, both because there is disagreement on what policies are best and because states and private organizations in developing countries allocate whatever assistance is provided. Those recipient institutions will vary greatly in their capacity to improve living standards and access to services in developing countries.

CONCLUSION: A FUTURE FOR THE NIEO?

We know that the NIEO disappeared from development policy discourse in the 1980s and is unlikely to make an immediate comeback now. The preceding analysis indicates multiple reasons for this, including changing international economic conditions and ideological changes originating in the more advanced countries. The analysis itself provides substantial reasons for thinking that demands for an NIEO corresponded, to some degree, to a fleeting moment in the history of the international political economy. The logic of the analysis also implies that this scenario could conceivably be repeated if material or ideological circumstances offered developing countries the power to once again attempt to assert control over the debate about the international allocation of resources. This could come from another oil crisis, another kind of commodity crisis, or the rise of political leaders in the more developed countries (and, in particular, in the United States) who favor greater redistribution. The latter is difficult to imagine, particularly given the fact that the United States is not likely to see its interests furthered by a global redistribution of resources. It is not impossible to imagine such a scenario, but it is highly unlikely.

It is difficult to imagine such a scenario because the NIEO was a fundamental challenge to the dominance of the North in the international political economy, and, as such, it was likely to be resisted at every opportunity by those in the North. There was a brief window of opportunity during the 1970s when it appeared to be possible to demand global redistributive justice. But economic and ideological circumstances made these demands short-lived, and they disappeared from the international radar screen with the rise of Thatcherism and Reaganism in the North and severe economic crises in many nations that were demanding these changes.

This does not mean that the demands will never reemerge. Nevertheless, demands for an NIEO were specific to a particular point in time, when demands for global redistribution encountered a more receptive environment. Such an environment might in fact reemerge, as a consequence of global economic or environmental crisis. Certainly there are politicians in developing countries who would be delighted to lead a new movement for more southern control in the global economy. Indeed, global turbulence in recent years has emboldened some of these politicians.

To put it differently, the demands for an NIEO (or whatever its next incarnation might be) are permanently latent in an international political economy that is profoundly unequal. Given the appropriate circumstances, these demands might spread. For the time being, however, market-based resource allocation reigns.

NOTES

I would like to thank Andrew Valls and an anonymous reviewer for their comments on a previous version of this chapter and David Daniel and Ayse Zarakol for their research assistance.

1. In his 1976 attack on the NIEO, Brunner writes, "We are addressed by a majority of members of the UN and 'intellectual and moral leaders' to accept in essence and initiate a transition into a socialist world and a socialist society" (1996, 175). This assertion is exaggerated, for those demanding an NIEO represented a wide range of political positions. It is, however, safe to say that most of them saw a significant role for the state in economic development.

2. See Evans (1979), for example, on the increased strength of the Brazilian state in negotiating with MNCs. Although Evans does not directly attribute this increased power of the Brazilian state to the capacity to borrow, clearly it was an important influence on Brazilian strength.

References

Adam, Hussein. 1996. Somalia: A Terrible Beauty Being Born. In *Collapsed States in Africa*, ed. I. William Zartman. Boulder: Lynne Reinner.

Adams, Valerie. 1990. *Chemical Warfare, Chemical Disarmament*. Bloomington: Indiana University Press.

Addington, Larry H. 1984. *The Patterns of War since the Eighteenth Century*. Bloomington: Indiana University Press.

Adelman, Howard. 1992. The Ethics of Humanitarian Intervention: The Case of the Kurdish Refugees. *Public Affairs Quarterly* 6: 61–87.

Aderiye, Segun. 1992. ECOMOG's Landing. In *ECOMOG: A Bold Attempt at Regional Peacekeeping*, ed. Margaret Vogt. Lagos, Nigeria: Gabumo Publishing.

Akehurst, Michael. 1984. Humanitarian Intervention. In *Intervention in World Politics*, ed. Hedley Bull. Oxford: Clarendon Press.

Alexander, Yonah, and Joshua Sinai. 1989. *Terrorism: The PLO Connection*. New York: Crane Russak.

Amdur, Robert. 1977. Rawls's Theory of Justice: Domestic and International Perspectives. *World Politics* 29: 438–62.

Ames, Roger T. 1997. Continuing the Conversation on Chinese Human Rights. *Ethics and International Affairs* 11: 177–205.

Anderson, Benedict. 1991. *Imagined Communities: Reflections on the Origin and Spread of Nationalism*. Rev. edition. London: Verso.

Anderson, Sean, and Stephen Sloan. 1995. *Historical Dictionary of Terrorism*. Metuchen, N.J.: Scarecrow Press.

Anscombe, Elizabeth. 1970. War and Murder. In *War and Morality*, ed. Richard A. Wasserstrom. Belmont, CA: Wadsworth.

Aquinas, Thomas. 1974 [1271]. Summa Theologica (Secunda Secundae, Quaestio XL De Bello). In *Aquinas: Selected Political Writings*, ed. A. P. D'Entreves. Oxford: Blackwell.

Archibugi, Daniele. 1995. From the United Nations to Cosmopolitan Democracy. In *Cosmopolitan Democracy: An Agenda for a New World Order*, ed. Daniele Archibugi and David Held. Cambridge: Polity.

Augustine, St. 1984. *City of God*. Trans. Henry Bettenson. London: Penguin Classics.

B'Tzelem. 1997. *Legitimizing Torture: The Israeli High Court of Justice Rulings in the Bilbeisi, Hamdan and Mubarak Cases*. Jerusalem: B'Tzelem.

Baier, Annette. 1989. Doing without Moral Theory? In *Anti-Theory in Ethics and Moral Conservatism*, ed. Stanley G. Clarke and Evan Simpson. Albany: State University of New York Press.

———. 1994. Violent Demonstrations. In *Moral Prejudices: Essays on Ethics*. Cambridge: Harvard University Press.

Ballingrud, David. 1998. It Didn't Happen . . . Like That. *New York Times*, 18 June.

Barry, Brian. 1991. *Liberty and Justice: Essays in Political Theory*. Vol. 2. Oxford: Clarendon Press.

———. 1998. International Society from a Cosmopolitan Perspective. In *International Society: Diverse Ethical Perspectives*, ed. David Mapel and Terry Nardin. Princeton: Princeton University Press.

———. 1999. Statism and Nationalism: A Cosmopolitan Critique. In *NOMOS*. Vol. 41, *Global Justice*, ed. Ian Shapiro and Lea Brilmayer. New York: New York University Press.

Barzilay, David. 1973. *The British Army in Ulster*. Vol. 1. Belfast: Century Books.

Beitz, Charles R. 1979a. Bounded Morality: Justice and the State in World Politics. *International Organisation* 33: 405–24.

———. 1979b. *Political Theory and International Relations*. Princeton: Princeton University Press.

———. 1980. Nonintervention and Communal Integrity. *Philosophy and Public Affairs* 9: 385–91.

———. 1983. Cosmopolitan Ideals and National Sentiments. *Journal of Philosophy* 80: 591–99.

———. 1988a. The Reagan Doctrine in Nicaragua. In *Problems of International Justice*, ed. Steven Luper-Foy. Boulder: Westview.

———. 1988b. Recent International Thought. *International Journal* 43: 183–204.

———. 1994. Cosmopolitan Liberalism and the States System. In *Political Restructuring in Europe: Ethical Perspectives*, ed. Chris Brown. London: Routledge.

Bell, Bowyer J. 1972. *The Secret Army: A History of the I.R.A., 1916–1970*. London: Sphere Books.

Benn, Stanley I., and R. S. Peters. 1959. *Social Principles and the Democratic State*. London: George Allen and Unwin.

Bennett, Ronan. 1998. Out of the Pound Loney. *London Review of Books*, 5 March: 25–26.

Berdal, Mats, and Michael Leifer. 1996. Cambodia. In *The New Interventionism 1991–1994: United Nations Experience in Cambodia, Former Yugoslavia and Somalia*, ed. James Mayall. Cambridge: Cambridge University Press.

Bhagavad Gita. 1968. Trans. Eliot Geutsch. New York: Holt, Rinehart and Winston.

Biersteker, Thomas. 1995. The "Triumph" of Liberal Economic Ideas in the Developing World. In *Global Change, Regional Response: The New International Context of Development*, ed. Barbara Stallings. Cambridge: Cambridge University Press.

Bishop, Patrick, and Eamonn Mallie. 1988. *The Provisional IRA*. London: Corgi Books.

Blumenfeld, S., and M. Meselson. 1971. The Military Value and Political Implications of the Use of Riot Control Agents in Warfare. In *The Control of Chemical and Biological Weapons*. New York: Carnegie Endowment for International Peace.

Booth, Ken. 1994. Military Intervention: Duty and Prudence. In *Military Intervention in European Conflicts*, ed. Lawrence Freedman. Oxford: Blackwell.

————. 1995. Human Wrongs and International Relations. *International Affairs* 71: 103–26.

Boutwell, Jeffrey, and Everett Mendelson. 1995. *Israeli–Palestinian Security: Issues in the Permanent Status Negotiations.* Cambridge, Mass.: American Academy of Arts and Sciences.

Bowen, Clay, and Robert Gard. 1998. Poison Gas Use by U.S.? Not Likely. *New York Newsday,* 22 June.

Bradshaw, James Stanford. 1978. Manley's Mistakes in Jamaica. *New Leader* 61: 9–11.

Brandt, Richard. 1979. Utilitarianism and the Rules of War. In *War, Morality and the Military Profession,* 1st edition, ed. Malham Wakin. Boulder: Westview Press.

Brewin, Christopher. 1978. Justice in International Relations. In *The Reasons of State,* ed. Michael Donelan. London: Allen & Unwin.

Broad, William J. 1997. Military Is Hoping to Test-Fire Laser against Satellite. *The New York Times,* 1 September: A1, A10.

Brown, Chris. 1992. *International Relations Theory: New Normative Approaches.* New York: Harvester Wheatsheaf.

————. 1993. International Affairs. In *A Companion to Contemporary Political Philosophy,* ed. Robert Goodin and Philip Pettit. Oxford: Blackwell.

————. 1997. Universal Human Rights: A Critique. *The International Journal of Human Rights* 1: 41–65.

Brownlie, Ian, ed. 1992. *Basic Documents on Human Rights,* 3rd edition. Oxford: Oxford University Press.

Bruce, Steve. 1997. Victim Selection in Ethnic Conflict: Motives and Attitudes in Irish Republicanism. *Terrorism & Political Violence* 9: 56–71.

Brunner, Karl. 1996 [1976]. The New International Economic Order: A Chapter in a Protracted Confrontation. In *Economic Analysis and Political Ideology.* Cheltenham, U.K.: E. Elgar.

Buchanan, Allen. 1991. *Secession: The Morality of Political Divorce from Fort Sumter to Lithuania and Quebec.* Boulder: Westview Press.

Buchanan, George. 1579. *On the Legitimate Kingdom of the Scots (De Iure Regni apud Scotos).* Edinburgh.

Buckingham, William A. 1982. *Operation Ranch Hand: The Air Force and Herbicides in Southeast Asia, 1961–1971.* Washington, D.C.: Office of Air Force History.

Bull, Hedley. 1984. Introduction. In *Intervention in World Politics,* ed. Hedley Bull. Oxford: Clarendon Press.

Burrowes, Carl. 1983. Who Rules Liberia? A Reconsideration of the Settler Class Thesis. Unpublished manuscript.

Burton, Frank. 1978. *The Politics of Legitimacy: Struggles in a Belfast Community.* London: Routledge, Kegan Paul.

Bush, George. 1992. *Public Papers of the Presidents of the United States.* Book 1. Washington, D.C.: U.S. Government Printing Office.

Calvert, Peter. 1982. *The Falklands Crisis: The Rights and the Wrongs.* London: Frances Pinter.

Campbell, David. 1993. *Politics without Principle.* Boulder: Lynne Rienner.

Campbell, T. D. 1974. Humanity before Justice. *British Journal of Political Science* 4: 1–16.

Caney, Simon. 1997. Human Rights and the Rights of States: Terry Nardin on Nonintervention. *International Political Science Review* 18: 27–37.

Carr, E. H. 1964. *Twenty Years Crisis, 1919–1939: An Introduction to the Study of International Relations.* New York: Harper Torchbooks.

Childress, James. 1986. Just War Theories: The Bases, Interrelations, Priorities and Functions of Their Criteria. In *War Morality and the Military Profession*, 2nd edition, ed. Malham Wakin. Boulder: Westview Press.

Chopra, Jarat, and Thomas Weiss. 1992. Sovereignty Is No Longer Sacrosanct: Codifying Humanitarian Intervention. *Ethics and International Affairs* 6: 95–117.

Christopher, Paul. 1999. *The Ethics of War and Peace.* 2nd edition. Englewood Cliffs, N.J.: Prentice Hall.

Clark, Ramsey. 1992. *The Fire This Time.* New York: Thunders Mouth Press.

Claude, Inis L. 1980. Just Wars: Doctrines and Institutions. *Political Science Quarterly* 95: 83–96.

Clausewitz, Carl von. 1976 [1816]. *On War.* Trans. and ed. Michael Howard and Peter Peret. Princeton: Princeton University Press.

Coady, C. A. J. 1985. The Morality of Terrorism. *Philosophy* 60: 47–69.

Coates, Anthony J. 1996. The New World Order and the Ethics of War. In *The Ethical Dimensions of Global Change*, ed. Barry Holden. London: Macmillan.

———. 1997. *The Ethics of War.* Manchester: Manchester University Press.

Cobban, Helena. 1984. *The Palestinian Liberation Organization: People, Power and Politics.* New York: Columbia University Press.

Cohen, Joshua, ed. 1996. *For Love of Country: Debating the Limits of Patriotism.* Boston: Beacon Press.

Coogan, T. P. 1987. *The I.R.A.* 3rd edition. London: Fontana.

Copson, Raymond. 1996. Africa's Internal Wars. In *Collapsed States in Africa*, ed. I. William Zartman. Boulder: Lynn Reinner.

Cranston, Maurice. 1973. *What Are Human Rights?* London: Bodley Head.

Curtis, Edmund. 1961. *A History of Ireland.* London: Methuen.

Danner, Mark. 1997. The US and the Yugoslav Catastrophe. *The New York Review of Books* 44: 56–64.

De Beauvoir, Simone. 1989. *The Second Sex.* New York: Vintage Books.

DeGeorge, Richard. 1993. *Competing with Integrity in International Business.* New York: Oxford University Press.

Diehl, Paul, Jennifer Reifschneider, and Paul Hensel. 1996. United Nations Intervention and Recurring Conflict. *International Organization* 50: 683–700.

Dillon, Martin. 1994. *The Enemy Within.* London: Doubleday.

Dingley, James. 1998. A Reply to White's Non-Sectarian Thesis of PIRA Targeting. *Terrorism & Political Violence* 10: 106–17.

Dobson, Christopher, John Miller, and Ronald Payne. 1982. *The Falklands Conflict.* London: Coronet.

Donaldson, Thomas. 1989. *The Ethics of International Business.* New York: Oxford University Press.

———. 1994. The Perils of Multinationals' Largesse. *Business Ethics Quarterly* 4: 367–71.

Donnelly, Jack. 1993. Human Rights, Humanitarian Crisis, and Humanitarian Intervention. *International Journal* 48: 607–40.

Doppelt, Gerald. 1978. Walzer's Theory of Morality in International Relations. *Philosophy and Public Affairs* 8: 3–26.

———. 1980. Statism without Foundations. *Philosophy and Public Affairs* 9: 398–403.

Doyal, Len, and Ian Gough. 1991. *A Theory of Human Need*. Basingstoke, U.K.: Macmillan.

Drake, C. J. M. 1998. The Role of Ideology in Terrorists' Target Selection. *Terrorism & Political Violence* 10: 53–85.

Dugard, John. 1982. International Terrorism and the Just War. In *The Morality of Terrorism: Religious and Secular Justifications*, ed. David C. Rapoport and Yonah Alexander. New York: Pergamon Books.

Duncker, Karl. 1939. Ethical Relativity? (An Enquiry into the Psychology of Ethics). *Mind* new series 48: 39–57.

Duvall, Raymond, and Michael Stohl. 1988. Governance by Terror. In *The Politics of Terrorism*, ed. Michael Stohl. New York: Marcell-Dekker.

Eddy, Paul, Magnus Linklater, Peter Gillman, and The Sunday Times Insight Team. 1982. *The Falklands War*. London: André Deutsch.

Edie, Carlene J. 1991. *Democracy by Default: Dependency and Clientelism in Jamaica*. Boulder: Lynne Rienner.

Eisenberg, Nancy, Janusz Reykowski, and Ervin Staub, eds. 1989. *Social and Moral Values: Individual and Societal Perspectives*. Hillsdale, N.J.: Lawrence Erlbaum Associates.

Elfstrom, Gerard. 1983. On Dilemmas of Intervention. *Ethics* 93: 709–25.

European Political Cooperation Press Release. 1992. *European Community: Declaration on Yugoslavia and on the Guidelines on the Recognition of New States*. 31 I.L.M. 1485. 16 December.

Evans, Michael. 1991. Bridge Bombing Campaign Tarnishes Allies' PR Image. *The Times*, 8 February.

Evans, Peter. 1979. *Dependent Development: The Alliance of Multinational, Local, and State Capital in Brazil*. Princeton: Princeton University Press.

Fay, Marie-Therese, Michael Morrissey, and Marie Smyth. 1999. *Northern Ireland's Troubles: The Human Costs*. London: Pluto Press.

Ferrill, Arther. 1985. *The Origins of War: From the Stone Age to Alexander the Great*. London: Thames and Hudson Ltd.

Finberg, Richard A. 1972. No More Chemical/Biological War. *The New Republic* 167: 21.

Finnis, John. 1996. The Ethics of War and Peace in the Catholic Natural Law Tradition. In *The Ethics of War and Peace: Religious and Secular Perspectives*, ed. Terry Nardin. Princeton: Princeton University Press.

———. 1998. *Aquinas: Moral, Political, and Legal Theory*. Oxford: Oxford University Press.

Fishkin, James. 1986. Theories of Justice and International Relations: The Limits of Liberal Theory. In *Ethics and International Relations*, ed. Anthony Ellis. Manchester: Manchester University Press.

Folger, Robert, ed. 1984. *The Sense of Injustice: Social Psychological Perspectives*. New York: Plenum Press.

Fotion, Nick. 1997. A Utilitarian Defense of Just War Theory. *Synthesis Philosophica* 23: 209–25.

Franck, Thomas, and Nigel Rodley. 1973. After Bangladesh: The Law of Humanitarian Intervention by Military Force. *American Journal of International Law* 67: 275–305.

Frankel, Benjamin. 1996. Introduction. In *Roots of Realism*, ed. Benjamin Frankel. London: Frank Cass.

Freedman, Lawrence, and Virginia Gamba-Stonehouse. 1990. *Signals of War: The Falklands Conflict of 1982*. London: Faber and Faber.

Frieden, Jeffry. 1981. Third World Indebted Industrialization: International Finance and State Capitalism in Mexico, Brazil, Algeria, and South Korea. *International Organization* 35: 407–31.

Friedman, Milton. 1990. The Social Responsibility of Business Is to Increase Its Profits. In *Business Ethics*, 2nd edition, ed. W. Michael Hoffman and Jennifer Mills Moore. New York: McGraw-Hill.

Fullinwider, Robert K. 1988. Understanding Terrorism. In *Problems of International Justice*, ed. Steven Luper-Foy. Boulder: Westview Press.

Gallup Opinion Poll. 1998. Latest Polls on Israel's May 29 Elections. Available at <http://www2.nando.net/net/newsroom/nt/527irpolls.html>, accessed 26 May.

Gardels, Nathan. 1992. Adam Smith Was Right. *New Perspectives Quarterly* 9–10: 46–51.

Genscher, Hans-Dietrich. 1995. *Errinerungen*. Berlin: Siedler Verlag.

Gertz, Bill. 1996. Powerful Foes Decry Chemical Arms Pact: Senate Is Likely to Vote Thursday. *Washington Times*, 9 September: A1.

Gibbs, John C. 1991. Toward an Integration of Kohlberg's and Hoffman's Moral Development Theories. *Human Development* 34: 88–104.

Gilbert, G. M. 1947. *Nuremberg Diary*. New York: New American Library.

Gilbert, Paul. 1994. *Terrorism, Security, and Nationality: An Introductory Study in Applied Political Philosophy*. New York: Routledge.

Gilpin, Robert. 1987. *The Political Economy of International Relations*. Princeton: Princeton University Press.

Glenny, Misha. 1993. *The Fall of Yugoslavia*. New York: Penguin Books.

Goodin, Robert E. 1988. What Is So Special about Our Fellow Countrymen? *Ethics* 98: 663–86.

———. 1990. Relative Needs. In *Needs and Welfare*, ed. Robert E. Goodin and Alan Ware. London: Sage.

Gordon, Neve, and Ruchama Marton, eds. 1995. *Torture: Human Rights, Medical Ethics and the Case of Israel*. London: Zed Books.

Gordon, Philip H. 1994. The Normalization of German Foreign Policy. *Orbis* 38: 225–42.

Gordon, Ruth. 1994. United Nations Intervention in Internal Conflicts: Iraq, Somalia, and Beyond. *Michigan Journal of International Law* 15: 519–89.

Greenberg, Jerald, and Ronald L. Cohen, eds. 1982. *Equity and Justice in Social Behavior*. New York: Academic Press.

Griffiths, Martin, Iain Levine, and Mark Weller. 1995. Sovereignty and Suffering. In *The Politics of Humanitarian Intervention*, ed. John Harriss. London: Pinter.

Grotius, Hugo. 1925 [1646]. *On the Law of War and Peace (De Jure Belli ac Pacis)*. Oxford: Clarendon Press.

Hallion, Richard P. 1992. *Storm over Iraq: Air Power and the Gulf War*. Washington, D.C.: Smithsonian Institution Press.

Harbour, Frances V. 1999. *Thinking about International Ethics: Moral Theory and American Foreign Policy*. Boulder: Westview Press.

Hardin, Garret. 1995. Lifeboat Ethics: The Case against Helping the Poor. In *World Hunger and Morality*, 2nd edition, ed. William Aiken and Hugh LaFollette. Upper Saddle River, N.J.: Prentice Hall.

Hare, R. M. 1979a. Can I Be Blamed for Obeying Orders? In *War, Morality and the Military Profession*, 1st edition, ed. Malham Wakin. Boulder: Westview Press.

———. 1979b. On Terrorism. *Journal of Value Inquiry* 13: 241–49.

Hart, Jeffrey. 1983. *The New International Economic Order: Conflict and Cooperation in North–South Economic Relations, 1974–77.* London: Macmillan.

Hart, Peter. 1996. The Protestant Experience of Revolution in Southern Ireland. In *Unionism in Modern Ireland: New Perspectives on Politics and Culture*, ed. Richard English and Graham Walker. Basingstoke, U.K.: Macmillan Press.

Hatch, Orrin. 1991. Turbulence Begging a Doctrine. *Washington Times*, 8 October.

Hauerwas, Stanley. 1986. Pacifism: Some Philosophical Considerations. In *War, Morality and the Military Profession*, 2nd edition, ed. Malham Wakin. Boulder: Westview Press.

Hayek, F. A. 1976. *Law, Legislation and Liberty.* Vol. 2, *The Mirage of Social Justice.* London: Routledge and Kegan Paul.

Hehir, J. Bryan. 1995. Intervention: From Theories to Cases. *Ethics and International Affairs* 9: 1–13.

Heidenrich, John G. 1993. The Gulf War: How Many Iraqis Died? *Foreign Policy* 90: 108–25.

Heikal, Mohamed. 1992. *Illusions of Triumph: An Arab View of the Gulf.* London: HarperCollins.

Held, David. 1995. *Democracy and the Global Order: From the Modern State to Cosmopolitan Governance.* Cambridge: Polity Press.

Held, Virginia. 1984. *Rights and Goods: Justifying Social Action.* New York: Free Press.

———. 1991. Terrorism, Rights, and Political Goals. In *Violence, Terrorism, and Justice*, ed. R. G. Frey and Christopher W. Morris. Cambridge: Cambridge University Press.

Held, Virginia, Sidney Morgenbesser, and Thomas Nagel, eds. 1974. *Philosophy, Morality, and International Affairs.* New York: Oxford University Press.

Hepburn, C. 1980. *The Conflict of Nationality in Modern Ireland.* London: Edward Arnold.

Hersh, Seymour M. 1968. *Chemical and Biological Warfare: America's Hidden Arsenal.* Indianapolis: Bobbs-Merrill.

Hewan, Clinton G. 1994. *Jamaica and the United States Caribbean Basin Initiative.* New York: Peter Lang.

Hodge, Carl Cavanagh. 1998. Botching the Balkans: Germany's Recognition of Slovenia and Croatia. *Ethics and International Affairs* 12: 1–12.

Hoffmann, Stanley. 1981. *Duties beyond Borders: On the Limits and Possibilities of Ethical International Politics.* Syracuse, N.Y.: Syracuse University Press.

———. 1984. The Problem of Intervention. In *Intervention in World Politics*, ed. Hedley Bull. Oxford: Clarendon Press.

———. 1995–96. The Politics and Ethics of Military Intervention. *Survival* 37: 29–51.

———. 1996. *The Ethics and Politics of Humanitarian Intervention.* South Bend, Ind.: University of Notre Dame Press.

Holmes, Robert L. 1989. *On War and Morality.* Princeton: Princeton University Press.

Horowitz, Donald. 1995. Self-Determination, Philosophy and Law. MacArthur Foundation Program in Transnational Security, Working Paper Series.

Huber, Jeff. 1997. Catch F-22. *Naval Institute Proceedings,* September: 368.

Human Rights Watch (HRW). 1993. *A License to Kill: Israeli Undercover Operations against "Wanted" and Masked Palestinians.* Washington, D.C.: HRW.

———. 1994. *Torture and Ill-Treatment: Israel's Interrogation of Palestinians from the Occupied Territories.* Washington, D.C.: HRW.

———. 1996. *Civilian Pawns: Laws of War Violations and the Use of Weapons on the Israel–Lebanon Border.* Washington, D.C.: HRW.

———. 1997. *Syria/Lebanon: An Alliance beyond the Law.* Washington, D.C.: HRW.

Jacobsen, Harold K., Dusan Sidjanski, Jeffrey Rodamar, and Alice Hougassian-Rudovich. 1983. Revolutionaries or Bargainers? Negotiators for a New International Economic Order. *World Politics* 35: 335–67.

Jervis, Robert. 1988. Realism, Game Theory, and Cooperation. *World Politics* 40: 317–49.

John of Salisbury. 1963. *The Statesman's Book.* Trans. John Dickinson. New York: Russell & Russell.

Johnson, James Turner. 1973. Ideology and the Jus ad Bellum: Justice in the Initiation of War. *Journal of the American Academy of Religion* 41: 212–28.

———. 1981. *Just War Tradition and the Restraint of War: A Moral and Historical Inquiry.* Princeton: Princeton University Press.

———. 1984. *Can Modern War Be Just?* New Haven: Yale University Press.

Johnson, James Turner, and George Weigel, eds. 1991. *Just War and the Gulf War.* Washington, D.C.: Ethics and Public Policy Center.

Jomini, Baron de. 1974. *The Art of War.* Trans. G. H. Mendell and W. P. Craighill. Westport, Conn.: Greenwood Press.

Jones, Peter. 1994. *Rights.* Basingstoke, U.K.: Macmillan.

———. 1996. International Human Rights: Philosophical or Political? In *National Rights, International Obligations*, ed. Simon Caney, David George, and Peter Jones. Boulder: Westview Press.

———. 2000. International Justice—amongst Whom? In *International Justice*, ed. Anthony J. Coates. Aldershot, U.K.: Ashgate.

Kahneman, Daniel, Jack L. Knetsch, and Richard H. Thaler. 1986. Fairness and the Assumptions of Economics. *Journal of Business* 59: S285–S300.

Kandeh, Jimmy. 1996. What Does the Militariat Do When It Rules? *Review of African Political Economy* 69: 387–404.

Keegan, John. 1993. *A History of Warfare.* London: Hutchinson.

Keith, Nelson W., and Novella Z. Keith. 1992. *The Social Origins of Democratic Socialism in Jamaica.* Philadelphia: Temple University Press.

Kennan, George. 1951. *American Diplomacy: 1900–1950.* Chicago: University of Chicago Press.

———. 1985–86. Morality and Foreign Affairs. *Foreign Affairs* 64: 205–18.

Kersch, Terrence Joseph Henry. 1995. The Idea of the National Interest: A Conceptual Analysis in the Context of the Gulf War. Ph.D. dissertation, University of British Columbia.

Khatchadourian, Haig. 1998. *The Morality of Terrorism.* New York: Peter Lang.

Kieh, George Klay. 1998. International Organizations and Peacekeeping in Africa. In *Peacekeeping in Africa: ECOMOG in Liberia*, ed. Karl Magyar and Earl Conteh-Morgan. London: Macmillan.

Kirton, Claremont. 1992. *Jamaica: Poverty and Debt*. Oxford: Oxfam Publications.

Kissinger, Henry. 1994. *Diplomacy*. New York: Simon and Schuster.

Kotsonouris, Mary. 1994. *Retreat from Revolution: The Dáil Courts, 1920–24*. Dublin: Irish Academic Press.

Krasner, Stephen. 1985. *Structural Conflict: The Third World against Global Liberalism*. Berkeley: University of California Press.

Kreinin, Mordechai E., and J. M. Finger. 1976. A Critical Survey of the New International Economic Order. *Journal of World Trade Law* 10: 493–512.

Kushner, Harvey W. 1996. Suicide Bombers: Business as Usual. *Studies in Conflict and Terrorism* 19: 329–37.

Kwanton, Luc. 1979. *Imperial Nomads: A History of Central Asia 500–1500*. Philadelphia: University of Pennsylvania Press.

Kymlicka, Will. 1995. *Multicultural Citizenship: A Liberal Theory of Minority Rights*. Oxford: Clarendon Press.

Langley, Winston. 1990. What Happened to the New International Economic Order? *Socialist Review* 20: 47–62.

Laws of Manu, The. 1991. Trans. Wendy Doniger and Brian K. Smith. New York: Penguin Books.

Lerner, Melvin J. 1975. The Justice Motive in Social Behavior: Introduction. *Journal of Social Issues* 31: 1–19.

Lerner, Melvin J., and Sally C. Lerner, eds. 1981. *The Justice Motive in Social Behavior: Adapting to Times of Scarcity and Change*. New York: Plenum Press.

Levy, Jack S., and Lily I. Vakili. 1992. Diversionary Action by Authoritarian Regimes: Argentina in the Falklands/Malvinas Case. In *The Internationalization of Communal Strife*, ed. Manus I. Midlarsky. London: Routledge.

Lewallen, John. 1971. *Ecology of Devastation: Indochina*. Baltimore: Penguin Books.

Lewis, Ioan, and James Mayall. 1996. Somalia. In *The New Interventionism 1991–1994: United Nations Experience in Cambodia, Former Yugoslavia and Somalia*, ed. James Mayall. Cambridge: Cambridge University Press.

Libal, Michael. 1997. *Limits of Persuasion: Germany and the Yugoslav Crisis, 1991–1992*. London: Praeger.

Lillich, Richard. 1967. Forcible Self-Help by States to Protect Human Rights. *Iowa Law Review* 53: 325–51.

———, ed. 1973. *Humanitarian Intervention and the United Nations*. Charlottesville: University Press of Virginia.

Lipton, Michael. 1977. *Why Poor People Stay Poor: Urban Bias in World Development*. Cambridge: Harvard University Press.

Locke, John. 1960 [1690]. *Two Treatises of Government*. Ed. Peter Laslett. Cambridge: Cambridge University Press.

Lopez, George A. 1995. Terrorism and Peace Studies. *Peace Review* 7: 261–66.

Luban, David. 1980a. Just War and Human Rights. *Philosophy and Public Affairs* 9: 160–81.

———. 1980b. The Romance of the Nation-State. *Philosophy and Public Affairs* 9: 392–97.

Lyons, F. S. L. 1973. *Ireland since the Famine*. Rev. edition. London: Collins, Fontana.

Lyons, Terrance, and Ahmed Samatar. 1995. *Somalia: State Collapse, Multilateral Inter-*

vention, and Strategies for Political Reconstruction. Washington, D.C.: Brookings Institution.

Macardle, Dorothy. 1968. *The Irish Republic.* London: Corgi Books.

Mahan, Alfred T. 1957 [1890]. *The Influence of Sea Power upon History: 1668–1783.* New York: Sagamore Press.

Makiya, Kanan. 1994. *Cruelty and Silence.* London: Penguin.

Manley, Michael. 1987. *Up the Down Escalator.* London: André Deutsch.

———. 1993. Caribbean Conversion. *The Wilson Quarterly* 17: 153.

Marable, Manning. 1993. Michael Manley. *The Progressive,* July: 23–27.

Margalit, Avishai, and Joseph Raz. 1990. National Self-Determination. *Journal of Philosophy* 87: 439–61.

Martin, F. X. 1993. Diarmait MacMurchada and the Coming of the Anglo-Normans. In *A New History of Ireland.* Vol. 2, *Medieval Ireland, 1169–1534,* ed. Art Cosgrove. Oxford: Clarendon Press.

Mason, Andrew, and Nick Wheeler. 1996. Realist Objections to Humanitarian Intervention. In *The Ethical Dimensions of Global Change,* ed. Barry Holden. London: Macmillan.

Maull, Hans. 1995. A German Perspective. In *Multilateralism and Western Strategy,* ed. Michael Brenner. New York: St. Martin's Press.

Maxwell, Mary. 1990. *Morality among Nations: An Evolutionary View.* Albany: State University of New York Press.

McCarthy, Richard. 1969. *The Ultimate Folly: War by Pestilence, Asphyxiation, and Defoliation.* New York: Vintage Books.

McGowan, Daniel A., and Marc H. Ellis, eds. 1998. *Remembering Deir Yassin: The Future of Israel and Palestine.* New York: Olive Branch Press.

McGuire, Michael T. 1991. Moralistic Aggression and the Sense of Justice. *American Behavioral Scientist* 34: 371–85.

McKinsey, Michael. 1981. Obligations to the Starving. *Nous* 15: 309–23.

McMahan, Jeff. 1986. The Ethics of International Intervention. In *Ethics and International Relations,* ed. Anthony Ellis. Manchester: Manchester University Press.

McMahan, Jeff, and Robert McKim. 1993. The Just War and the Gulf War. *Canadian Journal of Philosophy* 23: 501–41.

Meadows, Donella, and Dennis Meadows. 1974. *The Limits to Growth: A Report for the Club of Rome's Project on the Predicament of Mankind.* 2nd edition. New York: Universe Books.

Meinecke, Friedrich. 1962. *Machiavellism: The Doctrine of Raison d'État and Its Place in Modern History.* Trans. Douglas Scott. London: Routledge and Kegan Paul.

Mill, John Stuart. 1984 [1859]. A Few Words on Non-Intervention. In *Essays on Equality, Law, and Education: Collected Works of John Stuart Mill,* Vol. 21, ed. John Robson. Toronto: University of Toronto Press.

Miller, David. 1995. *On Nationality.* Oxford: Oxford University Press.

Minear, Larry, Thomas G. Weiss, and Kurt Campbell. 1991. Humanitarianism and War: Learning the Lessons from Recent Armed Conflicts. Occasional Paper, 8. Providence, R.I.: The Thomas J. Watson Jr. Institute for International Studies, Brown University.

Mitchell, Arthur. 1995. *Revolutionary Government in Ireland: Dáil Éireann 1919–1922.* Dublin: Gill & Macmillan.

Moore, John N. 1969. The Control of Foreign Intervention in Internal Conflict. *Virginia Journal of International Law* 9: 209–342.

Morgenthau, Hans J. 1950. The Mainsprings of American Foreign Policy: The National Interest vs. Moral Abstractions. *American Political Science Review* 44: 833–54.

———. 1952. *In Defense of the National Interest*. New York: Alfred A. Knopf.

———. 1967. To Intervene or Not to Intervene. *Foreign Affairs* 45: 425–36.

Morphet, Sally. 1995. UN Peacekeeping and Election-Monitoring. In *United Nations, Divided World: The UN's Roles in International Relations*, 2nd edition, ed. Adam Roberts and Benedict Kingsbury. Oxford: Clarendon Press.

Morris, Benny. 1987. *The Birth of the Palestinian Refugee Problem, 1947–1949*. Cambridge: Cambridge University Press.

Mufuka, K. Nyamayaro. 1978. The Jamaican Experiment. *Current History* 74: 70–73, 88–90.

Mühlen, Alexander. 1992. Die Deutsche Rolle bei der Anerkennung der Jugoslawischen Sezessionstaaten. *Liberal*, June.

Munck, Gerardo, and Chetan Kumar. 1995. Civil Conflicts and the Conditions for Successful International Intervention: A Comparative Study of Cambodia and El Salvador. *Review of International Studies* 21: 159–81.

Murray, A. J. H. 1996. The Moral Politics of Hans Morgenthau. *Review of Politics* 58: 81–107.

Nardin, Terry. 1983. *Law, Morality and the Relations of States*. Princeton: Princeton University Press.

Nardin, Terry, and David R. Mapel, eds. 1992. *Traditions of International Ethics*. Cambridge: Cambridge University Press.

Nasr, Kamel B. 1997. *Arab and Israeli Terrorism*. Jefferson, N.C.: McFarland & Co.

Neibuhr, Reinhold. 1932. *Moral Man and Immoral Society*. New York: Charles Scribner's Sons.

———. 1958. *The World Crisis and American Responsibility: Nine Essays*. New York: Association Press.

———. 1962. *The Irony of American History*. New York: Scribner.

Nielsen, Kai. 1984. Global Justice, Capitalism and the Third World. *Journal of Applied Philosophy* 1: 175–86.

Norman, Richard. 1995. *Ethics, Killing and War*. Cambridge: Cambridge University Press.

Nye, Joseph S., Jr. 1986. *Nuclear Ethics*. New York: Free Press.

O'Brien, Brendan. 1993. *The Long War: The IRA and Sinn Fein, 1985 to Today*. Dublin: O'Brien Press.

O'Brien, Conor Cruise. 1993. The Future of the West. *The National Interest* 30: 3.

O'Brien, William V. 1981. *The Conduct of Just and Limited War*. New York: Praeger.

O'Flaherty, J. Daniel. 1978. Finding Jamaica's Way. *Foreign Policy* 31: 137–58.

O'Neill, Onora. 1986. *Faces of Hunger: An Essay on Poverty, Justice and Development*. London: Allen & Unwin.

———. 1988. Hunger, Needs and Rights. In *Problems of International Justice*, ed. Steven Luper-Foy. Boulder: Westview Press.

Onwuka, Ralph I. 1986. The Illusions of the New International Economic Order. In *The Future of Africa and the New International Economic Order*, ed. Ralph I. Onwuka and Olajide Aluko. New York: St. Martin's Press.

Organization of Economic Cooperation and Development. 1998a. Oda5096.xls. Available at <http://ww.oecd.org/dac/htm/oda5096.htm>, accessed 18 November.

———. 1998b. Table3.xls. Available at <http://www.oecd.org/dac/htm/table3.htm>, accessed 18 November.

Pangle, Thomas L. 1976. The Moral Basis of National Security: Four Historical Perspectives. In *Historical Dimensions of National Security Problems*, ed. Klaus Knorr. Lawrence: University Press of Kansas.

Pangle, Thomas L., and Peter J. Ahrensdorf. 1999. *Justice among Nations: On the Moral Basis of Power and Peace*. Lawrence: University Press of Kansas.

Parekh, Bhikhu. 1997. Rethinking Humanitarian Intervention. *International Political Science Review* 18: 49–69.

Pasic, Amir, and Thomas G. Weiss. 1997. The Politics of Rescue: Yugoslavia's Wars and the Humanitarian Impulse. *Ethics and International Affairs* 11: 105–31.

Payne, Anthony. 1984. Jamaica: The "Democratic Socialist" Experiment of Michael Manley. In *Dependency under Challenge*, ed. Anthony Payne and Paul Sutton. Manchester: Manchester University Press.

Peffer, Nathaniel. 1945. Must It Be Power? *Political Science Quarterly* 9: 555–62.

Philpott, Daniel. 1995. In Defense of Self-Determination. *Ethics* 105: 352–85.

Physicians for Human Rights. 1995. *Shaking as a Form of Torture*. Boston: Physicians for Human Rights.

Pogge, Thomas. 1989. *Realising Rawls*. Ithaca: Cornell University Press.

———. 1992. An Institutional Approach to Humanitarian Intervention. *Public Affairs Quarterly* 6: 89–103.

———. 1994. Cosmopolitanism and Sovereignty. In *Political Restructuring in Europe: Ethical Perspectives*, ed. Chris Brown. London: Routledge.

Powell, Colin L. 1995. *A Soldier's Way*. London: Hutchinson.

Price, Richard M. 1997. *The Chemical Weapons Taboo*. Ithaca: Cornell University Press.

Priest, Dana. 1998. Pentagon Debunks Poison Gas Report; Probe Finds "No Hint" of Mission to Kill Defectors. *Washington Post*, 22 July.

Primoratz, Igor. 1990. What Is Terrorism? *Journal of Applied Philosophy* 7: 129–38.

Rabinovich, Itamar. 1991. Seven Wars and One Peace Treaty. In *The Arab–Israeli Conflict: Perspectives*, ed. Alvin Z. Rubenstein. New York: HarperCollins.

Rachel, Samuel. 1916 [1676]. *Dissertations on the Law of Nature and Nations (Dissertatio Prima De Jure Naturae, De Virtute Morali, De Bona Indole & Dissertatio Altera De Jure Gentium)*. Washington, D.C.: Carnegie Institution.

Rawls, John. 1971. *A Theory of Justice*. Cambridge: Harvard University Press.

———. 1993a. The Law of Peoples. In *On Human Rights: The Oxford Amnesty Lectures 1993*, ed. Stephen Shute and Susan Hurley. New York: Basic Books.

———. 1993b. *Political Liberalism*. New York: Columbia University Press.

Regan, Richard J. 1996. *Just War: Principles and Cases*. Washington, D.C.: Catholic University of America Press.

Rengger, N. J. 1993. Contextuality, Interdependence and the Ethics of Intervention. In *Political Theory, International Relations, and the Ethics of Intervention*, ed. Ian Forbes and Mark Hoffman. London: Macmillan.

Reyntjens, Felip. 1997. Rwanda: Recent History. In *Africa South of the Sahara*. London: Europa.

Richards, David A. J. 1982. International Distributive Justice. In *NOMOS*. Vol. 24, *Ethics, Economics and the Law*, ed. J. Roland Pennock and John Chapman. New York: New York University Press.

Riley-Smith, Jonathan. 1992. *What Were the Crusades?* 2nd edition. London: Macmillan.

Rock, William R. 1977. *British Appeasement in the 1930s*. London: Edward Arnold.

Rohter, Larry. 1997. Michael Manley, Ex-Premier of Jamaica, Is Dead at 72. *New York Times*, 8 March: 52.

Rosenthal, Joel. 1991. *Righteous Realists: Political Realism, Responsible Power, and American Culture in the Nuclear Age*. Baton Rouge: Louisiana State University Press.

Rousseau, Jean-Jacques. 1974. *The Social Contract: Or, Principles of Political Right*. New York: New American Library.

Samatar, Ahmed. 1988. *Socialist Somalia: Rhetoric or Reality?* London: Zed Press.

Sandel, Michael. 1982. *Liberalism and the Limits of Justice*. Cambridge: Cambridge University Press.

Schroeder, Paul. 1994. Historical Reality vs. Neo-Realist Theory. *International Security* 19: 108–48.

Schwartzkopf, H. Norman, and Peter Petre. 1992. *It Doesn't Take a Hero*. New York: Bantam.

Seale, Patrick. 1992. *Abu Nidal: A Gunman for Hire*. New York: Random House.

Sherman, William Tecumseh. 1892. *Memoirs*. Vol. 2, 4th edition. New York: Charles L. Webster and Co.

Shue, Henry. 1980. *Basic Rights: Subsistence, Affluence, and U.S. Foreign Policy*. Princeton: Princeton University Press.

Simons, Geoff. 1998. *The Scourging of Iraq*. London: Macmillan.

Simpson, Peter. 1986. Just War Theory and the IRA. *Journal of Applied Philosophy* 3: 73–88.

Singer, Peter. 1972. Famine, Affluence and Morality. *Philosophy and Public Affairs* 2: 229–43.

Slater, Jerome, and Terry Nardin. 1986. Nonintervention and Human Rights. *Journal of Politics* 48: 86–95.

Slim, Hugo, and Emma Visman. 1995. Evacuation, Intervention and Retaliation: United Nations Humanitarian Operations in Somalia, 1991–1993. In *The Politics of Humanitarian Intervention*, ed. John Harriss. London: Pinter.

Smith, Michael J. 1989. Ethics and Intervention. *Ethics and International Affairs* 3: 1–26.

———. 1998. Humanitarian Intervention: An Overview of the Ethical Issues. *Ethics and International Affairs* 12: 63–80.

Smith, Robert M. 1970. Nixon to Send Ban on Chemical War to Senate Today. *New York Times*, 19 August.

Smith, Ron C. 1991. *Ethics and Informal War*. New York: Vantage Press.

Spero, Joan, and Jeffrey Hart. 1997. *The Politics of International Economic Relations*. 5th edition. New York: St. Martin's Press.

Spiers, Edward M. 1989. *Chemical Weaponry, a Continuing Challenge*. New York: St. Martin's Press.

Stallings, Barbara. 1982. Euromarkets, Third World Countries and the International Political Economy. In *The New International Economy*, ed. Harry Makler, Alberto Martinelli, and Neil Smelser. Beverly Hills: Sage Publications.

————. 1987. *Banker to the Third World: U.S. Portfolio Investment in Latin America, 1900–1986*. Berkeley: University of California Press.

Sterns, Scott. 1994. Rwanda: An Uneasy Peace. *Africa Report* 39: 32–35.

Stohl, Michael. 1988. National Interests and State Terrorism in International Affairs. In *The Politics of Terrorism*, ed. Michael Stohl. New York: Marcell-Dekker.

Stohl, Michael, and George A. Lopez. 1988. Introduction. In *Terrible beyond Endurance? The Foreign Policy of State Terrorism*, ed. Michael Stohl and George A. Lopez. Westport, Conn.: Greenwood Press.

Suarez, Francisco. 1944 [1621]. A Work on the Three Theological Virtues Faith, Hope and Charity (De Triplici Virtute Theologicae Fede, Spe et Charitate). In *Selections from Three Works of Francisco Suarez*, Vol. 2, ed. John B. Scott. Oxford: Clarendon Press.

Sun Tzu. 1983. *The Art of War*. ed. James Clavell. New York: Dell Publishing.

Tamir, Yael. 1993. *Liberal Nationalism*. Princeton: Princeton University Press.

Taylor, P. 1997. *PROVOS: The IRA and Sinn Fein*. London: Bloomsbury.

Teichman, Jenny. 1989. How to Define Terrorism. *Philosophy* 64: 505–17.

Teson, Fernando. 1988. *Humanitarian Intervention: An Inquiry into Law and Morality*. New York: Transnational Publishers.

Thomas, Caroline. 1993. The Pragmatic Case against Intervention. In *Political Theory, International Relations, and the Ethics of Intervention*, ed. Ian Forbes and Mark Hoffman. London: Macmillan.

Thomas, Laurence. 1989. *Living Morally: A Psychology of Moral Character*. Philadelphia: Temple University Press.

Thomas, Raju. 1997. Self-Determination and International Recognition Policy: An Alternative Interpretation of Why Yugoslavia Disintegrated. *World Affairs* 160: 17–33.

Time-Life Editors. 1989. *Time Frame AD 1200–1300: The Mongol Conquests*. Alexandria, Va.: Time-Life Books.

Treitschke, Heinrich von. 1968 [1916]. Politics. In *Readings in Western Civilization: 1500 to the Present*, ed. George Knoles and Rixford Synder. New York: J. B. Lippincott Co.

UN Conference on Trade and Development. 1996. Midrand Declaration and a Partnership for Growth and Development.

U.S. Catholic Bishops. 1986. The Just War and Non-Violent Positions. In *War, Morality and the Military Profession*, 2nd edition, ed. Malham Wakin. Boulder: Westview Press.

U.S. Centers for Disease Control. 1992. Population-Based Mortality Assessment: Baidoa and Afgoi, Somalia. *Morbidity and Mortality Weekly Report* 41: 913–17.

U.S. Department of State. 1987. *Syrian Support for International Terrorism: 1983–86*. Washington, D.C.: Bureau of Public Affairs, Office of Public Communication.

————. 1996. *1996 Country Commercial Guide: Jamaica*. Washington, D.C.: U.S. Department of State.

————. 1998. *Patterns of Global Terrorism 1997*. Department of State Publication, 10321. Washington, D.C.: U.S. Department of State.

Valls, Andrew. 1996. Presidential Rhetoric: A Social Constructionist Approach. In *The Theory and Practice of Political Communication Research*, ed. Mary E. Stuckey. Albany: State University of New York Press.

van Heuven, Marten H. A. 1993. Testing the New Germany: The Case of Yugoslavia. *German Politics and Society* 11: 52–63.

Vann, Gerald. 1939. *Morality and War*. London: Burns Oates and Washbourne.

Vaux, Kenneth L. 1992. *Ethics and the Gulf War.* Boulder: Westview Press.

Velasquez, Manuel. 1995. International Business Ethics: The Aluminum Companies in Jamaica. *Business Ethics Quarterly* 5: 865–82.

Vincent, R. John. 1974. *Nonintervention and International Order.* Princeton: Princeton University Press.

———. 1986. *Human Rights and International Relations.* Cambridge: Cambridge University Press.

Vincent, R. John, and Peter Wilson. 1993. Beyond Non-Intervention. In *Political Theory, International Relations, and the Ethics of Intervention*, ed. Ian Forbes and Mark Hoffman. London: Macmillan.

Vitoria, Francisco de. 1991 [1539]. Relection on the Law of War (Relectio de Iure Belli). In *Vitoria—Political Writings*, ed. Anthony Pagden and Jeremy Lawrance. Cambridge: Cambridge University Press.

Wallace, Gerry. 1995. War, Terrorism and Ethical Consistency. In *Introducing Applied Philosophy*, ed. B. Almond. Oxford: Blackwell.

Waltz, Kenneth. 1979. *Theory of International Politics.* Reading, Mass.: Addison Wesley.

Walzer, Michael. 1980. The Moral Standing of States: A Response to Four Critics. *Philosophy and Public Affairs* 9: 209–29.

———. 1983. *Spheres of Justice.* Oxford: Blackwell.

———. 1988. Terrorism: A Critique of Excuses. In *Problems of International Justice*, ed. Steven Luper-Foy. Boulder: Westview Press.

———. 1992 [1979]. *Just and Unjust Wars: A Moral Argument with Historical Illustrations.* 2nd edition. New York: Basic Books.

———. 1994. *Thick and Thin: Moral Argument at Home and Abroad.* Notre Dame: University of Notre Dame Press.

Wayne, Stephen J. 1993. President Bush Goes to War. In *The Political Psychology of War*, ed. Stanley A. Renshon. Pittsburgh: University of Pittsburgh Press.

Weale, Albert. 1983. *Political Theory and Social Policy.* London: Macmillan.

Welch, David A. 1993. *Justice and the Genesis of War.* Cambridge: Cambridge University Press.

———. 1994. Can We Think Systematically about Ethics and Statecraft? *Ethics and International Affairs* 8: 23–37.

———. 1997. Remember the Falklands? Missed Lessons of a Misunderstood War. *International Journal* 52: 483–507.

Weller, Marc. 1992. The International Response to the Dissolution of the SFRY. *American Journal of International Law* 86: 569–607.

Wellman, Carl. 1979. On Terrorism Itself. *Journal of Value Inquiry* 13: 250–58.

Wellman, Christopher H. 1995. A Defense of Secession and Political Self-Determination. *Philosophy and Public Affairs* 24: 142–71.

West Africa. 1993. US Brute Force. *West Africa* 3956 (19–25 July): 1238–39.

Westmoreland, William. 1976. *A Soldier Reports.* Garden City, N.Y.: Doubleday.

Wheeler, Nick. 1992. Pluralist or Solidarist Conceptions of International Society: Bull and Vincent on Humanitarian Intervention. *Millennium* 21: 463–87.

White, Robert W. 1997a. The Irish Republican Army: An Assessment of Sectarianism. *Terrorism & Political Violence* 9: 20–55.

———. 1997b. The Irish Republican Army and Sectarianism: Moving beyond the Anecdote. *Terrorism & Political Violence* 9: 120–31.

———. 1998. Don't Confuse Me with the Facts: More on the Irish Republican Army and Sectarianism. *Terrorism & Political Violence* 10: 164–89.

Wicclair, Mark. 1979. Human Rights and Intervention. In *Human Rights and U.S. Foreign Policy: Principles and Applications*, ed. Peter G. Brown and Douglas Maclean. Lexington. Mass.: D. C. Heath.

———. 1980. Rawls and the Principle of Nonintervention. In *John Rawls' Theory of Social Justice: An Introduction*, ed. H. Gene Blocker. Athens: Ohio University Press.

Wilkins, Burleigh Taylor. 1992. *Terrorism and Collective Responsibility*. New York: Routledge.

Will, George. 1990. Lithuania and South Carolina. *Newsweek*, 29 January.

Wines, Michael. 1999. Two Views of Inhumanity Split the World, Even in Victory. *New York Times*, Section 4, 13 June: 1, 6.

Wolfers, Arnold. 1965. *Discord and Collaboration: Essays on International Politics*. Baltimore: Johns Hopkins University Press.

Wolff, Christian. 1934 [1764]. *Jus Gentium Methodo Scientifica Pertractatum*. Trans. Joseph Drake. Oxford: Clarendon.

Woodward, Bob. 1996. *The Choice: How Clinton Won*. New York: Simon & Schuster.

Woodward, Susan. 1993. Yugoslavia: Divide and Fail. *Bulletin of the Atomic Scientists* 49: 24–27.

———. 1995. *Balkan Tragedy*. Washington, D.C.: Brookings Institution.

World Bank. 1984. *World Development Report 1984*. New York: Oxford University Press.

Yoder, John Howard. 1996. *When War Is Unjust: Being Honest in Just-War Thinking*. New York: Orbis Books.

Zahn, Gordon. 1991. An Infamous Victory. *Commonweal*, 1 June: 366–68.

Zimmermann, Warren. 1996. *Origins of a Catastrophe: Yugoslavia and Its Destroyers— America's Last Ambassador Tells What Happened and Why*. New York: Times Books.

Index

About the Contributors

Simon Caney is a lecturer in politics and the deputy-director of the Centre for Political Thought at the University of Newcastle, U.K. His research focuses on contemporary analytical political philosophy, specifically liberalism, communitarianism, and global political theory. His articles have appeared in *Analysis, Political Studies, Utilitas, International Political Science Review, Oxford Journal of Legal Studies*, and *Journal of Political Philosophy*. He is currently completing a book entitled *Global Political Theory* for Oxford University Press.

Jeffrey Cason is an assistant professor of political science and the director of Latin American Studies at Middlebury College. He has written on trade policy in Brazil and economic integration in Latin America. He is coauthor (with Christopher Barrett) of *Overseas Research: A Practical Guide* (Johns Hopkins University Press, 1997) and coeditor (with Michael Carter and Frederic Zimmerman) of *Development at a Crossroads: Uncertain Paths to Sustainability after the Neo-Liberal Revolution* (Global Studies Program, University of Wisconsin Press, 1998).

Anthony J. Coates is a lecturer in politics at the University of Reading, England. His teaching and research interests are in political theory and the history of political thought. He is the author, most recently, of "The New World Order and The Ethics of War" (in *The Ethical Dimensions of Global Change*, ed. Barry Holden, Macmillan, 1996), *The Ethics of War* (Manchester University Press, 1997), and editor of *International Justice* (Ashgate, 2000).

Gerard Elfstrom is a professor of philosophy at Auburn University in Alabama. He has taught philosophy at Agnes Scott College, Emory University, and Morris Brown College and has written in the areas of the ethics of international relations, ethics and multinational corporations, military ethics, and political philosophy. His recent works include *International Ethics: A Reference Handbook* (ABC-

CLIO, 1998), *New Challenges for Political Philosophy* (ABC-CLIO, 1997), and *Moral Issues and Multinational Corporations* (ABC-CLIO, 1991). He is currently working on a project examining the context of moral agency.

Nicholas Fotion is a professor of philosophy at Emory University. He has published numerous articles on the philosophy of language, ethical theory, medical ethics, and military ethics. His recent publications include *Contingent Future Persons* (coedited with Jan Heller; Kluwar, 1997), *Toleration* (coauthored with Gerard Elfstrom; University of Alabama Press, 1992), *Military Ethics: Looking toward the Future* (Hoover Institution, 1991), and *Introduction to Medical Ethics* (Hyon-am Press, Korea, 1993). He is currently writing a book on the philosophy of John Searle.

David A. George is a lecturer in politics at the University of Newcastle, U.K. He is coeditor (with Simon Caney and Peter Jones) and contributor to *National Rights, International Obligations* (Westview, 1996) and has written numerous journal articles and book chapters on nationalism and terrorism. He broadcasts regularly on terrorism for the BBC and independent TV. Recently, he contributed twenty-four biographies of Middle East political leaders to the *Oxford Dictionary of Political Biography* (Oxford University Press, 1998). He is currently completing a book on jihad and Islamic international relations.

Neve Gordon is a lecturer in the Department of Politics and Government at Ben Gurion University, Israel. He is a former director of Physicians for Human Rights, Israel. His articles have appeared in a variety of journals, including *Polity, International Studies in Philosophy*, and *Peace Review*. He is also coeditor (with Ruchama Marton) of *Torture: Human Rights, Medical Ethics, and the Case of Israel* (Zed, 1995). He is currently working on a book analyzing methods of control in democratic societies.

Frances V. Harbour is an associate professor of government at George Mason University, where she teaches international relations. She is a founding member and served as secretary, vice chair, and chair of the International Ethics Section of the International Studies Association. Harbour is the author of several articles on the ethical implications of chemical weapons, as well as *Thinking about International Ethics: Moral Theory and Cases from American Foreign Policy* (Westview, 1999).

Peter Jones is a professor of political philosophy at the University of Newcastle, U.K. He has written on a variety of issues relating to democracy, freedom, justice, and human rights. He is the author of *Rights* (Macmillan, 1994) and coeditor (with Simon Caney and David George) of *National Rights, International Obliga-*

tions (Westview, 1996). He is currently working on strategies for dealing with diversities of belief and culture within societies and across cultures.

George Klay Kieh is an associate professor of political science and international studies at Morehouse College and was the founding director of the Morehouse Center for International Studies. His research and teaching interests are in foreign policy, conflict, international cooperation, political economy, and African politics. He is the author of numerous articles in academic journals and of *Dependency and the Foreign Policy of a Small Power: The Liberian Case* (Edwin Mellon, 1992). He is currently researching state collapse in Africa.

George A. Lopez is a professor of government and international studies and a fellow of the Kroc Institute at the University of Notre Dame. His research focuses on gross violations of human rights and other forms of state violence, especially economic sanctions. He is coeditor of two recent volumes, *Peace and Security: The Next Generation* (with Nancy Myers, 1997), and *Political Gain and Civilian Pain: Humanitarian Impacts of Economic Sanctions* (with Thomas G. Weiss, David Cortright, and Larry Minear, 1997), both published by Rowman and Littlefield.

Emil Nagengast is an assistant professor of international politics at Juniata College in Huntingdon, Pennsylvania. His area of expertise is German relations with East Europe. His articles have appeared in *Review of Contemporary German Affairs, European Studies Journal, International Politics, Peace Review, German Politics, East European Quarterly*, and *Current Politics and Economics of Europe*. His is currently working on a book that examines the ideological evolution of German *Ostpolitik*.

Andrew Valls is an assistant professor of political science at Morehouse College. His areas of interest include modern political thought, theories of social justice, applied ethics, and critical race theory. He is a contributor to several edited volumes, and his articles and reviews have appeared in *Social Theory and Practice, The Review of Politics, American Political Science Review*, and *Constellations*. He is currently working on a book on racial justice.

David A. Welch is an associate professor of political science at the University of Toronto. His publications include *Justice and the Genesis of War* (Cambridge University Press, 1993); *Cuba on the Brink: Castro, the Missile Crisis, and the Soviet Collapse* (with James G. Blight and Bruce J. Allyn; Pantheon, 1993); *Cuba on the Brink: Americans and Soviets Reexamine the Cuban Missile Crisis* (with James G. Blight; Hill & Wang, 1989); and articles in *Foreign Affairs, International Journal, International Security, Journal of Conflict Resolution, Ethics and International Affairs*, and *Security Studies*. He is currently working on decision making and the Vietnam War.